ARCHITECTURAL THEORY AND PRACTICE FROM ALBERTI TO LEDOUX

Dora Wiebenson

to Librarians

L'Origine des Chapiteaux des Colonnes.

II-6.

ARCHITECTURAL THEORY AND PRACTICE FROM ALBERTI TO LEDOUX

Edited by Dora Wiebenson

Foreword by Adolf Placzek

Contributions by

James S. Ackerman • Nicholas Adams • Etta Arntzen • Hilary Ballon • Bradley Barker • Robert W. Berger • John Bold • Paul Breman
John B. Bury • Joseph Connors • William J. Diebold • Richard A. Etlin • Steven Frear • Jörg Garms • George Hersey and Susan Ryan
Volker Hoffmann • Maurice Howard • Vladimir Juřen • Walter Kambartel • Diane Kelder • Cathie C. Kelly • Carol Herselle Krinsky
Elizabeth Lambeth • William L. MacDonald • Robin Middleton • Claude Mignot • Naomi Miller • Robert Neuman • John Newman
Werner Oechslin • John Onians • Martin C. Perdue • Jean-Marie Pérouse de Montclos • Lorendana Olivato Puppi • Elise M. Quasebarth
David Rosand • Kathleen Russo • Richard Ryan • Joseph Rykwert • Lucia Ciapponi Stadter • Barbara Maria Stafford • Christof Thoenes
David Thomson • Richard J. Tuttle • Patricia Waddy • Dora Wiebenson • Carroll William Westfall • John Wilton-Ely

Architectural Theory and Practice from Alberti to Ledoux
Architectural Publications, Inc. 1982
Distributed worldwide by the University of Chicago Press
Second edition, revised, 1983

©Architectural Publications, Inc.
All rights reserved. No part of this book may be reproduced by any form or means, electronical or mechanical, including photocopying, recording or by any information storage and retrieval system, without permission in writing from the publisher.

This book is published in association with exhibitions held at
Sterling Library, Yale University, 1 March-31 May, 1982
Low Memorial Library, Columbia University, 4 November-2 December, 1982
Art Library, University of California, Los Angeles, 26 May-4 August, 1983
Alderman Library, University of Virginia, 12 February-27 April 1984

The printing of this book is supported by a generous grant contributed by the Graham Foundation for Advanced Studies in the Fine Arts.

This book was set in nine point Palladium by E.M. Typesetting & Commercial Art, Charlottesville, Virginia, and was printed by Kaminer & Thomson, Inc., Charlottesville, Virginia in the United States of America.

Library of Congress catalog card number: 82-70938
ISBN 0—9608208—0—9

Cover: **III-B-13.**

ACKNOWLEDGEMENTS

This book is intended to be both an ideal catalog, supplementing exhibitions held at Yale University, Columbia University and the University of Virginia, and a survey and guide for those interested in the history of architectural theory. The entries included are more numerous than the holdings of any one library, but they are not, and could not be comprehensive. Some areas of architectural theory and practice are represented by only a few examples, other more peripheral areas such as garden structures and fortifications reclutantly have been omitted.

All credit is due the contributors. They, with their superb expertise, their interest, and their magnificent cooperation, have produced the substance of this book.

The publication of this book was made possible by a generous grant from the Graham Foundation for Advanced Studies in the Fine Arts. Support of the early work on the project was given by the Society of Architectural Historians, and the initial exhibition was mounted as a contribution towards an annual meeting of that Society. Damie Stillman must be credited with the idea for that exhibition, and thus as the source for all the later work connected with it, including this book.

The research and the preparing of the catalog could not have been undertaken without reference to the resources of libraries. Among those which deserve particular mention are Avery Library, Columbia University, where for many years, with the very generous assistance of Adolf Placzek and the staff, I was privileged to explore its vast holdings; Fiske Kimball Library, University of Virginia, where thanks to the continual kindness of Mary Dunnigan I have been able to undertake intensive study of the subject of architectural theory — her help and that of her staff have made possible much of the speedy and untroubled progress of this book; and the Yale Libraries, where Donald B. Engley kindly permitted me access to and assistance with that collection, and where Nancy Lambert's interest, help and enthusiasm has been indispensable in work on the exhibition and the organizing of the catalog.

Thanks are due to the translators, especially to Lavinia Lorch, whose assistance goes far beyond the brief mention that she receives in these pages, and to Carlo Pelliccia, whose superb translation of supplementary material is recognized only here. Among others who have helped are Barbara Chernow and Henry Millon, who recommended contributors; Ben Weinreb, who has produced so many fine catalogs and who has kindly supplied my students with copies of some of them; Pauline Page, who undertook a vast photographic project to produce illustrations for this book; Herbert and Mosette Broderick, who supplied additional photographic material on very short notice; and Bradley Barker, Steven Frear and Elizabeth Lambeth, and also Elise Quasebarth and Martin Perdue, who were available at all the right times.

I am deeply grateful to John Bury for sharing his bibliographical knowledge, and for other helpful comments in this revised edition.

Dora Wiebenson

FOREWORD

Theory and practice form the counterpoint of architecture. *Ratio-cinatio* and *Fabrica*, or *ars* and *scientia*, or even design and building, it is always out of this bi-polarity that architecture can be comprehended, that the story of architecture as idea and reality can be told. In the following pages this story is learnedly and clearmindedly presented for one of the most decisive phases of architecture, namely from the Italian Renaissance in the fifteenth century to the end of the eighteenth century. It is indeed in those highly literate centuries that theory and practice came to be most sharply defined and most perfectly interwoven. The defining and interweaving really started with one book which had been written fourteen centuries earlier: Vitruvius's *De architectura*. Now Gutenberg had come to the aid of the word of the Ancients, and the great dissemination could begin. We turn quickly to the Italian humanists, to Giovanni Battista Alberti above all, who bent his noble theoretical mind so lucidly to the demands of practice (his book was actually printed a year before the first printed Vitruvius came out). We then move on to Serlio, Palladio, Vignola, and Scamozzi — all theoreticians, all practitioners. The practical aspects are indeed coming into focus: the uses of perspective, the applications of geometry, the techniques of building. But for his *pragma* architectural man needs his *theoria:* the ever-loved Orders, the constant search for ideal proportions, the concepts of symmetry, harmony, perfection. This fine exhibition encompasses in addition variations on the theme: regional, as the Northern Renaissance with its own traditions of practice and its own accommodation to classical theory; and typological, as the amateur-architect-writer who, grounding himself in ancient theory, schooled himself and his fellow amateurs in the new complexities of practice. And there are the new types of books — ranging from the canonical textbook to the great architect's portfolio (as we would call it now), to the learned treatise, and to the modest but enormously useful handbook.

This exhibition reminds us once again (a reminder never offered too often) of the power and glory of the printed word. And to the word is added here the light and magic of the graphic illustration. Like practice and theory in architecture itself, these two — word and illustration — are essential interwoven elements in its dissemination. When Fra Giocondo, in 1511 — early in our story — added woodcuts to his Vitruvius edition, he took a vast step forward. And it was not really Vitruvius who was henceforth being illustrated, but classic design as the Cinquecento conceived it. Without these illustrations, without these books, Cinquecento architecture and, indeed, twentieth century architecture would have been very different, very much poorer.

There is, then, the text, there is the image — and there is, out of both, the sheer beauty of the books themselves. Architectural books, by the very fact of having to join image to word, are often among the wonders of book creation. Volumes such as Cesariano's or Perrault's Vitruvius, or Blondel's *Cours d'Architecture* can, in the subtlety and complexity of their lay-out, the variety and richness of their lettering, the clarity and logic of their illustrations, hardly be surpassed. And, as if by juxtaposition, next to these masterpieces of book-making, there rest the little books, also so attractive in their own way. Their careful simplicity and verbal enthusiasm gives them a charm that must not be overlooked.

For this splendid and thoughtful exhibition thanks must go to Dora Wiebenson who conceived, defined and articulated the project, and who, after many years, brought it to such fine fruition, and to her outstanding contributors. The book — books matter! — that accompanies this exhibition will remain a most valuable contribution to that fundamental topic of architecture: *Theoria* and *pragma, ars* and *scientia.*

Adolf K. Placzek
Avery Librarian Emeritus

INTRODUCTION

I. Vitruvius Discovered

At the time of the discovery of a manuscript copy of Vitruvius's *De architectura* in 1414, recorded information on architecture was devoted mainly to technology and engineering. Men concerned with architecture were not equipped to deal with the transposing of a difficult and forgotten language and profession into modern terms or with an architectural aesthetic based in large part on unfamiliar models, unfamiliar techniques, and an unfamiliar system for the designing of ornament. The task of making Vitruvius intelligible and thus of formulating principles of classical architecture fell at first to humanist scholars, to archaeologists, antiquarians, philologians and grammarians.

As interest in the classical past grew, artists, architects and their patrons also turned to Vitruvius's difficult and obsolete text. In the process of mastering it they were dependent for a time on the methodology and experience of the humanist scholars. For the early products of the collaboration of these two groups the authors were, then, familiar in some manner with Vitruvius's treatise, which they cited in their works. The manuscripts which they produced were extraordinarily varied and original.

Alberti's was the earliest of the treatises, conceived in the 1430's and printed posthumously in 1485. The task he set himself, that of a mastery of Vitruvius's treatise and of a practical and modern response to the classical work, resulted in the most profound of all these early essays, as well as one that was closest in spirit and in format — despite Alberti's criticism of the ancient author — to the original work. Unillustrated, written in a Latin prose that was modelled on the style of Cicero, it was rarely republished, despite the thorough grasp of both practical knowledge and of classical literature demonstrated by its author. However, Alberti's work, representing the challenge of modern man to the ancient past, would become one of the most consulted and cited of all the architectural treatises.

Other architectural treatises of this first group were illustrated. Filarete, who wrote with some of the same objectives as Alberti, was oriented towards crafts and the artisans. His intent was not to challenge the ancients, but to stimulate his patron to build. Francesco Colonna saw in Vitruvius's work those aspects that related to the visually delightful objects of an idealized and fantasized version of the fashionable late Gothic Venetian world. Of all the early works related to the classical treatise his may be the least immediately related to architecture, but it would provide decorative sources based on classical descriptions and classical remains, as well as a visual reconstruction of an ideal antiquity, imagined previously only from literary descriptions. The last of these early works, by Francesco di Giorgio Martini, may have been the most accessible of the writings of any of these early authors. Not only did Di Giorgio write in Italian, but he wrote within the framework of contemporary practice, and he included copious marginal illustrations with his interpretations and reworkings of the Vitruvian material. Di Giorgio represents the most direct link between the late medieval architect-artisan and the architect of the sixteenth century. He knew and was influenced by the work of the early fifteenth century engineer Taccola, and his treatises, although they remained in manuscript, were copied and referred to often. There is, through Peruzzi, a direct line from his work to that of Serlio.

Despite the interest of architects in the Vitruvian text, the first Vitruvius edition to be printed was produced by Fra Giovanni Sulpitius, a grammarian. His attention was focussed on the production of a correct Latin edition of the ancient text, based on his consultation of a single manuscript. Although versions of it appeared in two later editions it seems to have had little influence on architectural theory or practice, but this edition was followed by a wave of illustrated publications of the Vitruvius text that began to appear in 1511, and which by 1521 began to be translated into modern languages — Italian, French, German and Spanish. These editions appeared in response to a widespread popular demand for information on classical architecture. Both the translations and the illustrations are imaginative, inexact attempts to make Vitruvius's Latin text comprehensible to the modern, unlearned reader. In these editions the translators, editors and commentators published mainly for this readership, excluding the scholar, who, it was maintained, could refer to the original treatise for information.

I-6.

This group of treatises is centered on two works. The first is that of Fra Giovanni Giocondo, engineer and architect as well as archaeologist and internationally known scholar. Giocondo, consulting and collating several versions of the Vitruvian text, and also comparing it with the visual remains of antiquity, sought to clarify its discrepancies, and to relate the ancient work to his contemporary times. This Vitruvius edition was the first to be illustrated, and the selection of illustrations would be followed in later editions, where even the original woodblocks were copied, reused, and printed as late as 1648 in the final edition of Delorme's treatise. The second major work of this group is that of an artist-architect, Cesare Cesarinano. He, too, initiates major and lasting innovations in these editions — translation into a modern tongue (although his version was considered to be defective and was ignored by later editors), commentary (although his version was rambling and anecdotal), and imaginative and inexact illustrations, which would reappear in later Vitruvius editions, and would influence Northern architectural treatises of the sixteenth and early seventeenth centuries. Other illustrated vulgate versions based on these two followed in rapid succession. None were directed toward scholars, and all were edited by men who were not architects: Durantino, Caporali, Martin, and Ryff.

By the late 1530's the deficiencies of the earlier Vitruvius editions became apparent. They were too general and too uninformed to be useful either as a text on ancient architecture or as a treatise on which modern architecture could be based. In response, the first treatise on modern architecture independent of the Vitruvian text, by Sebastiano Serlio, began to appear in print before 1540. The format, in which the illustrations rather than the text was emphasized, and the planning of the treatise, in sections on specific architectural subjects, introduced the concentration on illustrations and the categorization of the elements architectural that would be typical of later sixteenth century treatises.

Slightly later, publications recording the ruins of ancient Rome began to be popular, and with these the possibility of the replacing of Vitruvius's treatise as a source of reference for classical architecture. The most influential of the early publications was Labacco's beautiful edition of Roman ruins, which may be a source for even Piranesi's eighteenth century views of antiquity, and which would be cited by later theorists, along with the treatises of Scamozzi, Vignola, and Palladio, as a major reference. The novel, unorthodox effects that would be achieved by a direct investigation of antiquity are suggested also in the early seventeenth century studies of Montano.

Simultaneously, scholars began to undertake critical editions of Vitruvius's treatise. The most important contribution to this new development is the work of the Roman-based Accademia della Virtù, composed of scholars who were concerned with the clarification of obscure passages in Vitruvius's treatise. Guillaume Philander's annotations to the *De architectura* may be the published outcome of this research. Philander was not only a scholar, but also an architect, and a pupil of Serlio. His work sheds light on Vitruvius's text, and with its simplified illustrations, suggests a selective and systematic interpretation in which information from classical literature and classical ruins are integrated. His annotations surely influenced later editions of Vitruvius's text, and may also have had some impact on those architectural theoreticians, such as Palladio, Vignola, and Delorme, who now would begin to master and interpret the classical material for modern practice.

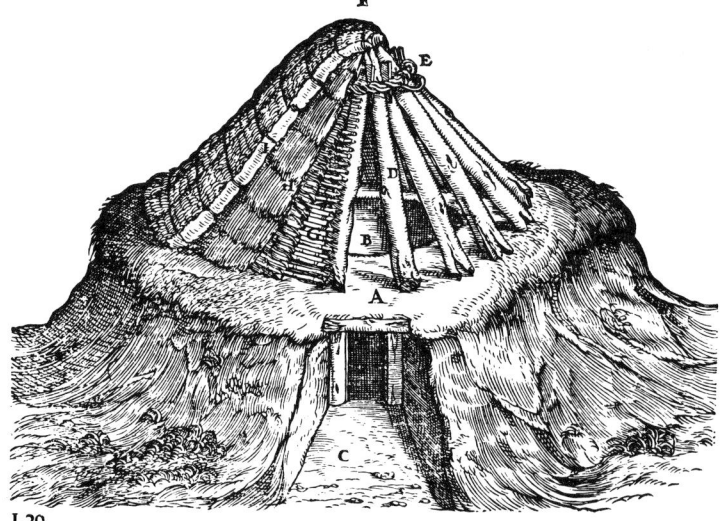

I-20.

The attitudes and methods developed during the years around the mid-century under the influence of scholarly research permitted the architects to begin to develop principles for their profession which now would become independent of external professional influence. Vitruvius editions were replaced by modern architectural treatises, systematically and selectively organized, each of which presented an original interpretation of the relation of the architectural profession to material from the classical past and a choice of topics important to its present development. The group of treatises produced in the last half of the sixteenth century provide the groundwork for architectural publications for the following two centuries. Only the treatises of Cataneo and the late work of Viola Zanini continue the pre-1540 popular tradition, and these are influenced by post-1540 developments. Philibert Delorme's work, with its learned and comprehensvie text, falls within the context of the work of the scholar-architect of the 1550's, and Scamozzi's *Idea* is its ultimate expression. Palladio, using the method of the scholar-architect, would select and synthesize the architectural material, presenting a personal theory that could be understood, like the early Vitruvius vulgate editions, by the unlearned. By the early years of the seventeenth century Wotton would still recall the scholar-architect when he stressed the need for the intellectual qualifications of the architect, in his "elemental" and "logical" work, now oriented toward the dilettante.

Although Vitruvius editions, along with the sixteenth century treatises, continued to be republished in the seventeenth century, new editions on the classical author were undertaken by scholars, who produced Latin-language lexicons and compendia rather than original interpretative works. The last great Vitruvius edition was the product of one of the last great architect-scholars, Claude Perrault, and it occurred only at the end of the seventeenth century. The work was a definitive text on the practice of the ancients and on that of the moderns. As a comprehensive interpretation of the Vitruvian material it is the product of a powerful and confident professional architect, capable of absorbing and developing much material from related disciplines. Perrault's interpretation would become the definitive edition of Vitruvius: consultation of this work by all later Vitruvius editors was mandatory. On the other hand, Perrault's abridged Vitruvius edition, in which he condensed and reorganized the original text, leads to the eighteenth century and to the amateur publications.

I-29.

I-31.

II. Architects and Amateurs

The production of major architectural treatises came to an end around 1600. In its place appeared a great number of new editions of these sixteenth century architectural publications, along with the reissues of the Vitruvius editions of Barbaro, Philander, Rusconi, and Martin. Serlio's complete treatise, which had been collected and published from the mid-sixteenth century, was popular in the first years of the seventeenth century, but, with the exception of one belated edition in 1663, disappeared. Palladio's complete *Quattro Libri* received a major edition in the mid-seventeenth century in a French translation; Delorme's treatise, to which Guarini's late seventeenth century treatise must be related, received two editions, in 1626 and 1648; Viola Zanini's late and retardataire work was reissued once. The prize for popularity must be shared between Wotton, whose *Elements,* oriented toward the amateur, was republished six times from 1649 to 1698 and continued to appear throughout the eighteenth and into the nineteenth century, and Scamozzi, whose *Idea,* a compendium suitable for a professional readership, was republished in full in two German editions and in three Italian ones up to 1714.

Whether encyclopaedic or summary, these books contained a series of architectural topics which might include the history and principles of architecture, perspective and geometry, building materials and technology, examples of civic and domestic architecture, and above all, the Orders, all of which would be continued and developed in many of the later treatises, which began to proliferate by the end of the seventeenth century.

A few seventeenth century handbooks continued this earlier tradition. Branca's early seventeenth century manual would become a standard textbook in Italy, and Capra's derivative treatise published as late as 1678, represent the provincial extension of the earlier works. However, innovation in architectural theory during the seventeenth century was the provenance of the non-professionals, the amateurs and dilettantes. Their contributions included the mystical association of classical architecture with Christianity in studies of the Temple of Solomon initiated with Villapando, which were continued by such writers as Caramuel de Lobkowitz and still preserved in the eighteenth century by John Wood; the rigorous adherence to the most severely correct principles of classical ornament such as those advocated by Gallaccini; and the developing of such handbooks on taste and architectural practice for the amateur and client as the 1660's works of Gerbier.

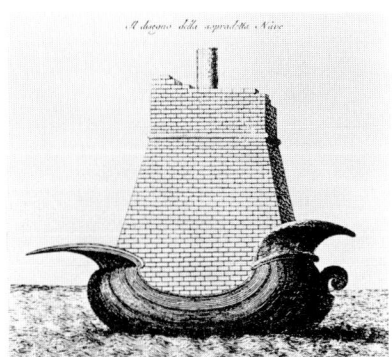

II-2.

The appearance of a new type of comprehensive architectural treatise is initiated mainly with the publication of the two great French *Cours d'architecture,* by François Blondel and Charles Daviler. Blondel's *Cours,* reflecting the education of the architectural student in the newly-formed Royal Academy of Architecture, is for the most part concerned with the Orders, and includes a comparative study of their proportional relationships developed by the great Renaissance theorists and modelled on the earlier work of Fréart de Chambray. His work reflects the conservative position of the Academy. However, even within this institution an alternate position, also rooted in sixteenth century tradition, and concerned with the authority of the visual remains of antiquity, would take place, despite the fact that allegiance to the developing of accurate information taken directly from classical ruins challenged the authority of Vitruvius and of modern theorists. The Roman archaeological study by the young academician Desgodets, sponsored by the Academy, did challenge these established authorities, and his work was not well received. But it would become one of the major influences on the later archaeological publications of the ancient architecture of the Levant, especially that of Stuart and Revett, which would, with its revelation of unorthodox ancient Greek systems of decoration, become a major cause of the undermining of the foundations of Renaissance architectural theory, and thus indirectly would pave the way for nineteenth century stylistic eclecticism.

However, the greatest impact on the development of the new comprehensive architectural treatise is that of Daviler's *Cours d'architecture.* This work, intended originally to be an annotated edition of Vignola's *Regola,* was developed and extended to include eventually a systematic topical exploration of the entire field of architecture. Reprinted in many editions in France, it received a German translation by Sturm, who also collected and published the material forming Goldmann's German architectural treatise. Through Sturm's translation Daviler's *Cours* had a considerable impact on German architectural publications. Paul Decker's *Ausführliche Anleitung zur Civil Baukunst* would include even plates taken from Daviler's work, and Christian Rieger's *Universae architectura* showed the same pragmatic and detailed organization of subject. The development of publications on domestic architecture of the first half of the eighteenth century in France also owes much to Daviler's *Cours.*

English architectural theory, while participating in the seventeenth century developments, remained close to a still-living sixteenth century tradition, with its dependence on both ancient ruins and classical texts. Wren's architectural notes, published posthumously in his *Parentalia,* and the unfinished contemporary treatise of Henry Aldrich, written in Latin, suggest a continuation of this earlier tradition.

The majority of publications on architecture, both those abbreviated versions put out for amateurs and those encyclopaedic versions produced for professionals, appeared during the eighteenth century. In the opening years of this century, and shortly after the publication of Perrault's popular abridged Vitruvius edition, a new type of amateur publication began to be produced. Authors would compose publications in new and literary formats, such as letters, essays and lectures, to produce works which were often eccentric, innovative, and iconoclastic. Some produced the most advanced thinking on architectural theory of the time. Michel Frémin challenged the priority of the Orders, substituting in their place the purely practical considerations of function and use; Jean-Louis Cordemoy based the use of the Orders on fundamental structural premises; and Robert Morris extracted the system of proportions from the Orders to apply to other architectural elements and to architectural spaces.

II-20.

At the same time simplified statements of the major architectural publications, written as elementary textbooks for students and amateurs, began to appear. Leclerc's abbreviated treatise of 1714 follows in the tradition of the Royal Academy of Architecture, concentrating on the Orders. Bardet de Villeneuve's 1740 architectural textbook for engineers, on the other hand, follows the more extended inclusion of topics of Daviler. These essays are examples of a flood of pocket-sized textbooks that would appear, summarizing the systematic exposition of material of the French *Cours*, and often written by scholars, clerics and mathematicians — men from professions which had played a major role in the formulating of the principles of the architectural profession in the sixteenth century, and would, with the production of these reduced works on architecture, again contribute to this field, but now by disseminating its established principles to a vastly expanded audience. The education of the architect by traditional methods and a thorough acquaintance with all aspects of the field is supported further in the pamphlet of J.F. Blondel's *Discours sur la necessité de l'étude de l'architecture*, where he discusses the principles and curriculum of his own prestigious and important architectural school, the Ecole des Arts, of the mid-eighteenth century.

The treatises of the mid-eighteenth century recapitulate the diversity of the earlier treatises. Laugier and Lodoli produced up-dated versions of Cordemoy's and Frémin's works; Briseux revived François Blondel's position on the Orders; the great eighteenth century treatises on civil architecture, by such architects as Ware, Chambers and J.F. Blondel, were oriented either toward François Blondel's emphasis on the Orders (as was Chambers' — and perhaps also Bibiena's earlier concern with the ornamental part of architecture along with the development of perspective theory), or toward Daviler's comprehensive survey of all the building arts (as were Ware's and J.F. Blondel's — and Milizia's later Neoclassical treatise). The authority of Vitruvius's treatise is questioned by Stuart and Revett who presented their empirical observations of the classical remains, using Desgodets' earlier work as a model. By the 1770's Neoclassical theory had crystallized in Italy to produce works in which concepts were extracted from even earlier treatises, with Pini's concentration on the simple geometric form, Visentini's support of Gallacini's early seventeenth-century "correct" classicism, and Preti's concern for musical proportion in architectural design.

Despite these recollections of earlier treatises, by the end of the century new ideals and methods introduced by the amateurs had become so dominant that they would influence both the form and the content of some of the major statements of architectural principles, and bring about the final rupture with the tradition that was based on the principles of Vitruvius. A new type of theoretical treatise, oriented toward the amateur and in a literary format, began to appear. The authors were architects: J.F. Blondel, Le Camus de Mézières and Viel de Saint-Maux. In their works the exploration of the means of producing an objective, rational environment is abandoned for the creation of a work of sensation, or of symbolism based on association. The architectural treatise, with its assumption of the integration of theory with practice and of the control of the external environment, based on rational ordering and empirical examination, is brought to a close. Treatises now will have different formats and different objectives.

II-30.

III. The Elements of Architecture
A. The Orders

The division of topics discussed in Vitruvius's work into handbooks on specialized subjects began to occur early in the sixteenth century. The first of these divisions was that of separate studies on the Orders. Publications on the Orders began to appear at the same time as the vulgate popular early sixteenth century Vitruvius editions. Like the Vitruvius editions, they were illustated — and the illustrations now began to dominate the rudimentary, vernacular texts. These books were produced as guides and explanations of the new style for both builder and client.

The first of these, Sagredo's *Medidas del Romano,* was written in the popular format of a dialogue: its contents were derived from Vitruvius's Books III and IV, on the Orders. Serlio's even more popular Book IV, on the Orders, may have been written simultaneously, although it was published just over ten years after Sagredo's Spanish first edition appeared. Both these works, but especially Serlio's, were extremely popular. Serlio's book would have the greatest influence on later publications on the Orders. His emphasis was on the recording of the visual remains of antiquity, and on the reduction of Vitruvian theory to simple, illustrated statements. Not least among the contributions of this book to later publications is the abstracting and application of ornament associated with the Orders to other architectural elements, such as doors, gates, and chimney-pieces.

III-A-1.

In Northern Europe Serlio's Book IV contributed to a vast outpouring of handbooks on the Orders. His very disparate disciples included Blum, Sambin, Vredeman de Vries, Shute, Bullant, Dietterlin and Mauclerc. Their products ranged from Blum's recording of the basic elements of the Orders to Dietterlin's exploitation of the Orders for their fantastic ornamental possibilities and the invention of vocabularies associated with the "character" of each Order, which he applied to every conceivable object. One late member of this group is the Italian Francine, whose book of illustrations of gates according to the Orders would achieve considerable popularity in English translation.

The main concern in the use of the Orders was with their proportions, as they could be developed from analogies with the human figure or from musical harmony, or by simplifying and standardizing the parts of the Orders for use in built architecture. Solutions to these problems were explored not in the North but in Italy, where the Orders were simplified into a standardized selection of vocabulary and proportions by Vignola, who also achieved a system of representation of the three-dimensional Orders on a two-dimensional page that would be adopted in all later architectural representations. Vignola's influence was profound. His *Regola* would achieve the greatest number of editions, whether translated, reproduced, or revised, of any architectural book published, including that of Vitruvius. The book corresponded to the needs of workmen, builders, architects and amateurs. In addition, handbooks on the Orders were excerpted from Palladio's and Scamozzi's treatises and published separately in many editions and many languages well into the eighteenth century. The simplification of the proportions of the Orders was also attempted by the invention of instruments (of limited practicality), such as Revesi Brute's *archisesto* for the determining of proportions appropriate to each Order, by the early seventeenth century.

Vignola's work also opened the door to the possibility of a selective analysis of the Orders. And, in fact, the invention of individual systems of the Orders by sixteenth century architects such as Palladio, Vignola, and Scamozzi, was followed in the seventeenth century by a retrospective period of analysis and reinterpretation of the earlier systems. By 1650 Roland Fréart de Chambray would present a comparison of all major systems of the Orders, both ancient and modern, in which he would conclude conservatively that the proportions of the ancients were the authoritative models. His comparative method was used in the majority of the books on the theory of the Orders, from the *Cours* of François Blondel to the diverse treatises and handbooks of Leclerc, Briseux, Bosboom and other Dutch writers, LeBlond, Nativelle, and Riou. All of these works would be centered on comparative investigations of the ornamental and proportional systems of at least some of the chief sixteenth-century theoreticians: in addition Riou included his friend James Stuart's Grecian findings in his study.

III-A-9.

III-A-14.

Fréart's was not the only direction which the study of the Orders would take. His work was followed by Claude Perrault's iconoclastic treatise in which he challenged one of the basic hypotheses associated with the Orders, that of their association with a presumed, unalterable system of universal proportions. Perrault introduced a single simplified system of the Orders, in which the proportions would be based on "common sense," and designed in easily comprehendible modular ratios which were determined by custom and use. The architectural part of the quarrel of the Ancients and Moderns centers on Perrault's concept of proportions as arbitrary and changeable, and on François Blondel's defense of the traditional belief that proportions were immutable and universal. In rejecting a proportional system which was imposed on architecture, Perrault spoke for the modern architect, self-sufficient, and independent of the authority of tradition. His position was the ultimate and logical expression of the development of the autonomy of the architectural profession. But it was restricted. In the next century it would be followed by a wide range of individual solutions, in which Perrault's concepts were simplified (Cordemoy and then Laugier), or modified and adapted in handbooks on the Orders which presented rule-of-thumb criteria for dilettantes (Morris) and rule-of-thumb methods for workmen (Langley, Halfpenny). Only Batty Langley's enormous and unselective compilation of the Orders and ornament of all modern architects in his encyclopaedic *Ancient Masonry* is a rare, but not very significant, exception to this development. And his application of the system of the five Orders to Gothic architecture is at the outmost edge of the Renaissance development of a theory of the Orders.

B. Geometry and Perspective

The main concern of the Renaissance architect was with the defining, ordering and controlling of his visible universe. This he would achieve by means of graphic representations. The most rudimentary graphic system, geometry, was an essential tool for the accurate recording of architectural information, the knowledge of which was considered by Serlio to be essential to all workmen so that they would be able to communicate information systematically and accurately. Instruction in basic geometry formed a small, essential and introductory part of many architectural treatises, especially those on civil architecture. Its applications were manifold. Geometry was useful not only for determining proportions related to human figures and the Orders, but also for dialling, according to Arphe y Villafame. One of the chief uses of

I-11.

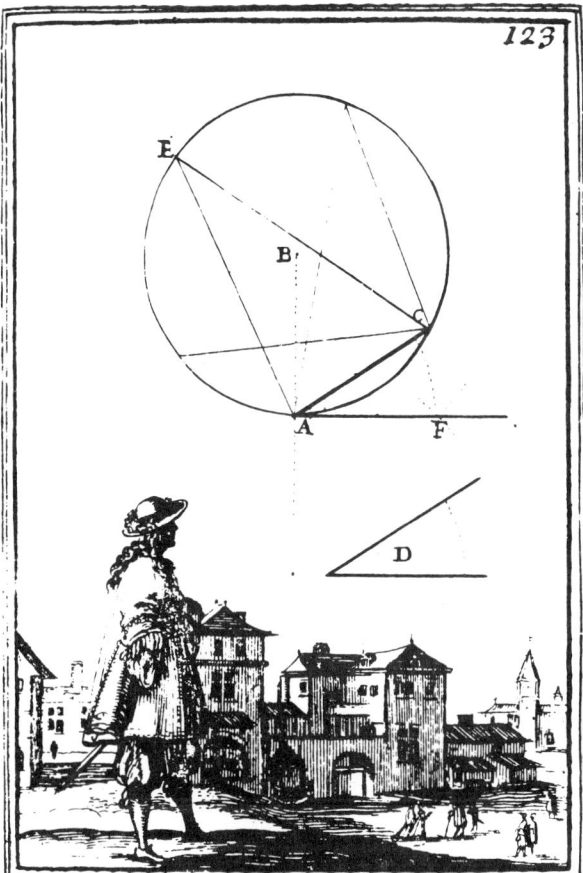

III-B-22.

geometry was for measuring. But this technique was restricted, until well into the seventeenth century, to simple Euclidian principles and to crude, inaccurate instruments. Manuals on measuring, such as Cosimo Bartoli's important mid-sixteenth century work (as well as Ryff's presentation of similar material in his German Vitruvius edition and his treatise), suggest the difficulty of transforming principles into practice even in the area of site measurement. Only gradually would instruments be developed with enough precision so that buildings could be measured accurately. The early geometry lessons of Serlio's Book I still continued to be included in architectural publications through the eighteenth century and in textbooks such as the charming one by Leclerc or in the simplified practical adaptations to field work by Halfpenny.

The chief attention of the treatise writers concerned with graphic representation was focussed on perspective, a method by which space can be rationally and architectonically organized from the view point of a person. Wren recommended that "the Architect ought, above all Things, to be well skilled in Perspective [because] a Model is seen from other Stations and Distances than the Eye sees the Building: what soever is good in Perspective, and will hold so in all the principal Views, whether direct and oblique, will be as good in great . . . "

I-12.

Perspective creates architectural space, and it is intimately connected with painting, by means of which architectural space can be extended and completed. While books on the Orders were developed from a study of the literary and visual evidence of the classical past, perspective, the most intellectual of all the disciplines associated with architecture, was developed from the modern methods of empirical examination and scientific experimentation. Its closest association is with mathematics. As a technique, perspective would be useful not only for architecture, painting and sculpture, but also for astronomy, surveying, cartography, ballistics, stereotomy, carpentry, crystallography, and gardening.

Perspective had it origins in the medieval science of optics, and with a possible "bifocal" pseudo-perspective developed by late medieval artist-artisans. The discovery of the vanishing point, which was critical to the development of perspective, is credited to the artist-architect Brunelleschi, who, in 1425, demonstrated a method for constructing a perspective space and an object (the Cathedral of Florence) within that space. It is not certain if he discovered the single-point system of perspective, but this system was described by Alberti in 1435. With this knowledge, the artist was able to place the viewer in total control of the object viewed: one of the most outstanding realizations of this objective is Bramante's Cortile of the Belvedere.

An additional relation between the viewer and the object viewed was achieved by Pèlerin in 1505 with his development of the two-point system of perspective. Both one- and two-point perspective were discussed by Serlio, and Vignola would develop a study of these two systems in a definitive exposition possibly begun as early as the 1550's, but published posthumously. The potential of perspective had already been fully realized by 1568 when Barbaro's manual on the subject, in which the author borrowed freely from the work of previous theorists, appeared. But perspective was far more than a method. Serlio in his Book II suggested the association of the artificial, rationalized architectonic and urban space created by perspective techniques with the theater, and its association with morality is suggested in the famous controversy initiated by Bassi, who objected to the production of an "inaccurate" perspective (with two ground lines) in a church.

After Pèlerin's simple and profound statement of the science of perspective, French perspective treatises, such as those by Cousin and Du Cerceau, as well as the French-oriented one by Johann II, instructed readers in easy, clear, simple, but visually elegant and appealing studies. At the same time German artists like Jamnitzer exploited the technical potential of perspective to depict objects in nature, rather than to rationalize space. Late sixteenth century studies, like Sirigatti's and Vredeman de Vries's, demonstrate full mastery of the field and become important text books for the following centuries.

Developments in perspective theory in the seventeenth century were centered on discoveries by mathematicians. The work of the first of these, Guidobaldo del Monte, who established the concept of the vanishing point, was disregarded in the practical perspective manuals. But the universal method, based on Cartesian geometry, of Girard Desargues, which resulted in the absolute, mathematical precision of the projection of three-dimensional objects on a two-dimensional surface, although supported by Bosse, was violently opposed by Lebrun and the Academy of Painting and Sculpture. The resulting controversy entered into the treatises of such perspective theorists as Vaulezard and Dubreuil, who wrote the most popular perspective treatise of the seventeenth century.

The seventeenth century also was the period in which the possibilities of perspective technique were exploited to include complex technical problems of anamorphosis (Niceron), of shades and shadows (Accolti), and of candlelight and reflection (Lamy), all of which received systematic studies.

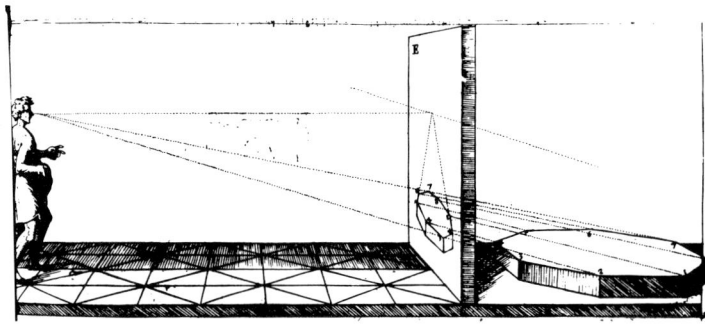
III-B-4.

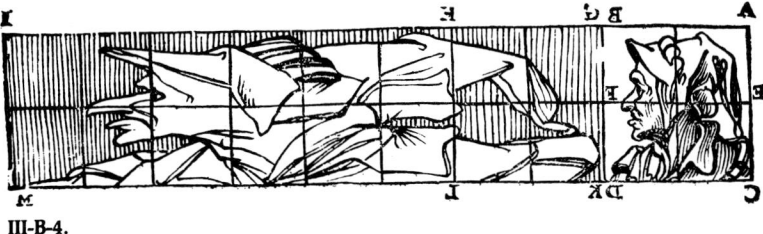

III-B-4.

In the last quarter of the century, the extension of architecture in painting is the point of departure for major perspective treatises. Troili (Paradosso) is the first of this group to publish, in 1672. Now, Vignola, an architect, in addition to demonstrating both one- and two-point systems, had indicated a preference for the single vanishing point, the system by which the viewer, and the creator, maintained total control over the area viewed. Painters, on the other hand, preferred the more flexible two-point system. The one-point system remained the most popular among architects and architectural and theatrical painters, and it was supported even by the late seventeenth century architectural painter Pozzo, whose work was the most influential of all baroque perspective treatises, being translated into English and eventually replacing Dubreuil's work. "Per angolo," two-point perspective, would emerge as the dominant perspective solution only in the eighteenth century, with Ferdinando Galli Bibiena's treatise.

But by this point in time the original, universal — and indeterminate — significance of perspective was fading. What had been an art now began to be considered simply as graphic technique. Elementary perspective books for students proliferated, such as the fine ones by Courtonne, Jeaurat, Lambert and Malton, and mechanical instruments were publicized, such as Halfpenny's perspective aid. Two important treatises, in which perspective is treated wholly as a technical field, deprived of its earlier extended context, appeared in the eighteenth century, by Brook Taylor, and by Gaspard Monge (the father of descriptive geometry). These works contributed extensively to nineteenth century perspective theory, and must be considered in that context.

C. Technology

The only major architectural discipline which does not have its roots in Italian theory is that of technology, although the influence of the Italian treatises on the Northern development of basic principles of the art of construction is deep. Most of the treatises and handbooks on technology are indebted to the work of Philibert Delorme. His *Nouvelles Inventions*, which develops principles for carpentry, is followed by the primitive studies in carpentry of Jousse and other treatise writers. Delorme's main contribution, which is specifically acknowledged by later authors on the subject, is to the field of stereotomy, which he explores in Books III and IV of his *Architecture*.

Stereotomy can be defined as a technique of "description" of vaulting in cut stone, demonstrated for the first time by Philibert Delorme. It is a process of representing the vault in construction, which permits the form of each of its voussoirs to be determined *a priori*. Stereotomy is developed from techniques of medieval drawing, notably that of the *art du trait*, or, in Spainish, *montea*. The *art du trait* is applied to carpentry and to the ribbed vault — to structures whose location in space is clarified by the separation of skeleton and infilling. In this manner all volume is reduced to the arch, so that the calculation of the outlines of the construction can be made. Delorme conceived the idea of turning to Italian studies of perspective to resolve in three-dimensional drawings a variety of problems posed by the installation of massive vaults. Since the *art du trait* was related to a style which had developed only in France and in Spain, stereometric treatises were only published in these two countries.

[Jean-Marie Pérouse de Montclos]

III-B-19.

I-24.

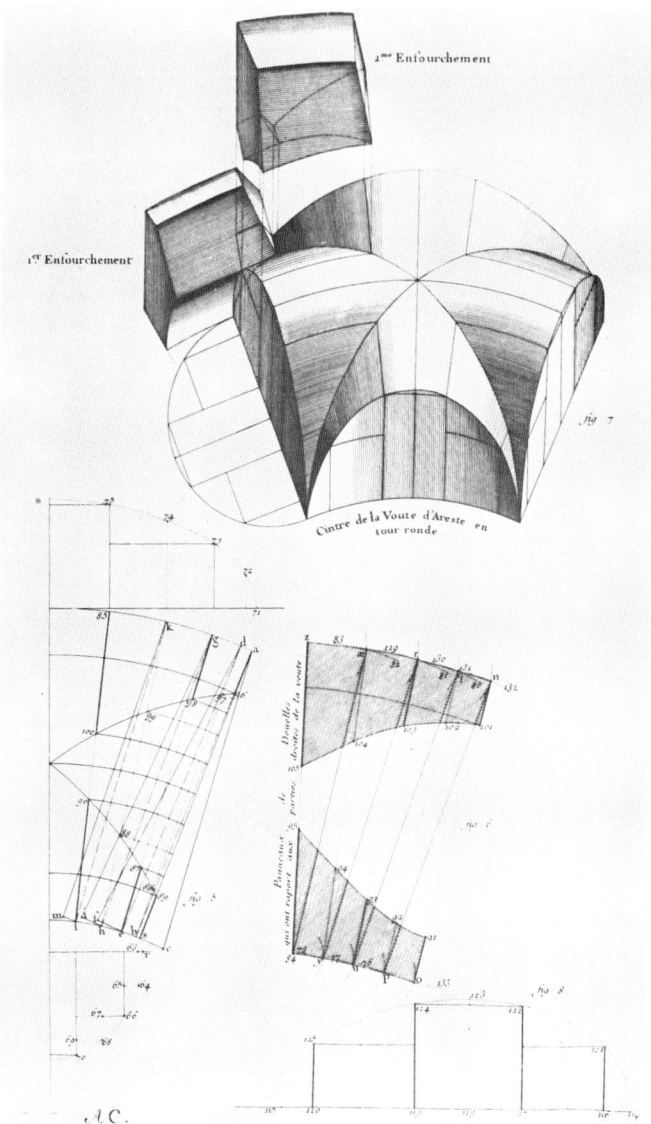

III-C-16.

Builder's manuals have a separate development, beginning with the early seventeenth century work of Louis Savot, who was concerned only with the application of building practices to house construction, and whose work should surely be associated with Pierre Le Muet's contemporaneous study on house types. When the Academy of Architecture became interested in building practice it would be with the determining of building standards and laws. The much-republished work of Bullet and the study of building laws by Desgodets are an outgrowth of this development. When Le Camus de Mézières returned to the study of building practice as related to house construction at the end of the eighteenth century, it would be within the format of the amateur publication, as it had been developed at the beginning of the century in such treatises as Frémin's *Mémoires,* but incorporating the expertise and accumulated knowledge developed from the building publications and the tradition of the previous two centuries.

Another type of amateur publication, associated with the defining and standardizing of terms related to the building crafts for the layman, and surely also, in France, with the development and control of standards of craft practice in mind, is Félibien's magnificent comprehensive study, published in 1676. This work is the end product of attempts to standardize building terminology which began already by the mid-sixteenth century. Félibien's work is echoed in Moxon's almost contemporary but by no means as inclusive English study of the same subject.

The English were not concerned, as were the French, with the establishing of principles for the field of technology but with supplying immediately useful manuals to those interested in building. English publications began in the late seventeenth century, and are, like the French comprehensive manuals, produced mainly for house construction. They consist of tables and charts of sizes and prices of materials by such authors as Wilsford and Salmon; manuals for bricklayers by, for instance, Halfpenny and Price; and designs for carpenters by Swan and by Pain, whose many repetitive volumes contain rudimentary information on masonry and carpentry construction. By the end of the eighteenth century even in France the earlier interest in the definition and explanation of structural principles was abandoned by, for instance, Monroy and Séguin, who, in the English manner, produced manuals for the immediate use of the practicioner.

The treatises of Chéreau, Vandelvira, Jousse, Derand, La Rue and above all Frézier, who produced a comprehensive summation of the work of two centuries in his three-volume treatise, all are deeply indebted to this earliest study. The only modification of this development is in the work of Desargues, whose application of the principles of Cartesian geometry to stereotomy, popularized by Bosse, was, as was his work in perspective, rejected because his method broke with established practice. Only in the last part of the eighteenth century would the theoreticians lose interest in the art of stereotomy, a decline that can be seen in the treatises of De Torija, Menand, and of Simonin.

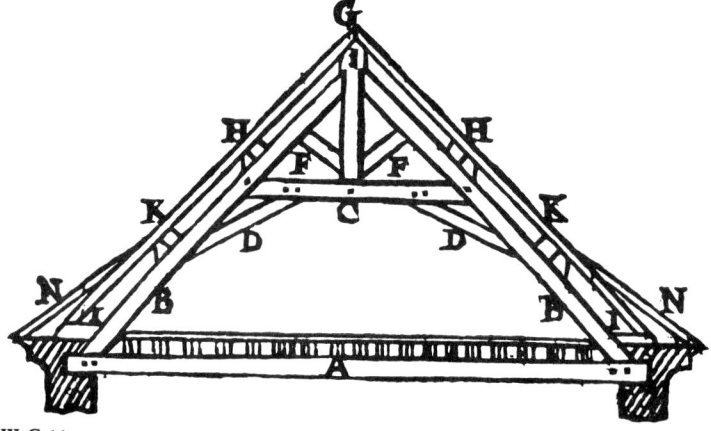

III-C-14.

D. Public and Private Architecture

In its most literal sense, civil architecture is concerned with public and private structures. It has it origins in those sections of modern civic buildings and domestic architecture included in sixteenth century treatises by, for instance, Serlio, Palladio, and Scamozzi. Its earliest independent published manifestation is with examples of built structures (mainly country houses) reflecting national style. These include Du Cerceau's *Bastiments;* the on-going *Architecture française* to which Marot, Mariette, and J.F. Blondel all contributed; and Colin Campbell's *Vitruvius Britannicus,* which would influence other similar eighteenth century "Vitruvius" editions, such as Thurah's work on Danish architecture.

German publications on modern civic buildings began in the early seventeenth century, and ranged from the practical projects of Fürttenbach to the more stylistically oriented eighteenth century studies of Decker and Schübler. By the mid-seventeenth century the work of an individual architect (Borromini) would be collected — although it did not appear in print until the eighteenth century — and this would be followed in the first half of the eighteenth century by such selective, theoretical publications of architects' projects as those by Boffrand and Peyre in France, and by such works publicising a specific style and taste as those by Gibbs and Adam in England.

Publications related to the house form a special branch of these publications on civil architecture, and have a special development. The ancestor of this group of works is Serlio's unpublished Book VI, which contains designs of houses for all ranks of people. It was followed by Du Cerceau's mid-sixteenth century study of house types and by his projects for country houses and fantastic villas. This last may have influenced Le Pautre in his publication of his works and projects a century later, which included several important fantastic villas. The imaginary restorations of Pliny's villas by Félibien and then by Castell around the turn of the eighteenth century must also be seen with this context.

Du Cerceau's study of house types, on the other hand, was surely a source for one of the most influential of all the publications on the house, Le Muet's *Manière de bastir,* which appeared in many French editions and in an English translation, and which introduced the awareness of an architectural expression for social classes that would dominate later works on this subject. However, not until the second quarter of the eighteenth century would French publications on the house develop the implications of Le Muet's work (perhaps with the example of the previous inclusion of domestic architecture in Daviler's *Cours* in mind), with the publication by Jombert of studies of houses for all classes of people, with the appearance of the comprehensive works on country houses by J.F. Blondel and Briseux, and, finally, with those cahiers which Neufforge, in his encyclopaedic *Recueil,* devoted to the house.

In contrast to the French house publications, English ones were focussed on basic types of rural domestic architecture, the farm and the cottage, and they were written either as handbooks for the builder or client, or as entertainment for the amateur. They form an extension of Campbell's promotion of Palladianism as a national style, and they began to appear around the middle of the eighteenth century, with Daniel Garrett's study of farmhouses, which was quickly followed by Morris's and Halfpenny's handbooks. From the mid-1750's the new publication type was exploited by craftsmen such as Swan, Lightoler, Crunden and Rawlins, and after 1780 large numbers of small volumes on houses appeared, at first produced from social concern (Wood's *Cottages* was based on the rural housing suggestions of the agrarian reformer, Nathaniel Kent). But after 1785 these publications became fashionably involved with the picturesque and the sentimental Rousseauian cottage, to the exclusion of earlier social or nationalistic concerns. The first of these publications is Plaw's *Rural Architecture,* which reappeared in five editions before 1804. The picturesque style was then defined by Malton to include thatched roofs, diamond-paned windows, rough posts, wood boarding, and even asymmetry. The popularity of the picturesque cottage book is attested by the fact that even large folio volumes on the country house, such as Richardson's, now included romanticized recreations of laborer's cottages in a landscape setting among the designs. Well-known architects did not publish in this genre, with the exception of Sir John Soane. The two styles, Palladian and picturesque, were united by Gandy in two books published in the first years of the nineteenth century. The house publication would continue to develop without a break in its production, and it would become one of the major types of architectural publication of the nineteenth century, and a record of the development of built domestic architecture.

On the other hand, publications on civic architecture already by the early eighteenth century began to encompass vast geographical and historical panoramas, in Fischer von Erlach's *Historischen Architektur,* which includes legendary monuments from history and from foreign lands. By the end of the century this type of the civil architecture publication had become a vehicle for the most advanced architectural theory of the time. It now included the extreme statements of unrealiseable projects reflecting the individual philosophies and ideals of the architects who designed them, specifically those of Boullée, who developed a universal

II-12.

III-D-12.

style based on an observation of effects in Nature, and of Ledoux, who developed a universal style based on the architectural expression of new social ideals and scientific discoveries. With the work of these men, in which theory and practice were severed, the civil architectural publication, replacing the comprehensive treatise as the treatise had replaced the Vitruvian editions, became a vehicle for the expression of the deepest and most progressive ideals of architectural principles of the time.

Dora Wiebenson

THE PUBLICATIONS

I Vitruvius Discovered

I-1.

Leone Battista Alberti (1404-1472), architect, painter, humanist), *Leonis Baptiste Alberti De re aedificatoria,* Florence, Nicolò di Lorenzo Alemanno, 1485 (crit. ed., Orlandi, Milan, 1966).

Alberti invented the modern notion of architecture and exemplified the role of architect in his broad range of intellectual and practical activities. Born in exile, his training in law opened a career as a professional humanist for the period's most illustrious popes and princes with whom he enjoyed an easy familiarity. He excelled in all manner of accomplishments from athletics to after dinner speeches, from singing to writing treatises on law, from contriving mechanical gadgets to demonstrating the suppleness of Italian for polite literature on a wide variety of topics. After his native Florence extended its hospitality to him he expanded his humanist interests to embrace architecture. From 1446 on came a series of buildings which showed how the important but relatively parochial new architecture of that bastion of republicanism could be made appropriate for use in a larger, princely world. By the time he died he had designed a wide range of building types throughout Italy—in Florence, Rimini, and Mantua, and almost certainly in Ferrara, Urbino, Pienza, Rome, and elsewhere. Each design satisfied a specific purpose and suited a particular place, but each also demonstrated the truths of universally valid principles. These he had uncovered from his extensive knowledge of classical antiquity and contemporary thought and developed with a unique, penetrating insight into the role of all the arts in the new, larger world of which we are the direct heirs.

De re aedificatoria is the capstone of Alberti's architecture. Begun perhaps as early as the later 1430s, its formal presentation to Pope Nicholas V occurred in 1452. The Latin treatise's debt to its only surviving predecessor, Vitruvius' *de architectura,* goes little beyond the division into ten books and the use of a few points which the Augustan architect had asserted but the Florentine first incorporated into a coherent presentation. For Alberti architecture is a learned discipline allied with the other arts of the mind and of the eye, buildings serve men gathered into societies, and design and construction bring the architect into direct confrontation with the forces of nature. With this Alberti had established architecture on principles articulated into reasons, on service to patrons, and on the manipulation of materials and construction techniques. These three aspects have ever since provided the substance of architecture. The treatise's manuscripts from Alberti's lifetime are unillustrated as is the *editio princeps* published posthumously. Its more than 23 subsequent publications include translations into a number of
languages: Italian (1546), French (1553), Spanish (1582), English (1726), German (1912), Russian (1935-37), Czech (1956), and Polish (1960). There is also an unpublished early sixteenth century Portuguese translation.

Carroll William Westfall

I-2.

Antonio Averlino, called Filarete, (c.1400-c.1465, artisan and architect), *libro architettonico* (facs. ed. New Haven, 1965).

Born in Florence, Filarete was active in Rome around 1440 and made a pair of bronze doors for St. Peter's. After a brief visit to Venice he arrived in Milan where he worked for Francesco Sforza from 1451 until about 1465 when his friend the Greek oriented humanist Francesco Filelfo wrote a letter of introduction to help him on a projected visit to Constantinople. During his stay in Milan his most important work was the design and construction of a new Hospital, the most ambitious yet planned.

The *libro architettonico,* as he called it, survives in few manuscripts. It was conceived in the mid-1450s and completed in twenty-four books by 1465. Initially intended for the Sforza duke, the treatise was subsequently also dedicated to Piero de'Medici with a twenty-fifth book added in praise of Medici buildings. The work is chiefly in the form of a dialogue between Filarete and a prince's son and deals with the construciton of a capital city Sforzinda and a port city Plousiapolis. Explanations are given not only of planning design and construction procedures but also of the organization of institutions such as prisons and schools. As an account of an imaginary state the treatise is modeled on a group of Platonic dialogues to which Filarete must have been introduced by Filelfo. Filelfo must also have been responsible for giving the writer his Greek name, Filarete 'lover of virtue' and for encouraging an emphasis on Greek artistic traditions. Filarete's book is the first treatment of architecture in a modern language and represents the first attempt to formulate a coherent theory of architecture which relates directly to the modern Christian world. The originality of his thought depends both on his ignorance and his independence. Lacking Alberti's profound knowledge of ancient architectural theory and practice he was forced to formulate his own rules both for the design of architectural forms and for their application. Unfortunately the irregularity and inelegance of his language has long obscured his susbtantial intellectual achievement.

John Onians

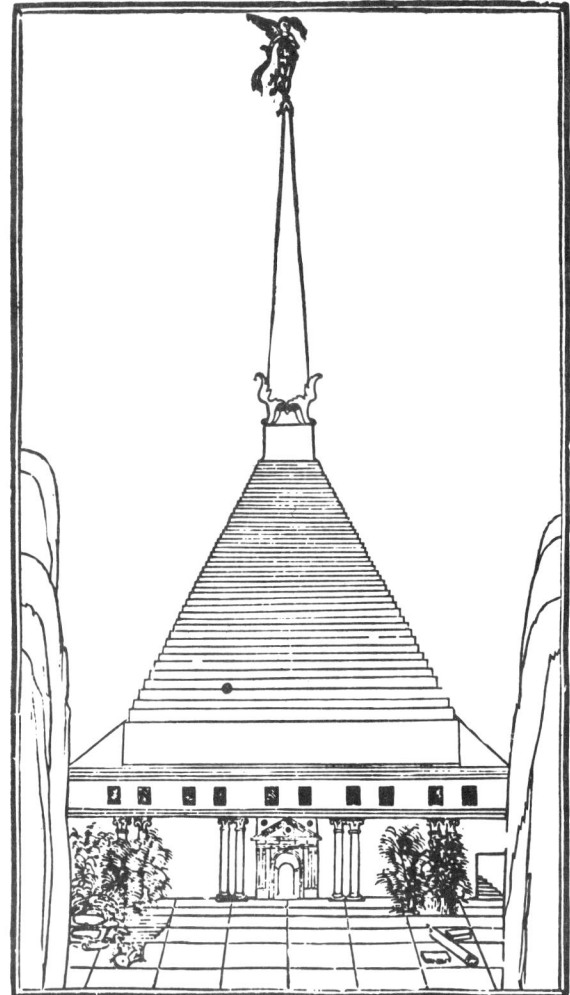

I-3.

I-3.

Francesco Colonna (1433?-1522?, Dominican friar), *Hypnertomachia Poliphili,* Venice, 1499, with many later editions and translations (crit. ed. G. Pozzi and L.A. Ciapponi, Padua, 1964, 2v.).

The identity of one Fra Francesco Colonna as the author of the *Hypnerotomachia* is only indirectly revealed in a cryptic sentence made by the first letters of succeeding chapters. He has been most plausibly recognized as a Dominican friar of Ss. Giovanni e Paolo in Venice. This Fra Francesco was born in 1433 and died in 1522, spending most of his life in Venice itself with occasional short stays in Treviso. The monastery records confirm an interest both in sex and art. His documented periods outside the monastery would have provided opportunities both for his amours and for contact with the many antiquarians then active in the Veneto.

The "Dream-love-fight of Poliphilus" is a Romance in two sections. The first and longer part tells the story of Poliphilus's search for his beloved Polia ending in a reunion which is brief but happy. The second tells the story of Polia herself. The work purports to have been written in Treviso in 1467 but the first part at least can only have been composed in the ten years or so before 1499 when it was published by Aldus Manutius in a beautiful edition illustrated with many woodcuts. It is a remarkable work using an Italian language rich in Latin forms. As a Romance combining architectural and erotic interests it depends on a medieval tradition. But the detailed knowledge and application of architectural theories deriving from Vitruvius and Alberti gives it a considerable importance as a document of architectural thought. Most revealing is the analysis of the gate in the bottom of the pyramid which constitutes a miniature treatise. The theme of this analysis is the equivalence between architectural and musical composition and a belief in this equivalence can be seen to underlie a repeated use of architecture for new expressive purposes.

John Onians

I-4.

Francesco di Giorgio Martini (1439-1501, painter, sculptor, architect, engineer), *Trattati di architettura, ingegneria e arte militare* (facs. ed., Maltese, Milan, 1967).

Francesco in fact produced two complete architectural treatises, (on architecture and on civil and military engineering, known as the *Trattati di architettura, ingegneria e arte militare*). Most of his career was spent in the employ of the dukes of Urbino, Federigo da Montefeltro and his son Guidobaldo, in the 1470s and 1480s, and in that of Alfonso, Duke of Calabria, in Naples after 1492. However, in 1490 he also worked in Milan, to advise on the construction of the dome of the cathedral, then traveled with Leonardo to Pavia, again to advise on the construction of the cathedral in that city. Among his principal architectural works are Santa Mario delle Calcinaio, Cortona; S. Bernardino, Urbino; and work on the Ducal Palace in that city. His most famous work as a sculptor is the group of bronze angel candlesticks made for the high altar of the Duomo, Siena.

The *Trattati* treat the entire scope of Renaissance architectural practice from the origins of building to the classical Orders, church and palace design, the qualifications of architects, site planning and military inventions. The earlier treatise dates before c. 1476 and the later was composed after Francesco had studied a reasonably accurate text of Vitruvius. The earlier one is uneven, unfinished and bolstered by passages translated from a corrupt Vitruvius text. All existing manuscripts of the *Trattati* are copies of Francesco's lost originals, except for parts of Codex Magliabechianus II.I.141 in Florence. The full text of each was published by Corrado Maltese. Richard J. Betts showed recently that 1476 is a more likely date for the earlier treatise on the basis of a manuscript in the Spencer Collection in the New York Public Library (Ms. 127).

The manuscript in the Yale collection incorporates the earlier version of the *Trattati,* and is particularly close to a version in the Biblioteca Laurenziana, Florence. It is slightly longer than the Laurenziana version, however, and was probably written in Siena in the 1480s. It has no author's name, title or headings, and is on paper 412mm x 236mm in double columns of 38 to 40 lines. It is written by a single scribe in brown ink, in a cursive Italic hand. The drawings are in brown ink, sometimes with green and pink washes. Often they have been pasted onto the leaves of the manuscript; they are probably by several hands. The flyleaf has a penciled note "Tommaso Obizzi 1776 Cremona."

Francesco's *Trattati* are notable for their emphasis on the human analogy in architecture and for their intricate mathematical formulas, both of which were to be used in the design of buildings. Francesco was the first architectural treatise writer to illustrate fully the functional requirements of different kinds of secular buildings. He had a strong influence on Leonardo, who owned a copy of the treatise and made notes in it.

George Hersey and
Susan Ryan

I-5.

Marcus Vitruvius Pollio [*De architectura*] [Rome, Heroldt, 1486/92] (ed. Johannes Sulpitius Verulanus, 2nd half 15c, grammarian).

The *editio princeps* of Vitruvius' *De architectura* does not have a title, the place of printing, the name of the printer, or the date. It begins directly with the letter of its editor to the reader: "Io. Sulpitius lectori salutem." However, from the following dedicatory letter to Cardinal Riarius, it can be safely supposed that the *editio princeps* of Vitruvius was printed in Rome between 1486 and 1492. The humanist, in fact, speaks there of himself as being in Rome, of a war just ended, and of Innocent VIII as the reigning Pope. The war between Rome and the kingdom of Naples, the only one of the time, ended in August 1486; Innocent VIII died in 1492.

Iohannes Sulpitius of Veroli was born in the middle of the XVth century. Very little is known of his life, except that he was a professor of grammar at the University of Perugia in the seventies before moving to Rome, where he founded his own school, belonged to the Accademia of Pomponius Laetus, and became a protegé of Card. Raphael Riarius, to whom he dedicated his edition of the *De architectura.* Together with Pomponius Laetus he prepared at the same time the *editio princeps* of Frontinus' *De aquaeductibus urbis Romae,* which immediately follows the text of the *De architectura.*

The manuscript tradition of Vitruvius is very corrupt. Sulpitius, a grammarian with a limited knowledge of architecture and engineering, was courageous to undertake the task of editing the *De architectura.* In his edition he followed the text of the more common manuscripts, but was forced to leave blank spaces for the Greek words and epigrams and for the illustrations (he attempted only one, a circle). Despite its weaknesses, his edition brought the Vitruvian text to the attention of scholars with more technical expertise who continued to work on the Vitruvian text throughout the following century.

Lucia Ciapponi Stadter

I-6.

Marcus Vitruvius Pollio, *M. Vitruvius per iocundum solito castigatior factus, cum figuris et tabula, ut iam legi et intelligi possit,* Venice, Tacuino, 1511 (ed. Fra Giovanni Giocondo, 1434?-1515, humanist, architect, engineer).

Giocondo was employed during his long life by Ferdinand King of Naples, by Charles VIII and Louis XII of France, the Venetian Republic, and Pope Leo X, who in 1513 appointed him architect of St. Peter's with Raphael and Bramante. In his later years he was also an editor of classical authors: for his friend Aldus Manutius he edited Nonius Marcellus (1513), Caesar (1513), and the *Scriptores Rei Rusticae* (1514). However, the most famous of his publications is this edition of the *De architectura* of Vitruvius printed in Venice by Iohannes Tacuinus of Trinus in 1511.

Fra Giocondo is the first editor to attempt a critical edition of Vitruvius. He used manuscripts of different families, corrected textual mistakes, filled *lacunae,* and restored the Greek in the text. For the first time the readers were provided with no less than 136 illustrations, a glossary, and a mathematical table to understand the text. The edition was popular: it was reprinted with the text of Frontius's *De aquaeductibus urbis Rome* in 1513 in Florence by the Giunta brothers in smaller size with four more figures (bringing the total to 140), in 1522 another Florence edition, and a final edition, which appeared in 1523, and does not give the place of printing, but is now thought to be a counterfeit of Lyon. Both the text and the illustrations of Giocondo's edition influenced successive editions of the *De architectura* throughout the sixteenth century.

Lucia Ciapponi Stadter

I-6.

I-7.

Marcus Vitruvius Pollio, *Di Lucio Vitruvio Pollione De architectura libri dece traducti de latino in Vulgare affigurati: Comentati: & con mirando ordine insigniti,* Como, Gotardus de Ponte, 1521 (ed. Cesare di Lorenzo Cesariano, 1483-1543, painter, architect) (facs. eds., New York, 1968; Munich, 1969).

Cesariano studied briefly as a youth with Bramante, and painted altarpieces and frescoes in Lombardy and Emilia before returning to his birthplace, Milan, where several minor but handsome works of architecture have been attributed to him. He never visited Rome itself. He began work on his Vitruvius edition c. 1513. Several illustrations bear dates of 1517-1520, and much of the commentary can be dated on internal evidence to 1519-1521. In the spring of 1521, his publishing collaborators commissioned others to finish the commentary, using materials taken from Cesariano by force. The commentary text after c. 154v is the work of Benedetto Giovio of Como and Bono Mauro of Bergamo, and is less informative than Cesariano's part.

Cesariano's edition is important historically because it was the first vernacular translation of Vitruvius to be printed, and it had the first printed commentary, also in Italian. Its illustrations are of un-precedented richness in Vitruvius editions. The format, the contents, and the pictures influenced subsequent editions in Italy, France, and Germany. The commentary, while incorrect from the viewpoint of modern scholarship, nevertheless contains information about local artists and taste, and about events and important people in northern Italy. The illustrations show how the precepts of the ancient Roman author were interpreted in localities outside Rome, creating local variants of Renaissance style.

Carol Herselle Krinsky

I-7.

I-8.

Marcus Vitruvius Pollio, *M. L. Vitruvio Pollione De architectura traducto di Latino in vulgare dal vero esemplare con le figure a li soi loci con mirando ordine insignito*... Venice, Ioañe Antonio & Piero fratelli di Sabio (ed. Francesco Lutio, of Durantino, 1st half 16c., painter).

Durantino was a painter of modest stature active in central Italy until the mid-sixteenth century. His most noteworthy accomplishment appears to have been this edition of Vitruvius's *Ten Books*, whose preface he signed.

This is the second earliest Italian translation of Vitruvius. The text, accompanied by a lengthy index, is a slightly improved version of the translation published by Cesariano at Como in 1521, while the woodcut illustrations are copied directly from Fra Giocondo's edition of 1511. In editing his volume, Durantino responded to the demands of an expanding readership. With little effort he produced a volume that was attractive to a growing number of non-Latinist patrons, artists and builders. The enterprise was successful enough to call for a second printing, with further textual revisions, in 1535.

Richard J. Tuttle

I-9.

Marcus Vitruvius Pollio, *Architectura, con il suo commento et figure. Vetruvio in volgar lingua raportato per M. Gianbattista Caporali di Perugia*. Perugia, Stamparia del conte Iano Bigazzini, 1536 (ed. Giovanni Battista Caporali, c. 1475-1555, painter and architect).

Caporali was a collaborator of Pietro Perugino and Pinturicchio, through whom he seems to have met Bramante in Rome around 1508-9. His intellectual pursuits, which included historical and musical studies, were supported by Count Giano Bigazzini, who edited the *Architectura*. Little is known of his architectural oeuvre, but tradition credits Caporali with having been the first teacher of Galeazzo Alessi.

The *Architectura* is an Italian translation of the first five books of Vitruvius with an extensive polemical commentary aimed at correcting errors in Cesariano's edition of 1521. Caporali's work, despite its erudition, is essentially derivative, as are many of the illustrations, which are based on Cesariano's. The incomplete translation undoubtedly discouraged wide diffusion and influence, but it is noteworthy that Daniele Barbaro consulted this edition in preparing his important Vitruvius of 1556.

Richard J. Tuttle

I-10.

Marcus Vitruvius Pollio, *Architecture, ou Art de bien bastir*, Paris, Jacques Gazeau, 1547 (ed. Jean Martin (?-c. 1553, translator, publisher) (facs. ed., Ridgewood, New Jersey, 1964).

Martin, secretary of Monseigneur le Cardinal de Lenoncourt, was a popularizer who helped to spread the vocabulary of the Italian Renaissance architecture north of the Alps. He was in charge of décor for the classical Renaissance entries of Henri II to Lyon and Paris in 1548 and 1549. As a professional translator, he played an important role in making architectural works known in France: from 1545 on, he was preparing a French version of Serlio; in 1546, he published a translation of F. Colonna's *Hypnerotomachia Poliphili* with new engravings by French artists; in 1547, this Vitruvius edition; and in 1553, Alberti's *L'Architecture* which appeared posthumously and includes the following "Epitaph for Jean Martin" by Ronsard:

> Tandis qu'à tes edifices
> Tu faisois des frontispices,
> Des termes, des chapiteaux,
> Ta truelle et tes marteaux
> N'ont seu de ta destinée
> Rompre d'heure terminée.

Dedicated to King Henri II, this is the first complete French translation of Vitruvius. The first eight books may have been translated by Abel Foulon, who may also be responsible for the glossary of architectural terms appended to the book. Martin's preface acknowledges the new illustrations by Jean Goujon "formerly architect of monseigneur the Connestable, and now one of yours." Most of the woodcuts, however, are from the Durantino Italian edition, copying Giocondo's work, or based on illustrations from Cesariano's edition; theatrical illustrations are from Barbé's Serlio of 1545. The woodcut portrait on the title page is probably of Jean Martin, although Vitruvius and the printer Jean Barbé have been suggested. A second edition of Martin's translation was published in Paris in 1572, a third edition, in which the Philander illustrations replaced those by Goujon, and some of the Philander annotations were translated, appeared in Tours in 1618.

Naomi Miller

I-10.

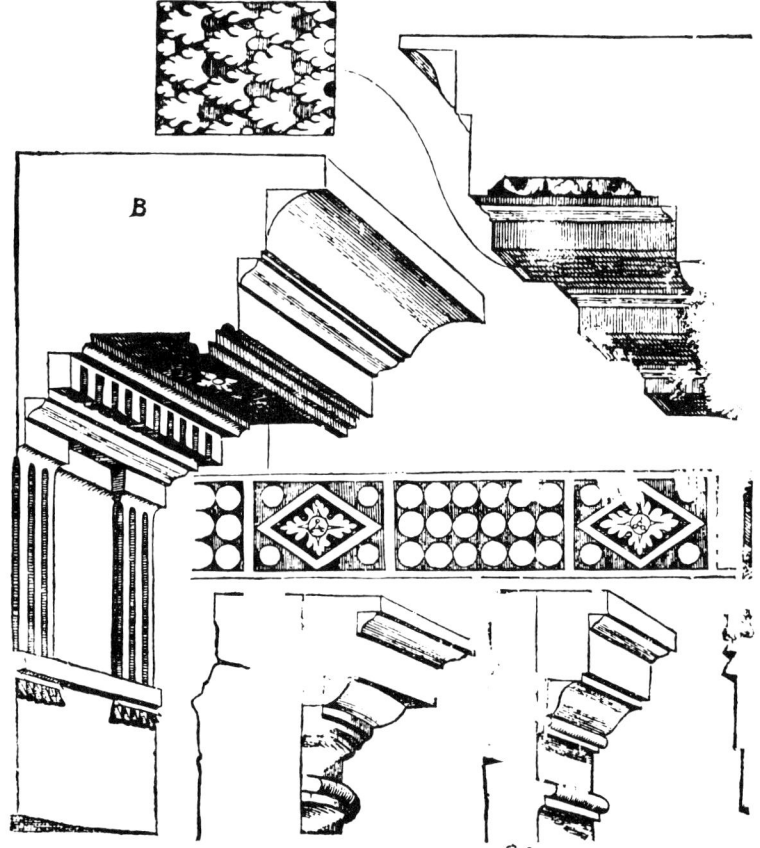

I-12.

I-11.

Marcus Vitruvius Pollio, *Vitruvius Teutsch. Nemlichen des aller Namhafftigisten uñ Hocherfarnesten Roemischen Architecti und Kunstreichen Werck oder Bawmeisters Marci Vitruvij Pollionis Zehen Buecher von der Architectur und Kunstlichem Bawen*, Nurnberg, Johannes Petreius, 1548 (ed. Walther Hermann Ryff, fl. 1550, physician, mathematician, writer) (later eds., Basil, 1574, 1582, 1614) (facs. ed., Hildesheim, 1973).

Ryff was a prolific author. Among his many publications are several Vitruvius editions and an architectural treatise. In these books, Ryff emphasizes his interest in applied mathematics, illustrating the tools and methods used in measuring.

This first German-language annotated edition of Vitruvius, in which Cesariano's commentary to his 1521 Italian-language edition was translated and appended to the end of each chapter, was intended for "craftsmen, builders, stonemasons, architects, military and civil engineers, hydraulic engineers, metal workers and painters, sculptors, goldsmiths, cabinet-makers, and all those who use artful circles and rectangles . . ."

Dora Wiebenson

I-12.

Sebastiano Serlio (c. 1475-1554/5, painter, architect, architectural theoretician), *Tutte l'opere d'architectura* (facs. 1584 ed. Lib. I-VII, Ridgewood, 1964; 1611 Eng. ed. Lib. I-V, New York, 1970; 1552 Span. ed. Lib. III-IV, Valencia, 1977).

Son of an obscure painter, Serlio worked as a painter in Pesaro (1511-1515) and at Bologna (1525). During this period or before, he spent several years at Rome and studied architecture under the direction of Baldassare Peruzzi. From 1528 to 1541 he worked in Venice as an architect, and conceived the idea of an illustrated treatise on architecture divided into seven books, and published two of them: Book IV (on the Orders) (1537), and Book III (on the antiquities of Rome) (1540). In 1541 he went to France to enter the service of François I and, after a period in Paris, worked at Fontainebleau up to the accession of Henri II (1547). During this period he prepared the first version of Book VI (on houses) (the ms. is now in New York). Conforming to the original project, the publication of his treatise continued in Paris with the appearance of Books I and II (on geometry and perspective) (1545), and of Book V (on temples) (1547). After leaving Fontainebleau, Serlio worked in Lyon, where he executed several minor works and published in 1551 a collection of engraved models of rustic gates, which, as the title *Libro extraordinario* indicates, was not a part of the unpublished Book VI in editions of Serlio's collected works. In Lyon Serlio developed a second version of Book VI (the ms. is now in Munich), finished Book VII (on models of palazzi and examples of restorations) and completed his treatise with Book VIII (on the architecture of the military camps of the ancients). Book VII would be published in Italian and Latin in 1575 in Frankfurt by the antiquarian Jacopo Strada, who purchased the manuscript from Serlio in 1552/3 (the date of 1550 that Strada gives in the preface is not compatible with the chronology of his travels). As for Book VIII, also sold to Strada, it remains in manuscript. After having passed six years in Lyon, Serlio returned to Fontainebleau where he died.

Vladimir Juřen
Dora Wiebenson, translation

I-13.

Claudio Tolomei (1481-1556, humanist, diplomat, writer), *De le lettere lib. sette*, Venice, G. Giolito de Ferrari, 1547 (Tolomei to Count Agostino de' Landi, 14 November 1542).

In this letter Tolomei outlines the activity and the goals of the Roman *Accademia della Virtù*. The *Accademia*, originally established to implement the transposing of literary forms, grammar and vocabulary from classical Latin to modern Italian, turned after 1539 to a study of Vitruvius's treatise. At this time it was composed of humanists, grammarians, philologians, antiquarians and archaelogists. According to the letter, the *Accademia* had formulated an eight-point program:
1) a Latin commentary on the difficult passages of Vitruvius,
2) a new critical edition of Vitruvius,
3) a Latin lexicon of terms used in Vitruvius,
4) a Greek lexicon of terms used in Vitruvius,
5) an edition of Vitruvius rewritten in good Latin style,
6) a translation of Vitruvius's text into the Tuscan language followed by a lexicon of Tuscan terms,
7) a collection of the principles and examples taken from Vitruvius,
8) a study of the ancient buildings of Rome, and of its sculpture, medals, and works of hydraulic and military engineering.

Despite the removal of this group from active participation in architecture, it may have had considerable impact on the establishing of the selective methodology and the intellectual rigor of later architectural theoreticians. Among its members were Guillaume Philander and for a short period Vignola. Palladio, Delorme, Barbaro and Rusconi all may have visited the *Accademia* or have had contact with its members.

Dora Wiebenson

I-14.

Guillaume Philander (1505-1565, scholar, philologian, architect), *Gulielmi Philandri Castilioni Gall. Civis Ro. In decem libros M. Vitruvii Pollionis De architectura annotationes ad Franciscum Valesium Regem Christianissimum. Cum indicibus Graeco et Latino locupletissimis*, Rome, Go. Andrea Dossena, 1544 (later eds. 1545, 1557).

Educated by a philologian, Philander entered the circle of Georges d'Armagnac, bishop of Rodez, in 1533, and accompanied him to Venice in 1536, where he became Serlio's pupil. After removing to Rome in 1539, Philander participated with the Accademia della Virtù in its discussions on Vitruvius's text, and in 1544, just before departing for France, published his annotations to that text. He continued his previous architectural work on his return to Rodez, his major contribution being the classical additions to the Gothic Cathedral at Rodez.

Of all editions related to Vitruvius's treatise, Philander's commentary was republished the most; first without the Vitruvian text, but from 1550 including it. His work was an attempt to clarify the meaning of the ancient text, and he stated in his dedication to François I: "I purged it from so many mistakes that I dare to assert that I have a firm interpretation except for a few places which not even Apollo could have deciphered." Although Philander wrote in Latin and his work is still representative of philological and scholarly interst in the classical world, he also selected and synthesized material that he would have received from Serlio. He is the first of the "scholar-architects" of the mid-sixteenth century.

Dora Wiebenson and
Elise M. Quasebarth

I-15.

I-15.

Leone Battista Alberti, *L'architettura di Leonbatista Alberti: tradotta in lingua Fiorentina da Cosimo Bartoli*, Florence, L. Torrentino, 1550 (ed. C. Bartoli, 1503-1572, humanist, connoisseur, translator, writer).

Bartoli was in the service of the Church and the Medici for the greater part of his life: his friendship with Vasari may have established his patterns of taste. His fortunate inheritance of a group of fifteenth century manuscripts, among them writings of Alberti and the Zibaldone of Buonaccorso Ghiberti, caused him to undertake one of his major enterprises — the translating of Alberti's *De re aedificatoria*, which, despite its fame and probably because of its profundity, was seldom published. Bartoli's version is the first illustrated edition, and the second translation of his work. His uncritical and freely interpreted text caused his work to be not highly regarded by scholars. The illustrations with their emphasis on contemporary building practice, and their simple even derivative character reflect mid-century concerns on relating practice to theory. This translation would become the standard edition of Alberti's treatise and the source of the eighteenth century Leoni folio English editon.

Dora Wiebenson

I-16.

Marcus Vitruvius Pollio, *M. Vitruvii Pollionis viri suae professionis peritissimi De architectura libri X*, Strasbourg, Officina Knoblochiana, 1550 (ed. Georgio Machaeropieo).

Using the 1543 Latin Strasbourg edition of Vitruvius, and those illustrations (which were taken mainly from Cesariano), this Vitruvius edition included Philander's Latin annotations and illustrations at the end of each chapter along with Philander's dedication to François I, his Life of Vitruvius, and the "Architecti Virtutes."

Dora Wiebenson

I-17.

Marcus Vitruvius Pollio, *M. Vitruvii Pollionis De architectura libri decem*, Lyon, Jean de Torneas, 1552 (annotations, G. Philander).

With the text of the 1513 Giocondo edition, and including an enlarged and revised version of Philander's commentary and illustrations (sometimes attributed to Serlio), this edition also includes Philander's epitome of George Agricola's *De mensuris et ponderibus libros*.

Philander was considerably embarrassed at the discovery of an unkept promise about this publication, as Tomaso Spica records in 1549 in a letter to his friend Diogeni Atanagi: "Regarding the work of Philander, allow me to excuse myself to you, for it can no longer be advanced. When we arrived here I asked him to give it to me according to the agreement we made in Rome. He immediately stiffened and holding onto his beard with one of his hands he stroked it many times, and with his other he snapped his fingers as Spaniards do when they dance, and turning his eyes up he kept them fixed for a while on the vault of the loggia, and finally said that he had changed his mind and that he now intended to send it to Lyon to be printed."

This revised version of Philander's commentary and illustrations was reprinted in 1586, and then appeared in altered form in a French (1618) and a Latin (1648) edition.

Dora Wiebenson

I-18.

Antonio Labacco, (c. 1495-1580, architect), *Libro d'Antonio Labacco appartenente a l'architettura nel qual si figurano alcune notabili antiquita di Roma*, Rome, 1552, in Casa nostra, and many later editions.

A student of Sangallo the younger, Labacco is best known for his construction of the grand wooden model of St. Peter's after Sangallo's designs of 1547. He also worked with Sangallo on the fortifications of Parma and Piancenza in the 1520's. He is believed to have died c. 1580 in Rome.

A product of the revived interest in antiquities and archaelogy of the Renaissance, *Libro d'Antonio Labacco* consists of 36 plates, including frontispiece, etched by his son Mario. They show views and reconstructions of ancient Rome buildings such as the Trajan arch, the temple of Castor and Pollux, a centralized plan for S. Giovanni dei Fiorentini, and plans of the port of Hadrian. Despite some inaccuracies this book was widely popular. No two copies appear to be the same, and the history and extent of these many republications remains unclear.

Martin C. Perdue

I-18.

I-19.

Jean Gardet (fl. 1550's, philologian) and Dominique Bertin (fl. 1550's, architect), *Epitome, ou extrait abrégé des dix livres d'architecture de Marc Vitruve Pollion*, Tolouse, Guion Boudeville, 1559 (later eds. 1565, 1568, 1597).

This abridged edition of Vitruvius includes all the most recent innovations associated with the classical treatise: annotations (for the first three Books only), illustrations related to the practice of architecture, the collaboration of scholar and architect, and also a popular abridged format. However, it makes no original contribution to the Vitruvius editions, other than that of being the first edition to incorporate engraved illustrations in an architectural treatise. Despite the three subsequent editions within the next four decades, the work was all but forgotten during the seventeenth century.

Dora Wiebenson

I-20.

Marcus Vitruvius Pollio, *Della architettura, di Gio. Antonio Rusconi, con centosessanta figure dissegnate dal Medesimo. Secondo i precetti di Vitruvio, e con chiarezza, e brevità dichiarate. Libri Dieci*, Venice, Giolito, 1590 (ed. Giovanni Antonio Rusconi (c. 1520-1586/9, architect and engineer) (facs. ed., Farnborough, 1968).

Rusconi studied with the mathematician Niccolo Tartaglia, and probably designed the illustrations for his *Quesiti et inventioni diversi . . .* , a work on problems in pure and applied science published in 1546 in Venice. Rusconi worked as an architect and engineer in the Veneto, collaborating with Palladio on several projects. He probably began work on his book, an Italian translation and commentary with illustrations, in the early 1540's: a letter from Claudio Tolomei (the chief member of the Accademia della Virtù) to Rusconi, dated before 1553, describes the work as nearly completed, and praises Rusconi for his interpretation of the text.

The text and commentary of Rusconi's manuscript are now lost, the illustrations, published posthumously with summaries of the contents of Vitruvius's ten books by the publisher Giolito, are unique solutions to the problem of the visual communication of complex architectural information. Rusconi turns to the more developed methods of pictorial communication of the fields of anatomy and botany. He may have been directly influenced by Vesalius's *De humani corporis fabrica*, Basel, 1543, and by such works as Fuch's *De historia stirpium*, Basel, 1542.

Dora Wiebenson

I-21.

Marcus Vitruvius Pollio, *I dieci libri dell'architettura di M. Vitruvio tradutti et commentati da Monsignor Barbaro eletto patriarca d'Aquileggia*, Venice, Francesco Marcolini, 1556 (ed. Daniele Barbaro, 1514-1570, Venetian patriarch and humanist).

Barbaro's career was one of remarkable diversity. Educated at the University of Padua, where he studied a range of subjects, including classical philology and moral philosophy, mathematics and natural science, he received his first official state appointment in that city, when, in 1547, he was charged with the creation of the research-oriented botanical garden. From 1548 to 1551 he served as Venetian ambassador to the English court; during his absence he was appointed patriarch elect of Aquileia, a position that he would never fully assume but which led to his active participation at the Council of Trent in 1562-1563. In Venice he is credited with the iconographic program for the ceiling of the Sala del Consiglio dei Dieci in the Ducal Palace, painted by Paolo Veronese and others between 1553 and 1555. By then Barbaro had already initiated his greatest project as a patron, the family villa at Maser, designed by Andrea Palladio and frescoed by Veronese. Barbaro's publications reflect the variety of his early studies, essentially Aristotelian, as well as his subsequent theological concerns; his books include a treatise on Porphyry's *Isagoge* (1542), a commentary on the Latin translations by Ermolao Barbaro, his great uncle, of Aristotle's *Rhetoric* and the *Nichomachean Ethics* (1544), a dialogue on eloquence (1557), and a commentary on the Psalms of David (1569).

Barbaro's most sumptuous and significant publication was his translation of and commentary on Vitruvius's ten books *De architectura*. Although it had been preceded by other editions of Vitruvius — most notably those of Fra Giocondo (1511) and Cesare Cesariano (1521) — Barbaro's appears as the splendid culmination of the Renaissance tradition of Vitruvian studies. In the preparation of the volume, which may have begun as early as 1547, Barbaro enjoyed the active collaboration

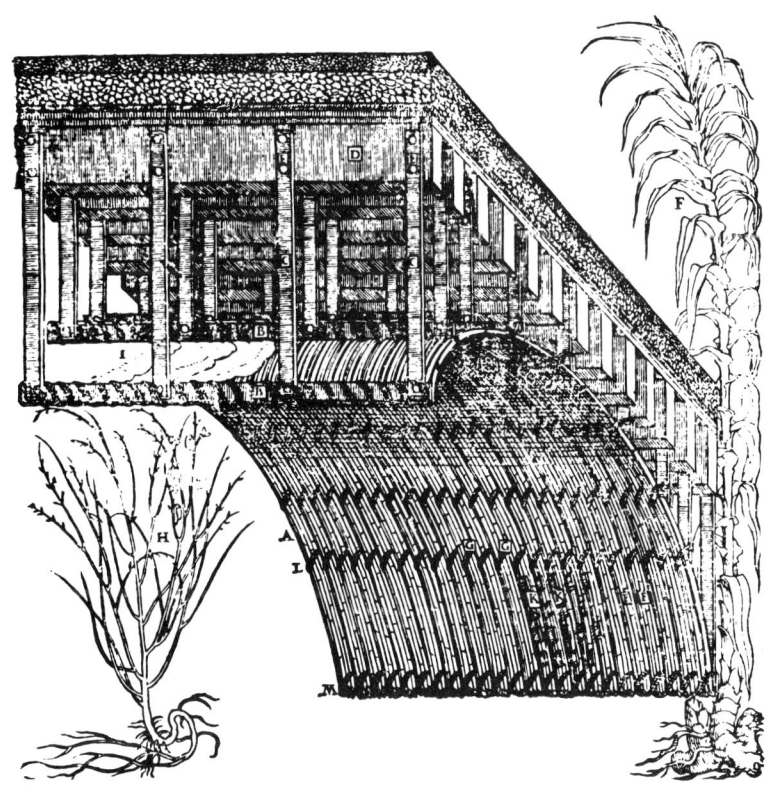

I-20.

of Palladio himself, who not only designed the most important illustrations but also contributed his own fund of experience and expertise, archaeological as well as architectural. Barbaro's acknowledgement of Palladio's help specifically cites his work on the ancient Roman theater. As impressive as the illustrations is Barbaro's own commentary, basically Aristotelian, in which a single line or even word of Vitruvius's text becomes the occasion for a full disclosure; the extensive learning of the commentator is evident throughout. Taking his cue from Vitruvius, Barbaro ranges widely. His commentary includes a broad philosophical discussion of the arts, in which pride of place is given to architecture, since it is so closely based on mathematics and hence approximates to the pure intellect; on less exalted levels, the commentary extends to the more practical matters of building and machines. A second edition, revised and expanded, although of smaller format, was published in Venice in 1567 by Francesco de Franceschi and Giovanni Chreigher, who also issued a Latin edition in the same year. Later editions appeared in 1584, 1629, and 1641, all in Venice.

David Rosand

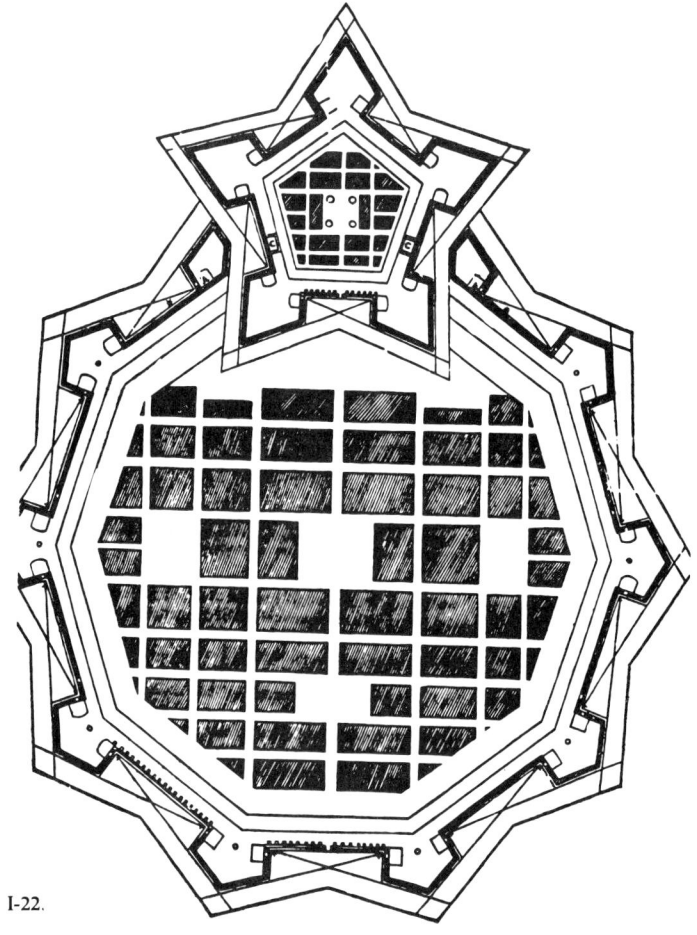

I-22.

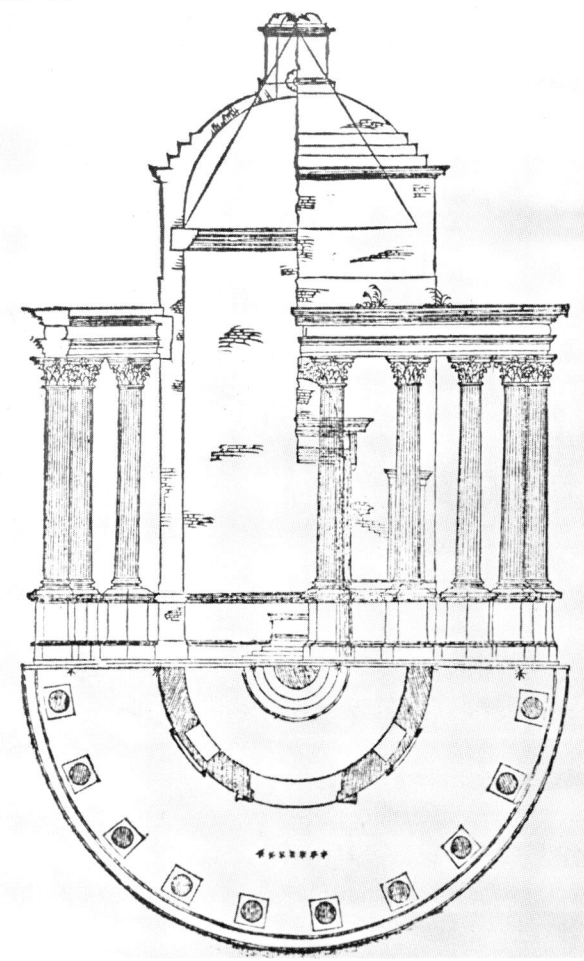

I-21.

I-22.

Pietro Cataneo (1510-1569, artist, architect, engineer), *L'architettura di Pietro Cataneo Senese,* Venice, figliuoli di Aldo, 1567 (facs. 1554 ed., Ridgewood, 1964).

Cataneo was probably trained in the circle of Baldassare Peruzzi in Siena (c. 1527-1535) and had close relations with other Sienese artists; a sister was married to the painter Domenico Beccafumi. We know relatively little about his work in Siena; there is no painting or sculpture attributed to him and no securely documented building. It is likely that he worked closely with Peruzzi, possibly superintending his works. During the 1540's and early 1550's, after Peruzzi's death (1536), Cataneo was active throughout the Sienese republic as a fortification engineer and visited many of the outlying contado towns (Talamone, Campagnatico, Asinalunga). During a lull in the Sienese wars, possibly during the summer of 1553, Cataneo moved to Venice where his first treatise, *I Quattro Primi Libri di Architettura* was published in 1554.

Cataneo was deeply indebted to the *Trattati* of Francesco di Giorgio Martini and the *Architettura* of Sebastiano Serlio and to his years with Peruzzi. *L'architettura* was composed of eight books, four from the 1554 treatise and four new works. The four original books deal with fortifications, building materials, churches, palaces and private houses. Cataneo is the last of the Renaissance architectural treatise writers to consider military and civil architecture together. The most original of the chapters is that on military architecture. Using pentagonal and star plans Cataneo shows how city plan, walls and topography can form a unified defence organism. This combination makes Cataneo's work an especially valuable tool for the study of actual fortifications rather than merely for theories of defence; it is rich in references to the Sienese wars. The four books added in 1567 deal with ornament, water resources, geometry and perspective and largely reflect Cataneo's later experiences in Venice.

Published by Aldo Manuzio in Venice many of the illustrations use an unusual perspective presentation. Although Canateo's treatises were much admired at the time and he was, personally, in contact with Palladio, his works did not gain the kind of distribution or exert the kind of European-wide influence of either Palladio or Serlio. There are, so far as I know, no translations of his works.

Nicholas Adams

I-23.

Walter Hermann Ryff, *Der Furnembsten Notwendigsten der Gantzen Architectur Angehörigen Mathematischen und Mechanischen Kunst eygentlicher Bericht und vast klare Verstendliche Unterrichtung zu Rechtem Verstandt der Lehr Vitruvii in drey furneme Bücher abgetheilet,* Nurnberg, Johannes Petreius, 1547.

This treatise includes a composite of illustrative material from Serlio (mainly on perspective), Giocondo, and other sources including Ryff's own *Vitruvius Teutsch*. It is divided into three books, with many inserts on related material, on the "new perspective," on practical geometry (especially on its application to ballistics), on building materials and technology and on geometrical instruments and proportions.

Dora Wiebenson

I-24.

Philibert Delorme (c. 1510-1570, architect, mason), *Le premier tome de l'architecture,* Paris, Federic Morel, 1567 (facs. ed., Ridgewood, 1964).

Delorme was born in Lyon, the son of a master mason. From 1533-36, he was in Rome, where he studied and measured antiquities, became acquainted with modern works, and enjoyed the society of other architects and humanists, including Rabelais and the Cardinal Du Bellay. His first important commission was the Château of Saint Maur-les-Fossés in 1541-45 for the Cardinal, notable for its Italianate features. With the accession to the throne of Henri II in 1547, Delorme became architect to the King and superintendent of all royal buildings with the exception of the Louvre. By far the most innovative architect of the sixteenth century in France, only fragments of his works survive, the most significant being the Château of Anet, built for Diane de Poitiers, the mistress of Henri II. Following the latter's death in 1559, he fell from royal favor and turned to writing on architecture. His first work,

I-24.

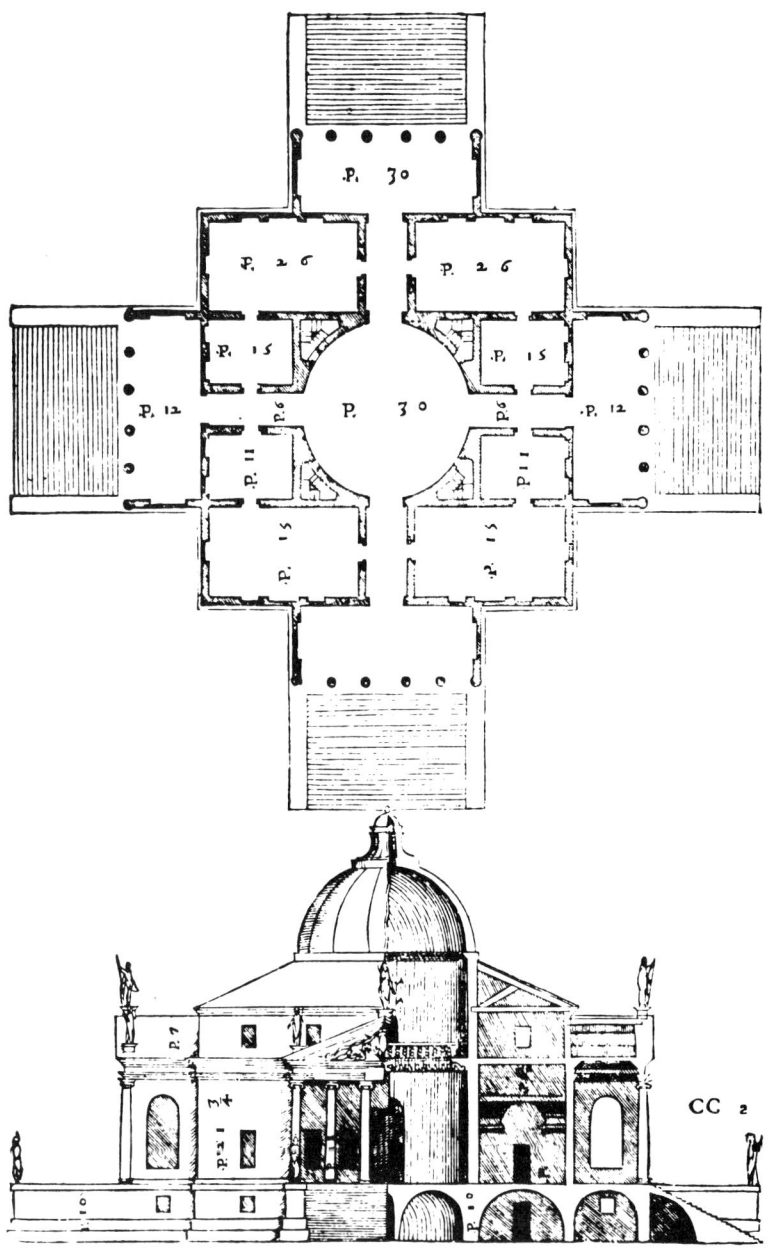

I-25.

Nouvelles inventions pour bien bastir et à petit fraiz was a practical tract embodying his inventions for the construction in wood of vaulting and roofing.

Considered the most modern architectural treatise of the Renaissance, Delorme's *Architecture* is an amalgam of theory and practice. It comprises nine books and 205 woodcuts, and was dedicated to Catherine de' Medici. It owes much to Vitruvius, Alberti, and Serlio, as well as to the writings of contemporary humanists. In addition to its display of erudition, the treatise is remarkable as a personal statement, for the light it sheds on Delorme's own works, on the profession of architecture, and as a practical guide to building of the day. Here, as in *Nouvelles inventions* . . . , Delorme emerges as an artisan. His chapters on stereotomy confirm his ties with the stone work tradition of medieval France, and do his explications of his inventions such as the French order and in particular *trompes*. Cast in the medieval mode, too, are the three allegorical woodcuts, with their exegesis on the profession of the architect. Delorme frequently alludes to a planned second volume dealing with Divine Proportions, as transmitted by the Old Testament. This projected work was interrupted by his death. A second issue of *Architecture* appeared in 1568 and a third in 1576. A 1626 edition included *Nouvelles inventions pour bien bastir* . . . as Books X and XI, and a final 1648 edition, published in Rouen by David Ferrand, contains around 40 additional illustrations, many from the Giocondo edition of Vitruvius and from Serlio's treatise.

Naomi Miller

Books III and IV of Delorme's treatise are almost entirely devoted to stereotomy. This is the first known text on this subject. Delorme represents himself here as the inventor of this technique and he was recognized as such by all his French successors. With a few improvements the method of Delorme was used in France until the eighteenth century. Delorme presents stereotomy as one of the principal applications of geometry to architecture and as an essential technique of the growth of a new art, liberated from medieval empiricism.

Jean-Marie Pérouse de Montclos
Dora Wiebenson, translation

I-25.

Andrea Palladio (1508-1580, architect), *I quattro libri dell'architettura*, Venice, Domenico de' Franceschi, 1570 (facs. ed., Milan, 1968) (facs. Ware ed., New York, 1965).

Palladio's *Four Books of Architecture* cover general principles and the classical orders, palaces, villas, bridges and civic buildings, and temples (including churches). They really constitute one book, more cohesive than the seven published at various times by Sebastiano Serlio during the early years of Palladio's career (1537-50). There is little abstract theory: Palladio was a practical and straightforward writer who used words economically and liked to discuss actual situations. Most of the text relates to issues raised by existing buildings, partly ancient and partly modern — the latter being primarily of Palladio's own design. The manuscript was underway already in 1555, when it was mentioned by A.F. Dion, and Giorgio Vasari saw a revised text in Venice in 1566. The year after Palladio's death in 1580, his sons were preparing an expanded edition with a fifth book completed by their father, but it was never published.

The *Quattro Libri* exerted an astonishing impact on the architects and architecture of the centuries following its publication, and helped to make Palladio the most imitated architect of all time. In part this was due to Palladio's useful canon for the ancient orders, but to a far greater degree it was due to the illustration, in rather heavy-handed woodcuts, of Palladio's own civic and domestic buildings (in depicting his own work, Palladio occasionally altered the design used in the construction of the actual building, either to eliminate irregularities caused by the specific site, or to record his afterthoughts). The symmetry and harmony of Palladio's designs, effectively conveyed by his spare conception of the didactic image, appealed to future generations, particularly in Protestant Northern Europe, and stimulated the building of Palladian houses, palaces and villas. The *Quattro Libri* does not contain illustrations of Palladio's churches.

The book was republished frequently in Italy and abroad. The lavish London edition of 1715 translated by Giacomo Leoni was the harbinger of a second widespread Palladian revival in England (the first was launched by the work of Inigo Jones a century before). Peter Harrison and Thomas Jefferson, who both knew Palladio only from books, were the chief American exponents of the Palladian revival.

James S. Ackerman

I-26.
Vincenzo Scamozzi (1552/7-1616, architect, architectural theorist), *Dell'Idea dell'architettura universale di Vincenzo Scamozzi divisa in X Libri,* Venice, by the Author, 1615 (later eds. and translations) (facs. ed., Farnborough, 1964, 2v.).

After receiving his early education from his father, an architect, and in the intellectual circles of the Accademica Olympica and the Scuola di Seminaria, Scamozzi left Vicenza for Venice where he began a prestigious architectural career. By 1582, when he published his *Discorsi sopra l'antichita di Roma,* he was considering the publication of an encyclopaedic treatise on architecture in twelve books, on which he began work by 1591. By 1607 when he began the first draft he reduced his twelve books to ten, and by publication of the edition he had further reduced them to six: on the history and theory of architecture, town planning, civic and domestic architecture, the Orders, building materials, and construction. When Scamozzi died shortly thereafter, his extensive collections and unpublished material were dispersed, finding their way into libraries, collections, and into some of the many later editions of his work.

In the *Idea,* Scamozzi assumes that architecture "is a science which has its own certain and indisputable laws, which can be taught and demonstrated as with mathematics and other learned disciplines." But this apriorism, which replaces the objective foundation of architectural theory, results in a universal systematization in which all data from architectural experience (even Gothic) are included, opportunely dehistoricized, however, and neutralized. Although functional preoccupations and technical interests are included in the *Idea,* Scamozzi is intent on an eclectic presentation of abstract models which are purified of subjective judgment and reduced to the articulation of objective and scientific reality.

Loredana Olivato Puppi
Lavinia Lorch, translation

I-26.

I-27.

Giovanni Battista Montano (1534-1621, carpenter, architect), *Li cinque libri di architettura*, Rome, G. J. de Rossi, 1684-1691.

A reedition of four earlier volumes:
Scielta di varii tempietti antichi, Rome, 1624.
Diversi ornamenti capricciosi per depositi o altari, Rome, 1625.
Tabernacoli diversi, Rome, 1628.
Architettura con diversi ornamenti cavati dall'antico, Rome, 1636.

Montano was a Milanese carpenter who moved to Rome and took up architecture, doing a number of organs, a coffered ceiling, and a wooden model for Giacomo della Porta's project for a Cappella Medici at San Lorenzo in Florence. His one purely architectural commission was the facade of San Giuseppe dei Falegnami, designed in 1597. He is famous for his many studies after ancient ruins in the Roman countryside, which he drew partly from his own observations on the site, and partly from his "exquisite imagination," fueled by the reading of Serlio, Palladio, Duperac, and Ligorio. He had an acute sense of the complexities of Roman structure and planning, and often his plates convey the mystery of exploration in ruins, where the spectator progresses down dark tunnels into floodlit chambers, or through winding staircases to forgotten crypts and sepulchers.

Montano left behind a large corpus of drawings after the antique and at least part of a treatise on the Orders, which eventually found their way into the papers of Robert Adam and John Talman, but which first were entrusted to Montano's student Giovanni Battista Soria for publication. Soria began with a volume of Antique Temples in 1624 and concluded with a volume called Diverse Ornaments in 1636; the entire series was republished, though now divided into five rather than four volumes, between 1684 and 1691. The printed edition exerted a strong influence over the architecture of Bernini, Borromini and Cortona.

Joseph Connors

I-27.

I-28.

Sir Henry Wotton (1568-1639, diplomat, scholar, author, connoisseur), *The Elements of Architecture*, London, John Bill, 1624 (facs. ed., Charlottesville, Virginia, 1968).

Wotton, a favorite of James I, was knighted and sent to Venice as ambassador; his definition of that office is often cited — "An ambassador is an honest man sent to lie abroad for the good of his country." Although more widely known as a poet, Wotten reflects Elizabethan interests in architecture which were nurtured by his travels and diplomatic assignments from 1604-1624 and his observations and studies in Italy.

Wotton considers himself to be "but a gatherer and disposer of other mens stuffe at my best value." He acknowledges his debt to Vitruvius and to Alberti. But the *Elements* is not a paraphrase of Vitruvius; rather it is a compilation of Wotton's observations and studies of Italian architecture. Divided into two parts, the first deals with architecture, the second with ornament, i.e. painting and sculpture. The *Elements* is the first English text on architecture in the genre of handbook or treatise. As such, it is a record of the most sophisticated English taste of the time, a taste already on the wane in Italy where it was born. In its time, Wotton's treatise provided inspiration and advice for the practicing architect. As a fairly early especially charming and enthusiastic document marking the English preoccupation with Venetian architecture, the *Elements* is as appealing today as it was to the seventeenth-century cognoscenti. For us, it provides a theoretical parallel to the introduction of Palladianism in England manifest in Inigo Jones's almost contemporary Banqueting House. The book was translated into Latin in 1649 and into Spanish in 1698; it was reprinted many times: six reprints between 1649 and 1698, and five reprints between 1723 and 1825, and in 1901 and 1903.

Naomi Miller

I-29.

Giuseppe Viola Zanini (c. 1575-1629/31, painter, architect), *Della architettura di Giuseppe Viola Zanini padovano pittore et architetto libri due*, Padua, Francesco Bolzetta, 1626.

Viola Zanini was educated by his father, a building constructor. He remained a poor man all his life, mainly practicing painting to support himself and his family rather than his preferred field of architecture.

Zanini was working on his treatise by 1623 when it was planned to consist of three books. The last book, on fortresses, churches, fora, porticos and roads, was not published. The two published books (Book I on geometry, building materials, proportions and construction; Book II on the Orders) appear to be incomplete, possibly owing to Zanini's death before completion of final work on the text.

Although his treatise does not have the philosophical breadth, the rigorous doctrine, or the strong control of the subject of earlier treatises, from which it quotes repetitiously, its occasional concern with technical and functional problems suggests the climate of transition from the sixteenth century to the seventeenth century which was prevalent in the ambience of the University of Padua.

Loredana Olivato Puppi
Lavinia Lorch, translation

I-30.

Ioanne de Laet (1593-1649, editor), *M. Vitruvii Pollionis De architectura libri decem. Cum notis, castigationibus & observationibus Guilielmi Philandri integris; Danielis Barbari excerptis, & Claudii Salmasii passim insertis. Praemittuntur Elementa architecturae collecta ab . . . Henrico Wottono . . . Accedunt Lexicon Vitruvianum Bearnardini Baldi Urbinatis . . . et ejusdem Scamilli Impares Vitruviani. De pictura libri tres absolutissimi Leonis Baptistae Albertis. De Sculptura, excerpta maxime animadvertenda ex dialogo Pomponii Gaurici Neapolit. Ludovici Demontiosii Commentarius de sculptura et pictura. Cum variis indicibus copiosissimis*, Amsterdam, Ludwig Elzevir, 1649.

This extensive collection of Vitruviana and related subjects consists of, among other material, Vitruvius's text with excerpts from the commentaries of Philander and Barbaro, and the only Latin translation of Wotton's *Elements of Architecture*. De Laet used the 1552 edition of Philander's commentary, and included copies of illustrations from it in this work.

Dora Wiebenson

I-31.

Marcus Vitruvius Pollio, *Les dix livres d'architecture de Vitruve corrigez et traduits nouvellement en François, avec des notes et des figures*, Paris, J. B. Coignard, 1673 (ed. Claude Perrault, 1613-1688, physician, architect).

Perrault was the brother of Charles, chief assistant of Colbert, and Superintendent of Buildings of the King from 1664-80. Claude is now acknowledged by most scholars to be the leading designer, together with LeVau and Lebrun, of the east facade of the Louvre. Its antique conception, archaeological references and engineering feats are surely due to him. Unparalleled in its classicism, the east facade reflects Perrault's theoretical interests, also evident in his annotated edition of Vitruvius of 1673, enlarged in 1684, and in his *Ordonnance des cinq especes de colonnes selon la méthode des ancients* of 1683. A member of the Académie des Sciences, his ideas and research are included in *Mémoires pour servir a l'histoire naturelle des animaux* (1671-76) and *Essais de physique* (1680-88). Claude Perrault also designed the Observatoire in 1667 for the Académie des Sciences, began a model for a triumphal arch at the Porte St. Antoine in 1669, and designed the Château of Sceaux for Colbert in 1674.

Perrault's Vitruvius edition is a large folio of 325 pages with a 12 page index to text and notes; there are copious notes and numerous woodcut illustrations and explanatory diagrams on text pages, and 65 engraved plates, mostly after Le Pautre, of excellent quality. The book opens with a beautifully engraved frontispiece after a design by S. Leclerc, depicting the presentation of "The Ten Books of Architecture of Vitruvius," before a background where the newly built east facade of the Louvre is viewed across parade grounds. Dedicated to Louis XIV, this is the first authoritative translation and well-annotated commentary of Vitruvius; it became a standard work throughout Europe until the mid-nineteenth century. Perrault's original ideas, which were the subject of meetings of the Academy and generated an architectural version of the "Quarrel between the Ancients and the Moderns" with François Blondel, are stated in his preface. While acknowledging the authority of the rules, he asserts that they are derived from custom, rather than from reason or nature, according to the ancients. As he stated in his preface, "Beauty has hardly any other foundation than fantasy" and since everyone has different ideas of perfection "rules are necessary for forming and rectifying these ideas" . . . and thus he calls for "a definite authority taking the place of reason." In this context, the authority is Vitruvius.

Naomi Miller

I-32.

Claude Perrault, *Abregé des dix livres d'architecture de Vitruve*, Paris, J. Baptiste Coignard, 1674 (many later editions and translations).

In this epitome Perrault reorganizes and condenses the Vitruvian text into a thoroughly modern theory of positive and arbitrary beauty. To this he adds a selection of major classical monuments taken from the plates of his own folio Vitruvius edition. Perrault's folio edition marks the end to the development of a long tradition of the interpreting of the Vitruvian text; the epitome the beginning of a new one. Published in at least five languages and eleven editions over the following century, this small, popular book is oriented toward the amateur and the tastemaker.

Dora Wiebenson

I-33.

Marcus Vitruvius Pollio, *L'architettura di M. Vitruvio Pollione colla traduzione italiana e comento del Marchese Berardo Galiani*, Naples, Simoniana, 1758 (ed. Berardo Galiani, 1724-1774, archaeologist, scholar, theoretician, writer), (2nd ed. Italian text only; Naples, Siena, 1790).

Galiani was from a celebrated family. His famous brother, Fernando, was a distinguished political economist, and also known as the little Italian *abbé* who charmed his fellow *philosophes* in Paris with his brilliant and witty conversation. The uncle, Celestino Galiani, was director of studies at the University of Naples. Winckelmann wrote that his palace was the meeting place of the intellectuals of Naples; Berardo Galiani served as Winckelmann's guide to the excavations at Herculaneum. The Galiani brothers were influential members of the Accademia Ercolanese, founded by Charles III for the purpose of publishing the findings at Herculaneum. Berardo Galiani is remembered for his fine edition of Vitruvius; his work on aesthetics and his unfinished treatise on architecture have not been published. Upon his death in 1774 he left a manuscript on beauty in the fine arts, an unfinished treatise on architecture, and a large library of books.

The Galiani Vitruvius, a small folio volume in Latin and Italian, and beautifully illustrated, is a comprehensive summary of all previous Vitruvius editions. The work is easy to use, for it has a detailed table of contents, an analytical chart which organizes the material according to general subject matter, an index of places, an index of Greek words, and a good general index of names and subjects.

The most valuable section for the historian is the scholarly commentary in the footnotes, in which Galiani summarizes previous explanations of the text and adds his own. These notes provide the architectural historian with a convenient summary of the various interpretations of certain passages, in particular those of Daniele Barbaro and Claude Perrault. No architectural theorist was unfamiliar to him; he even mentioned the little cabin of Laugier. A study of Galiani's agreement and disagreement with his predecessors would tell us more about the classical climate of Naples (and Rome) in the middle of the eighteenth century.

Etta Arntzen

I-32.

II. Architects and Amateurs

II-1.

Juan Bautista Villalpando (1552-1608, Jesuit, mathematician, architectural theorist), *Hieronymi Pradi et Ioannis Baptistae Villalpandi e Societate Iesu, In Ezechielem Explanationes et Apparatus Urbis ac Templi Hierosolymitani. Commentariis et Imaginibus Illustratus, opus tribus tomis distinctum,* Rome, Zannetti, 1596 (I); 1604 (II); 1604 (III).

Villalpando studied mathematics under Juan de Herrera. He joined the Society of Jesus in 1575 and was occasionally employed to supervise building operations at Jesuit establishments in Andalusia (1578-1587). In 1592 he gave designs for the College at Baeza. From about 1583 he was collaborating with Father Jerónimo del Prado S.J. (1547-1595) on a commentary on the Book of Ezekiel — first in Spain and then, from 1592 onwards, at Rome. Prado was not only a notable theologian but also a sculptor and he possessed some knowledge of architecture too.

Their joint (incomplete) work was eventually published at Rome in three volumes, issued together in 1605 — as the inscription at the foot of page 655 of Vol. II makes clear — despite the dates on the title pages. Prado was responsible for the commentary on chapters 1-26 of Ezekiel and Villalpando for that on chapters 27, 28, 40, 41 & 42. The special studies in Vol. III were written in collaboration. Vol. II is solely concerned with the vision in which God reveals to the prophet a holy city containing a temple of which detailed measurements are given by "a man whose appearance was like the appearance of brass." This structure is identified as Solomon's temple and a comprehensive reconstruction of it is presented. This exercise was recognized at the time to be of the utmost importance because Solomon's temple had been built under the direct inspiration of God and the reconstruction would therefore reveal the principles of divine, that is, perfect architecture.

The magnificent plates illustrating the temple were executed in the Spanish Netherlands: Villalpando was given special permission in 1594 to travel there in order to supervise the task of engraving them.

John B. Bury

II-2.

Teofilo Gallaccini (1564-1641, mathematician, architectural theorist), *Trattato di Teofilo Gallaccini sopra gli errori degli architetti,* Venice, Pasquali, 1767 (facs. ed., Farnborough, 1970).

Gallaccini studied rhetoric, philosophy, and theoretical medicine in his native city of Siena. He lived in Rome from 1585 to 1602; there he studied architecture and engineering and made drawings of what he considered to be licenses in Roman architecture. In 1602 he returned to Siena; from 1621 on he taught mathematics, logic, and philosophy at the University of Siena. Gallaccini did not practice architecture. His treatise on the errors of architecture is dedicated to his compatriot, Giulio Mancini, a physician who wrote on painting.

The manuscript of the treatise was published for the first time by the partnership of Giambattista Pasquali and Joseph Smith, British consul in Venice. The text is prefaced with a life of Gallaccini by Giovanni Antonio Pecci; another *notizie,* with a detailed summary of the treatise, is in G. della Valle, *Lettere sanesi,* III, 1786.

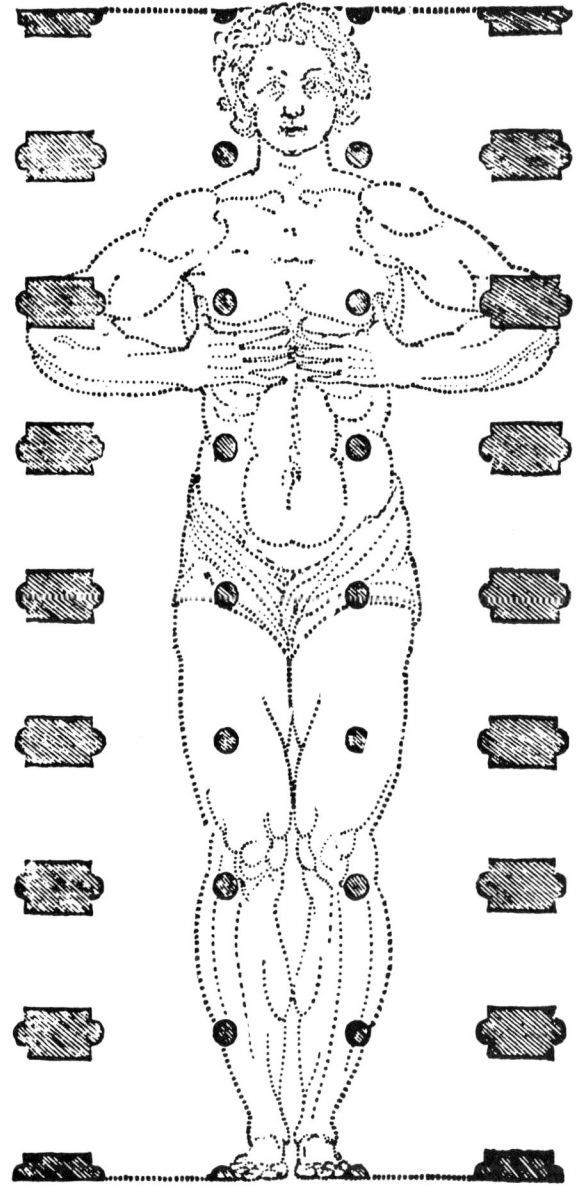

II-1.

Gallaccini's treatise follows a Vitruvian framework; his principal mentors were Vitruvius and Alberti. But instead of giving rules, he points to errors. His criticism is grounded in classical cannons such as anthropomorphic proportion, decorum, and the appearance of solidity. As a young man he had studied medicine and anatomy, and it would seem that he used the methods of a physician to diagnose illnesses and deformities of buildings and features of buildings, e.g. errors in proportion, broken pediments, arches without supports, solids over voids. He found many mistakes in late sixteenth and early seventeenth century architecture in Rome, including Michelangelo's Porta Pia and Maderno's facade of St. Peter's. One can see why his rational approach to architecture and his critical method appealed to the Venetian followers of Lodoli. The Gallaccini *trattato* was continued by Visentini, *Osservazioni* (1771).

Etta Arntzen

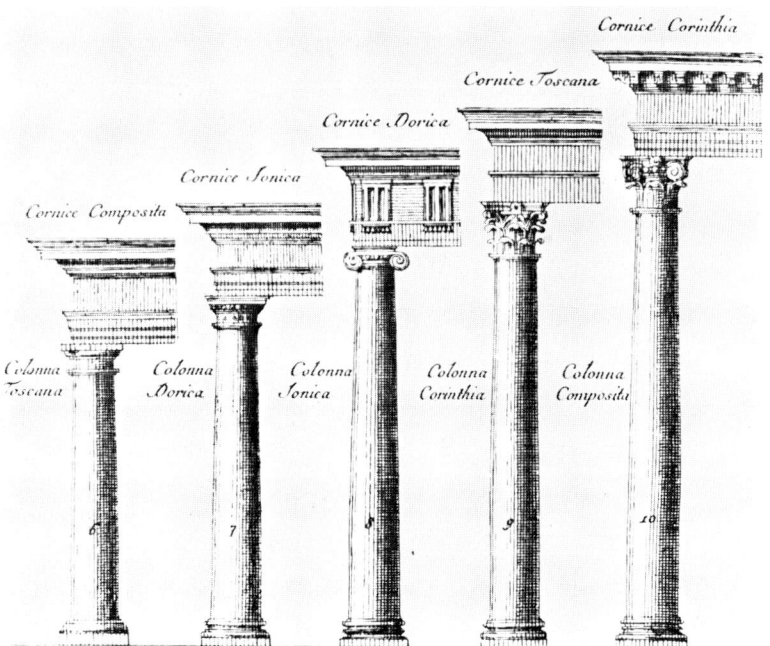

II-2.

II-3.

Giovanni Branca (1571-1645, architect, engineer), *Manuale d'architettura, breve, e risoluta pratica*, Ascoli, Salvioni, 1629 (later eds., Rome, 1718, 1757, 1772, 1783; Modena, 1789).

Branca was born in Sant'Angelo (Pesaro). He studied mathematics and architecture in Rome and was honored with Roman citizenship. From 1616 to 1645 he was architect of the Santa Casa in Loreto, and, during the papacy of Urban VIII, designed the five pentagonal bastions of the sanctuary. Branca is best remembered for his *Manuale d'architettura* and *Le machine*, both of which were published in 1629.

Throughout most of the seventeenth and eighteenth centuries *Manuale d'architettura* served as the standard practical handbook for Italian architects and students of architecture. This one-volume compendium of established rules and practices is divided into six books treating materials and methods of building, the five Orders, vaults, doors, windows, stairways, fireplaces, etc., the rules of arithmetic and geometry. The text is followed by an appendix of thirty-two aphorisms on the reclamation of rivers. The first edition is sparsely illustrated with woodcuts.

The manual was revised and brought up to date, with new illustrations, in several eighteenth century editions.

The revival of Branca in the eighteenth century reflects a conscious return to the classical tradition of design; the revisions and commentaries incorporate the new research in building technology.

Etta Arntzen

II-4.

Sir Balthasar Gerbier (1592-1667, courtier, diplomat, architect), *A Brief Discourse concerning the Three Chief Principles of Magnificent Building: viz. Solidity, Conveniencey and Ornament*, London, Thomas Mabb, 1662 (facs. ed., Farnborough, 1969).

Counsel and Advice to all Builders; for the choice of their surveyours . . . and other work-men . . . as also in respect to their Works, Materials, and Rates thereof. Together with Several Epistles to Eminent Persons, Who may be concerned in Building, London, Thomas Mabb, 1663 (facs. ed., Farnborough, 1969).

Gerbier was born at Middleburg in Zeeland, the son of a Huguenot emigré. He was possibly a pupil of Hendrik Goltzius. It was as a man of diverse artistic and diplomatic talents that he served successively the Duke of Buckingham and King Charles I of England as foreign envoy, miniature painter, art collector, military engineer and architect. During the Civil War and Interregnum he sought to support himself by various means including setting up an academy in east London, banking in Paris and prospecting for gold in America. Disappointed of royal appointment at the Restoration of 1660, he became actively involved in architecture again (previously, he had worked on York House for the Duke of Buckingham in the 1620's), designing a house at Hampstead Marshall in Berkshire in the years before his death. Gerbier's publications, which also included several lectures of which one was on fortification, were largely opportunist, seeking to advertise his skills to potential patrons at court and beyond.

The *Brief Discourse* and the *Counsel and Advice* both offer practical ideas on building in the English tradition from Andrew Boorde (*Dyetary of Helth*, 1542) and Sir Henry Wotton (*Elements of Architecture*, 1624). Like those texts, they are small, pocket-sized handbooks rather than the ilustrated, theoretical treatise such as was first produced in England by John Shute (1563). Gerbier does, however, discuss the Orders and their proportions and his comments on buildings are informed, by way of comparison, by his familiarity with contemporary European architecture. The dedication to King Charles II and the description of a royal palace in the *Brief Discourse* are aimed at a possible commission. The *Counsel* outlines the duties of the chain of command on the building site from surveyor to master workmen and also lists current prices of materials and services. The two books were reprinted as one volume in 1664.

Maurice Howard

II-5.

Nikolaus Goldmann (1611-1665, mathematician, architectural educator), *Nicolai Goldmann's Vollständige Anweisung zu der Civil-Bau-Kunst,* Leipzig, Jeremiae Wolffens, 1696 (facs. ed., Baden-Baden, 1962).

Goldmann published treatises on fortifications and the proportions of columns during his lifetime, but his major work, the *Vollständige Anweisung zu der Civil-Bau-Kunst,* appeared posthumously. A manuscript of Goldmann's work, which was finished just before his death, was owned by a friend of Leonhard Christoph Sturm (1669-1719) who revised and expanded the manuscript for publication. Sturm, the son of a mathematics professor, was a true polymath, being director of buildings in Mecklenburg, a mathematics professor at Wolfenbuttel, and a theologian. He published prolifically on all of his interests.

Nicolai Goldmann's Vollständige Anweisung zu der Civil-Bau-Kunst is an amalgamation of much of the architectural knowledge of the seventeenth century. Not surprisingly, considering the interests of its author and editor, the book stresses the importance of mathematics in architecture. Particular emphasis is placed on the use of a module in building and on the theory of proportions, but the *Civil-Bau-Kunst* also contains an illustrated multilingual glossary of architectural terms, a brief history of architecture, and a series of plans and elevations of model buildings. There was a second Leipzig edition of the *Civil-Bau-Kunst* in 1708 and the work was the subject of more than a dozen contemporary published commentaries.

William J. Diebold

II-6.

François Nicolas Blondel (1617-1686, engineer, mathematician), *Cours d'architecture enseigné dans l'Académie Royale d'Architecture. Première partie. ou sont expliquez les termes, l'origine & les principes d'architecture, & les pratiques des cinq Ordres suivant la doctrine de Vitruve & de ses principaux Sectateurs, & suivant celle des trois plus habiles Architectes qui ayent écrit entre les Modernes, qui sont Vignole, Palladio & Scamozzi.* Paris, Lambert Roulland, 1675 (Part 1); Paris, chez l'Auteur, 1683 (Parts 2-3, 4-5) (new ed., 1698).

Born in Ribemont, Blondel began his career as naval engineer. From 1652 to 1655 he was employed as a travelling tutor to the son of Loménie du Briene, secretary of State, and then as a diplomatic envoy to Berlin, and later, in 1658, to Constantinople. From 1662 Blondel worked for the Crown as military and civil engineer. In 1669 he was enobled Seigneur de Croiselles et de Guillardon, and became a member

II-6.

of the Academy of Science. When the Royal Academy of Architecture was founded in 1671, he was its first Director. The same year Colbert entrusted his son, the Marquis de Seignelay, to the care of Blondel and the architect Mignard, on a tour to Italy. On his return in 1672, he was appointed tutor to the Dauphin. Among his Paris designs was that of a scheme for the improvement of Parisian public buildings, the Porte S. Bernard, and the Porte S. Antoine. In 1673 he designed his masterpiece the Porte S. Denis: its construction was carried out by Pierre Bullet. In 1673 he wrote a brief treatise entitled *Resolutions des quatre principaux problemes d'architecture,* and in 1683, as Maréchal des Camps, he wrote *Nouvelle manière de fortifier les places; l'art de jeter les bombes.*

Consisting of lectures given at the Academy, Blondel's *Cours d'Architecture* initiated a new genre of architectural treatise. The bulk of the writing is devoted to a scholarly discussion and comparison of the Orders of Vitruvius, Alberti, Vignola, Palladio and Scamozzi. This theme is evident throughout; the sections on columns, pedestals, entablatures, architraves, cornices, etc., are accompanied by tables and complicated diagrams of comparative ratios. A single chapter concerns bridges, gateway and aqueduct design and construction. It is illustrated with such examples as the Rialto and Palladian bridges as well as with Blondel's works. The product of a scholastic engineer, *Cours d'Architecture* is rigidly classical and conservative in comparison with the works of Perrault and other contemporaries. It contributed greatly to the systematic study of the Orders.

Martin C. Perdue

II-7.

Juan Caramuel de Lobkowitz (1606-1682, nobleman, scholar, linguist, mathematician, writer), *Architectura civil, recta y obliqua considerada y dibuxada en el Templo de Ierusalen,* Vigevano, Corrado, 1678 (3v.).

Caramuel was a universally gifted man with a wide sphere of activity from Spain to Prague. He made his mark in architectural history with the design of the square and facade of the Cathedral of Vigevano, where he was bishop at the end of his life, and especially with his treatise. This remarkable work, rich in original ideas and strange notions, attracted the attention of many people of consequence. Caramuel advocated the importance of "architettura obliqua" including both sloping capitals and balusters as well as oval columns. These forms were much criticized by Guarini, who carried on with Caramuel intensive discussions as he did with no other theorist. The controversy clearly characterizes Caramuel's position in architectural history. He appears as the representative of the dilettante architects who indulged in intellectual experiments and geometric fantasies without regard for practical considerations of architecture.

Werner Oechslin

II-8.

Alessandro Capra (1633-1683, architect), *La nuova architettura famigliare di Alessandro Capra architetto, et cittadino cremonese. Divisa in cinque libri corrispondenti à cinque Ordini, cioè Toscano, Dorico, Ionico, Corintio e Composito,* Bologna, Giacomo Monti, 1678.

Alessandro Capra spent his life in the town of Cremona. He was a student of Jacopo Erba, and he worked on the Cathedral of Pontremoli. He is known principally through this book, and his *La nuova architettura militare d'antica rinovato* which was published in 1683.

The division of *La nuova architettura* into books corresponding to the Orders was entirely symbolic; the emphasis in the text was placed on construction and mechanics. Volume V contains many full page plates on machines.

Steven Frear

II-9.

René Ouvrard (1624-1694, cleric, music theorist), *Architecture harmonique ou application de la doctrine des proportions de la musique à l'architecture.* Paris, Robert Jean Baptiste de la Caille, 1679.

Born near Chinon, Ouvrard joined the Church and wrote several books on music. He served as Maître de Chapelle to the cathedrals of Bordeaux and Narbonne and, finally, at Ste.-Chapelle in Paris.

This book was brought to the attention of the architectural comunity in François Blondel's *Cours d'Architecture.* Ouvrard felt that without harmonic proportions architecture was nothing more than a confused mass of stones. He demonstrated how harmonic proportions could be applied to actual buildings. In this short book with few illustrations Ouvrard quoted extensively from Vitruvius.

Steven Frear

II-10.

Antoine Babuty Desgodets (1653-1728, architect, teacher), *Les Edifices antiques de Rome, dessinés et mesurés tres exactement,* Paris, 1682 (later eds., Paris, 1695, 1697, 1779; London, 1771; Eng. trans., London, 1795; Paris, 1800; Rome, 1822, 1843) (facs. of 1682 ed., London, 1969).

Born in Paris, Desgodets was among the first students of François Blondel at the *école* established by the *Académie Royale d'Architecture.* At the age of twenty he was commissioned by Louis XIV to measure the ancient monuments in Rome. While traveling by sea to Rome, Desgodets and his companion Daviler were kidnapped and taken to Algiers by Turkish pirates. After being ransomed by the King, they proceeded on to Rome where Desgodets was to complete his task in an incredible sixteen months! Returning to Paris in 1677 he presented his drawings to the Academy for their review; "un fort grand et fort beau travail" was the comment. After the presentation of a copy of the book in 1682, however, the Academy made no comment and ignored the work until 1693. Desgodets was Contrôleur des Bâtiments du Roi at Chambord in 1680; later, he held the same post in Paris. He was made a member of the Academy in 1698 and in 1719 he became the first professional architect to be made professor there. Although his *Traité des Ordres d'Architecture* and his *Cours d'Architecture* were never published, the manuscripts were well known and not without influence.

Published by order of Colbert, the *Edifices Antiques* was the first accurate representation of Roman architecture and began the long tradi-

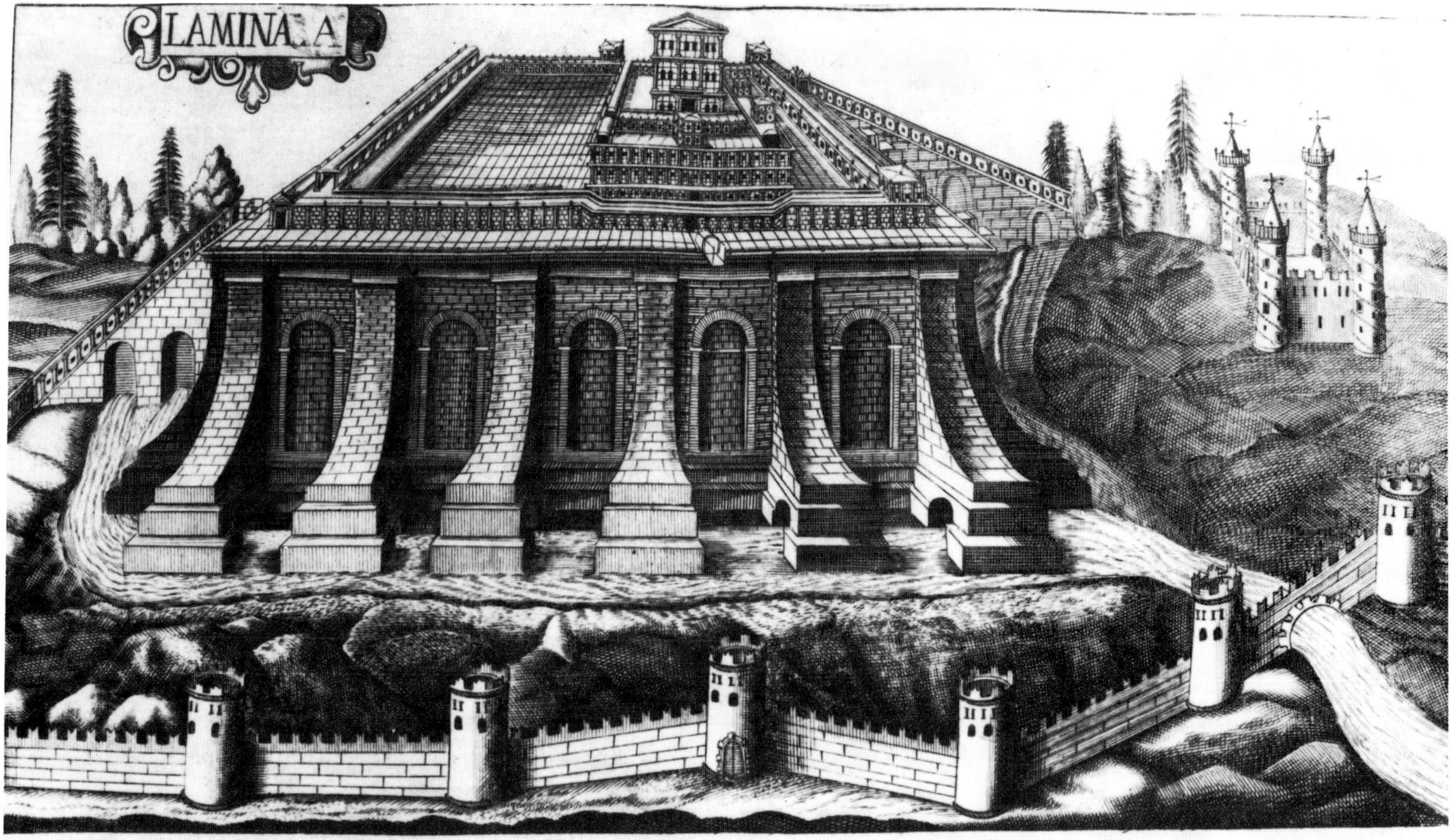

TEMPLI HIEROSOLYMITANI ACCVRATA DESCRIPTIO

Cæsar de Laurentijs fecit

II-7.

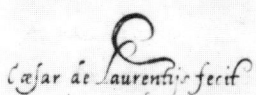

II-11.

tion of measured drawings in French architecture. The book includes plans, sections, elevations and details of the major monuments. Along with a description of the plates, the text points out errors of Serlio, Palladio, and Fréart de Chambray. Herrmann attributes the Academy's silence to several factors. First, the Academy found it difficult to accept a person of Desgodet's youth challenging the accepted masters and revealing significant errors that they themselves had overlooked. Secondly, Blondel had used the proportions of the monuments as shown by these masters as the means to justify his theory of harmonic proportions. The official recognition of these errors would have seriously undermined the foundation of Blondel's theory. On the other hand, Perrault often referred to Desgodet's work. After the death of Blondel, the Academy was to rely on the work more and more; it would become the reference work on the Roman monuments until the twentieth century.

Steven Frear

II-11.

Guarino Guarini (1624-1683, mathematician, philosopher, architect, Theatine), *Architettura civile del padre D. Guarino Guarini, Opera postuma dedicata a sua Sacre Reale Maesta,* Turin, Mairesse, 1737 (facs. ed., Turin, 1966).

Guarini was born in Modena; while living in Rome (1639-47), where he served as a novice in the Order of the Theatines, he became interested in architecture, old and new. Before settling in Turin in 1666, he taught mathematics and philosophy in Modena and Messina, supervised construction of the Theatine church in Modena, and designed churches in Messina. Perhaps he traveled to Spain and Portugal. From 1662 to 1666 Guarini lived in Paris, where he taught theology at the Sorbonne, designed the Theatine church, Sainte-Anne-la-Royale, and wrote *Placita philosophica* (1665). There he saw the Gothic buildings which "seemed to require miraculous intervention for support;" his idea on structure matured with the study of French methods of calculating complex structural forms in stone; he studied the stereotomy of Philibert Delorme, and must have been familiar with the geometry of Descartes as well as the writing of Desargues, in which Cartesian geometry is applied to stereotomy. In 1666 Carlo Emanuale II of Savoy called Guarini to Turin; he remained there until 1681. The Turin years were his most productive, in building, and in writing. His writings related to architecture are *Modo di misurar le fabbriche* (1674), *Euclides adauctus et methodicus* (1671; 1676), *Trattato di fortificazione* (1674), and his treatise on civil architecture. Only the engravings for the treatise, *Disegni d'architettura civile ed ecclesiastica* (1686) were published in his lifetime.

Architettura civile, published posthumously in 1737, was edited by Bernardo Vittone. The text is divided into five books: I. *Dell'architettura in generale* (observations on the nature, purpose, and principles of architecture); II. *Ichnografia* (sites, foundations, and plans); III. *Ortografia elevata* (sections, vaults, elevations, the orders); IV. *Ortografia gettata* (methods of projecting plans on surfaces); V. *Geodesia* (methods of transforming one geometric form into another, methods of subdividing geometric figures). The illustrations on 79 plates are coordinated with the text; some of the plates are signed by Guarini, Abbiati, and Fayneau. The engravings consist of mathematical drawings, architectural details, and sections, plans, and elevations of Guarini's buildings in Turin, his churches in

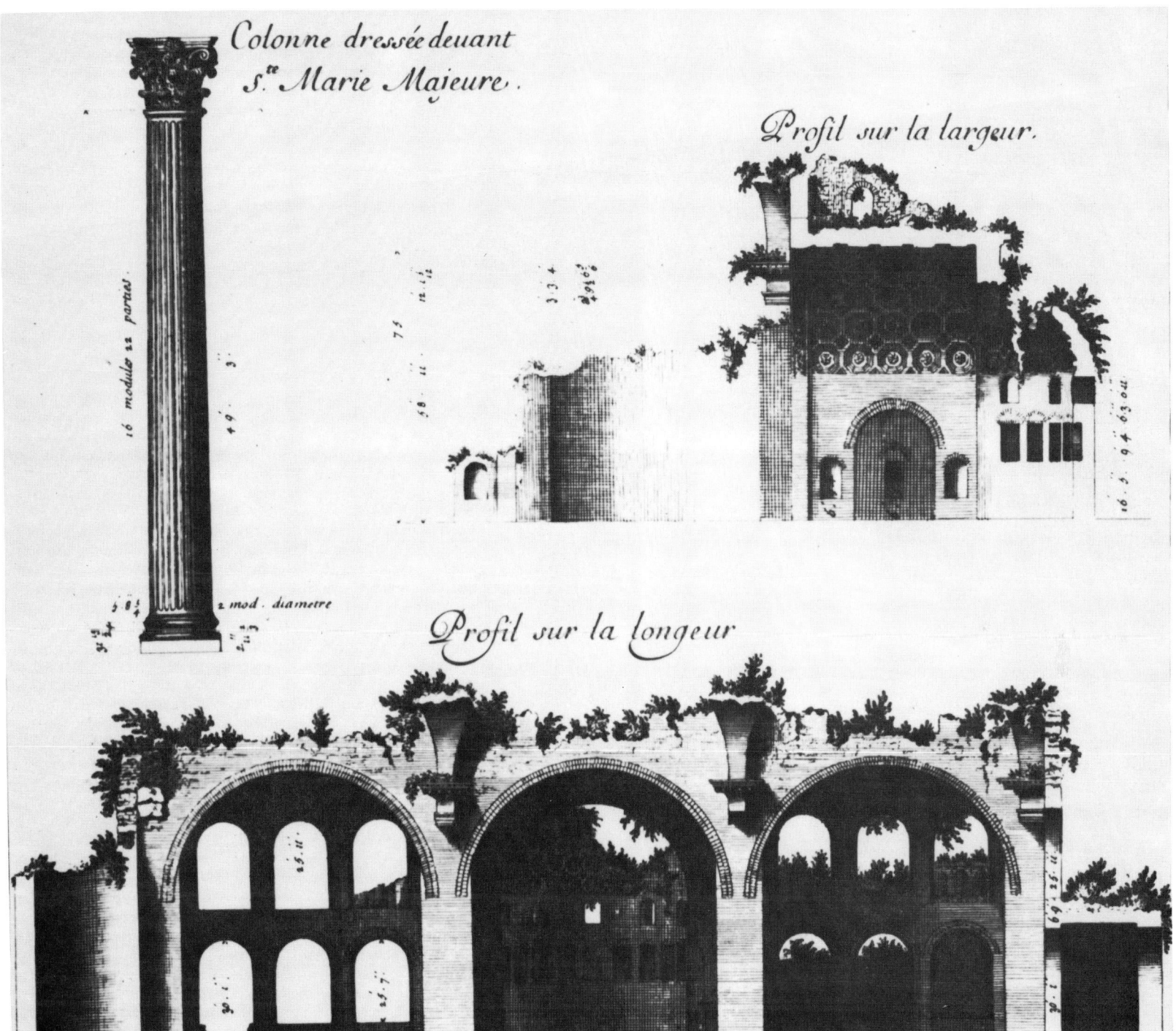

Paris, Lisbon, Messina, Prague, and his projected works in Vicenza, Verona, and Oropa. Guarini knew the literature of architecture and mathematics; he used, in a critical way, passages from the treatises of Vitruvius, the Renaissance theorists, Delorme, as well as those of contemporary writers, e.g. J. de Caramuel and C.F. Millet de Chales.

In the opening address of the Guarini symposium of 1968 Rudolf Wittkower summarized the ideas in *Architettura civile* and the methods of its author; Wittkower remarked on the clarity of the treatise's organization, Guarini's critical judgment in his correcting of traditional rules, his new inventions, his profound erudition, his admiration for the Gothic, and his use of the lessons in stereotomy and projective geometry which he learned from the French. The average art lover who sees one of Guarini's marvelous, expanding domes neither understands, nor cares to understand the complicated geometry of its construction. Guarini's general rule is fulfilled: he observed that although architecture depends upon mathematics, its end is to flatter and please the viewer (*Architettura civile*, I, 3).

Etta Arntzen

II-12.

Charles Augustin Daviler, or d'Aviler (1653-1700, architect), *Cours d'Architecture qui comprend les ordres de Vignole . . . avec une ample explication de tous les termes*, Paris, Nicolas Langlois, 1691-1693 (2v.) (many later eds., among which are: J. B. Le Blond, 1710, 1720; and, P. Mariette, 1750; German trans., L.C. Sturm, Amsterdam, 1699; and later eds.) (facs. ed., Geneva, 1973).

Daviler, one of the first students at the newly-formed Royal Academy of Architecture, was nominated in 1674 as a Royal Pensionary for the Academy at Rome. In 1684 he entered the office of Jules Hardouin-Mansart where he continued till 1689. In 1685 Daviler published a French translation of the Book VI of Vincenzo Scamozzi's architectural theory. In 1691 followed his *Cours d'Architecture*. Accepting an invitation from the town of Montpelier he undertook the supervision of the so-called "Port de Peyrou," a triumphal arch to Louis XIV, to be built from the designs of François d'Orbay. Daviler settled in Montpelier where in 1693 he was appointed "architecte de la province" of Languedoc. As provincial architect Daviler designed buildings for the Catholic church as the archbishop's palaces in Toulouse and Béziers. In addition he designed such profane buildings for the urban aristocracy of Montpelier as the "Hôtels" of Jean Deydé, of Bonnier d'Alco and of Beaulac. Characteristic details of Daviler's architecture are the so-called "courbe Davilerte," a sort of flattened arch, and beautiful sculptured portals. Otherwise Daviler's designs correspond to the strong classicism demanded in his *Cours*.

Daviler's *Cours d'Architecture* includes a life of Vignola, a description of buildings by Vignola and by Michelangelo and a dictionary of architectural terms, and practical advice for the design and the construction of buildings. His book contains plans and elevations of a typical house and designs of all architectural details as doorways, entrances, windows, etc., including even the design of gardens. Daviler refers to the architectural works of Jacques Lemercier, Salomon de Brosse, both the Mansarts and Pierre Bullet. In his dictionary of terms Daviler notes the modern distinction between "Simmetrie respective" (symmetry) and "Simmetrie uniforme" (proportion). In the eighteenth century Daviler's

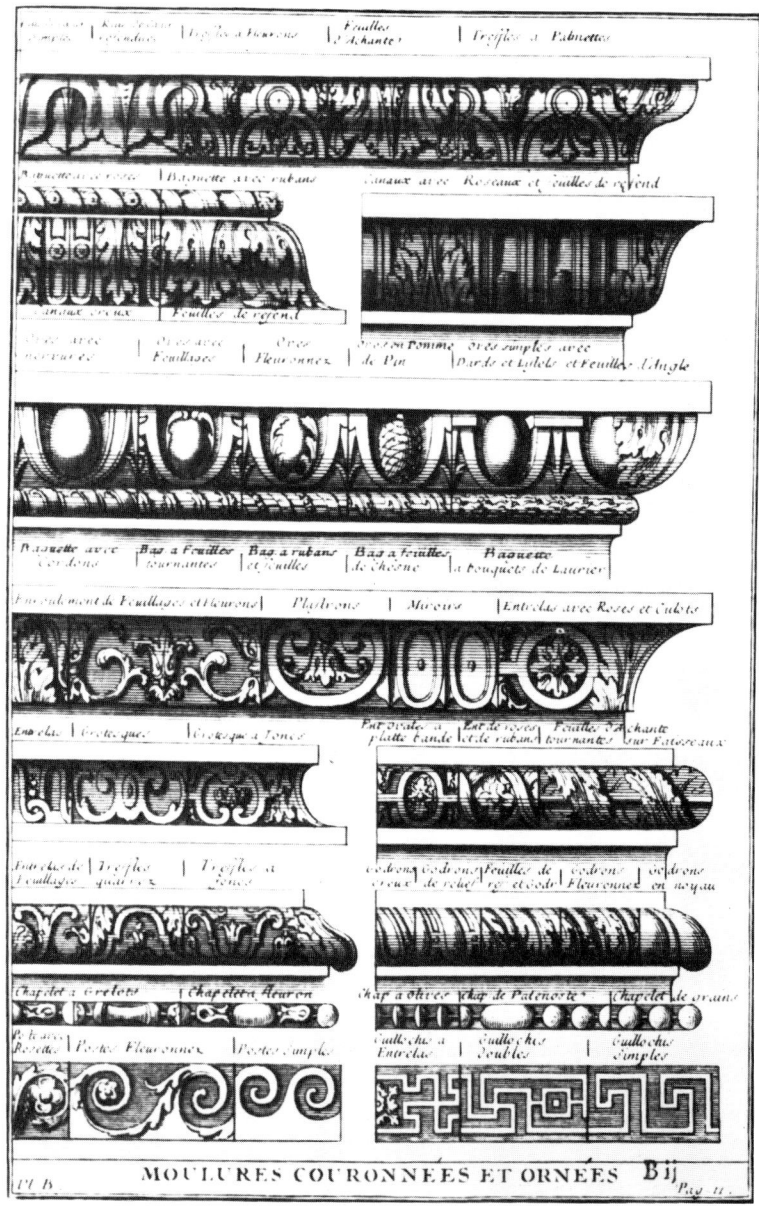

II-12.

book was received as a standard work for architects, many revised editions and translations were published.

Walter Kambartel

II-13.
Michel de Frémin (active 1665-1704, administrator), *Mémoires critiques d'architecture contenans l'idee de la vraye et de la fausse architecture,* Paris, Charles Saugrain, 1702 (facs. ed., Farnborough, 1967).

Frémin was not a trained architect but a high official in the Department of Bridges and Dikes of the city of Paris who possessed a practical knowledge of financial administration and engineering. He may have been involved in the designing of bridges since he is documented as having supervised the reconstruction of the Pont-sur-Yonne (1684-1686). Apparently he engaged in real estate speculation. But it was his own secure financial position, as well as a keen interest in experimentation with inventions, that led him to assume the role of lay spokesman for architectural clients in general in his *Mémoires critiques.* He also published the more esoteric *Exposition des coutumes sur la largeur des chemeins, sur la destination des péages, sur la question: "si la voyerie estune suitte de la haute justice," et sur la durée de la garantie des ouvrages publics* (Paris, 1686; 2nd ed. 1687).

Frémin wrote the *Mémoires critiques* as a means of popularizing his personal rules on the art of building and of debunking the offical doctrines dispensed by the Academy. Since the book was written exclusively for laymen and not for professionals, it assumed a form different from the standard architectural treatise — a pocket-sized volume without illustrations consisting of forty-eight chatty letters written to an imaginary correspondent on such diverse subjects as the principles of true architecture, frauds perpetrated by masons, the nature of building materials, and Frémin's own inventions. Frémin insisted that the basis of good architecture was not a concern for the Orders, which to the Academy represented the ultimate truth, but for the needs of the patron and the circumstances of the site. He criticized modern classical architecture as false and held up examples of Gothic as models of architectural prudence; in so doing he reflected the opinions expressed in Félibien's *Dissertation touchant l'architecture antique et l'architecture gothique* (1699), and he anticipated the thesis of Laugier's *Essai sur l'architecture* (1753).

Robert Neuman

II-14.
Jean Louis de Cordemoy (fl. 1709-1714, cleric), *Nouveau traité de toute l'architecture ou l'art de bastir utile aux entrepreneurs et aux ouvriers,* Paris, Jean-Baptiste Coignard, 1706 (facs. ed., Farnborough, 1966).

Nothing, almost, is known of Jean-Louis de Cordemoy. The dates of his birth and death given in works of reference are incorrect, though it seems likely that he was the fifth son of Gerauld de Cordemoy (1626-1684), the Cartesian philosopher and author of the *Discours physique de la parole* (1668) and also of the *Histoire de France* (1685, 1689), which was finished off by the eldest son, Louis Gerauld (1651-1722). Jean-Louis, as the title page of his book reveals, was "prieur curé" at St. Nicholas in La Ferté-sous-Jouarre and canon at St. Jean-des-Vignes in Soissons, not too far distant. He is also known to have been a friend of Bossuet and his brother.

Though his life is unrecorded his one publication was a work of the highest import. The theory of architecture that he proposed was not coherent, indeed it emerged rather in the letters he exchanged between 1709 and 1712, in the *Mémoires de Trévoux* with his far more forceful and aggressive opponent, the architect A.F. Frezier. Cordemoy's replies were appended to the second edition of his work, published in 1714. Therein the novelty of his ideas is at once apparent. He took up the lead of Claude Perrault to put forward an ideal of architecture that was based on the notion that both Greek and Gothic architecture — the classical and national sources of architecture — consisted of an array of structural elements that were efficiently and honestly expressed. He thought that contemporary building should be based on such principles, and considered thus in particular church building. He liked neither arches nor acute angles; he aimed at an orthogonal architecture. His ideas were not at once taken up, though they were to form the basis of Laugier's far more famous *Essai sur l'architecture* of 1753, and even towards the end of the century were sufficiently stimluating to Sir John Soane to be translated for his own use and his students'. Cordemoy's notions later informed the doctrines of Viollet-le-Duc and survived thus into the twentieth century, in particular in the work of Auguste Perret.

Robin Middleton

II-15.
Henry Aldrich (1648-1710, educator, amateur, architect), *Elementa architecturae civilis,* Oxford, W. Baxter, 1789.

Henry Aldrich, Dean of Christ Church, Oxford, had a considerable reputation for learning in several fields. In addition, the two volumes of his drawings which survive show him to have been a skilled draughtsman. Our knowledge of his architectural activities is limited as all his personal papers were destroyed, in accordance with his will, but his one authenticated work, the Peckwater Quadrangle (1707-1714) at Christ Church, is extraordinary in the context of baroque Oxford in being a conscious, learned piece of early Palladianism.

The *Elementa Architecturae* was intended to have been in two parts, of three books each, dealing with civil and military architecture, but only Book 1 and part of Book 2 of the civil section were completed. These, resting heavily on Vitruvius and Palladio, deal first with various general introductory rules (the 'apparatus,' foundations, walls and roofs, the Orders, proportions, etc.) before discussing public and private buildings (their location, the aspect of rooms, the columned hall, private city houses both ancient and Palladian, the villa and country house, and various Roman houses by architects of the High Renaissance). Although Aldrich makes many practical points, particularly applicable to English usage, on for example the placing of chimneys and the use of back stairs, the general tenor of the work is scholarly. It is addressed in Latin to an educated audience. The text was first printed with some illustrations in an undated, small edition during the author's lifetime as *Elementorum Architecturae.* The first published edition, with 55 plates, appeared in 1789 with Aldrich's Latin text followed by an English translation by the Revd. Philip Smyth, who also added introductory "notices, concerning Architecture and Architects" and a brief biography of Aldrich. Further editions, omitting the Latin text, appeared in 1818 and 1824.

John Bold

II-16.

Ferdinando Galli Bibiena (1657-1743, painter, stage designer, architect), *L'architettura civile preparate su la geometria, e ridotta alle prospettive*, **Parma, P. Monti, 1711 (facs. ed., New York, 1971).**

Bibiena was born in Bologna, where he studied painting with Viane and *quadratura* with Mauro Aldrovandini, Jacopo Mannini and Andrea Seghizzi. Active in Emilia-Romagna as an illusionistic fresco painter and stage designer, he settled in Parma in 1680 and was subsequently made *pittore di corte* (1687) and *primo architetto ducale* (1697) by Ranuccio Farnese, Duke of Parma. His activities as a stage designer and renovator of theaters took him to Genoa, Milan, Turin, Venice, Rome and Naples, and in 1708 he was called to Barcelona to supervise the festivities for the wedding of Charles III. Four years later the Spanish prince, then Emperor Charles VI, summoned him to Vienna. As *primo architetto teatrale* to the Hapsburg court, Ferdinando, assisted by his sons Giuseppe and Antonio, was probably the most active and certainly the most influential stage designer of the century. Returning to Bologna, he served as director of architecture of the Accademia Clementina from 1719 to 1731. Most of his architectural projects have not survived; two notable extant works are the Church of Sant'Antonio Abate in Parma (1712-1760), completed after his death, and Villa Paveri-Fontana in Caramello di Piacenza (1739).

L'architettura civile is a five-part treatise illustrated with diagrams and engravings that deals with the history, theory and practice of perspective and of *quadratura*. After reviewing the contributions of the major architectural theorists and painters involved in the development of perspective, Ferdinando concentrates in Part IV on documenting his various perspective techniques including the revolutionary *veduta per angolo* or angle view that replaced the central perspective inherited from Renaissance painting. Ferdinando's claim that he was the first to employ the *per angolo* has been disputed by most historians, but there is no question that his historical importance is mainly due to the wide influence of his illustrated text.

Direzione a'giovani studenti nel disegno dell'architettura civile, nell'Accademia Clementine dell'Istituto delle Scienze, **Bologna, 1725.**

As the change in title indicates, Ferdinando conceived this smaller, economical edition of *L'architettura civile* as a practical manual for his students at the Institute. It enjoyed considerable success and was reedited by the author and printed again in 1731.

Diane M. Kelder

II-17.

Sébastien Leclerc (1673-1714, engraver, graphic artist), *Traité d'architecture, avec des remarques et des observations très utiles pour les jeunes gens*, **Paris, P. Giffart, 1714 (2v.).**

Leclerc, one of the most prolific engravers of the seventeenth century — over 3000 prints by him are known — was born in Metz where he studied geometry, perspective, and mathematics with the intention of becoming an engineer. In Paris by 1664, he entered the service of Louis XIV as draftsman and engraver at the Hôtel des Gobelins. Between 1680 and 1699 he taught geometry and perspective at the Academy of Architecture and from 1691 life drawing at the Gobelins. His pedagogical bent fully emerged in several studies of instructional prints, such as the *Figures d'académie* (c.1665), *Caractère des passions* (after Lebrun; c. 1692), and the *Principes de dessin* (1700), as well as in a vast number of illustrations for books by other writers, many on architectural topics (e.g., Antoine Desgodets' *Les Edifices antiques de Rome.*

In his *Traité d'architecture* Leclerc strove to provide in a portable format a synthesis of information published on the Orders in seventeenth century France. In his introduction, Leclerc stated that he would provide a survey to the field of architecture for students and amateurs. The pair of volumes, one each for text and plates, was divided into sections on architectural principles, the Orders of columns and pilasters, and other classical motifs. While he felt the creation of good architecture lay in the correct use of the Orders, Leclerc admitted that the diversity of rules set down by previous generations indicated that "cez beautez n'etant qu'arbitraires." Thus the book marked an important point of transition from the academic insistence on established rules to a new emphasis on personal taste and the rejection of rigid systems. Leclerc was working on the treatise the year of his death and probably was unable to give the plates the embellishment which characterizes his other work. An English translation, *A Treatise of Architecture*, went through three editions early in the eighteenth century; the book appeared in German and Dutch versions later in the century.

Robert Neuman

II-18.

Sir Christopher Wren (1632-1723, anatomist, mathematician, astronomer, professor, inventor, architect, city planner, bureaucrat, politician, writer), *Parentalia: or Memoirs of the Family of the Wrens: . . . Compiled by his son Christopher: Now published by his grandson Stephen Wren Esq. With the Care of Joseph Ames F.R.S. and Secretary of the Society of Antiquities, London,* **London: T. Osborn in Greys Inn, and R. Dodsley in Pall Mall, 1750 (facs. ed., Farnborough, 1965).**

Christopher Wren was born at East Knoyle, Wiltshire, where his father was Rector. He studied classics at Westminster, mathematics at Bletchington parsonage, and anatomy in London. His scientific works and inventions were numerous. In 1667 he was named one of the Surveyors for the Rebuilding of the City of London, and submitted a plan for the redesign of the city. He was appointed Surveyor General of the King's Works in 1669. Wren was well acquainted with Italian and French architectural books. He travelled in France, where he met Bernini, saw his plan for the Louvre, and studied the work of Mansard and LeVau. His London City Churches, St. Paul's Cathedral, the Royal Hospitals at Greenwich and Chelsea, and the academic buildings at Oxford and Cambridge, classically grammatical, often Baroque in expression, sometimes incorporating elements of the Gothic, constituted a synthesis of Continental architectural thought and English sensibility, unprecedented in English building. Wren built little after the completion of the City Churches. He was twice elected Member of Parliament (1686-87, 1701-02). With the accession of George I in 1714, he lost the Surveyorship.

Parentalia was edited, and, in part, written by Wren's son, Christopher. Much of the biography and commentary on Wren's architecture was taken from Camden's *Britannia* and Echard's *History of*

II-16.

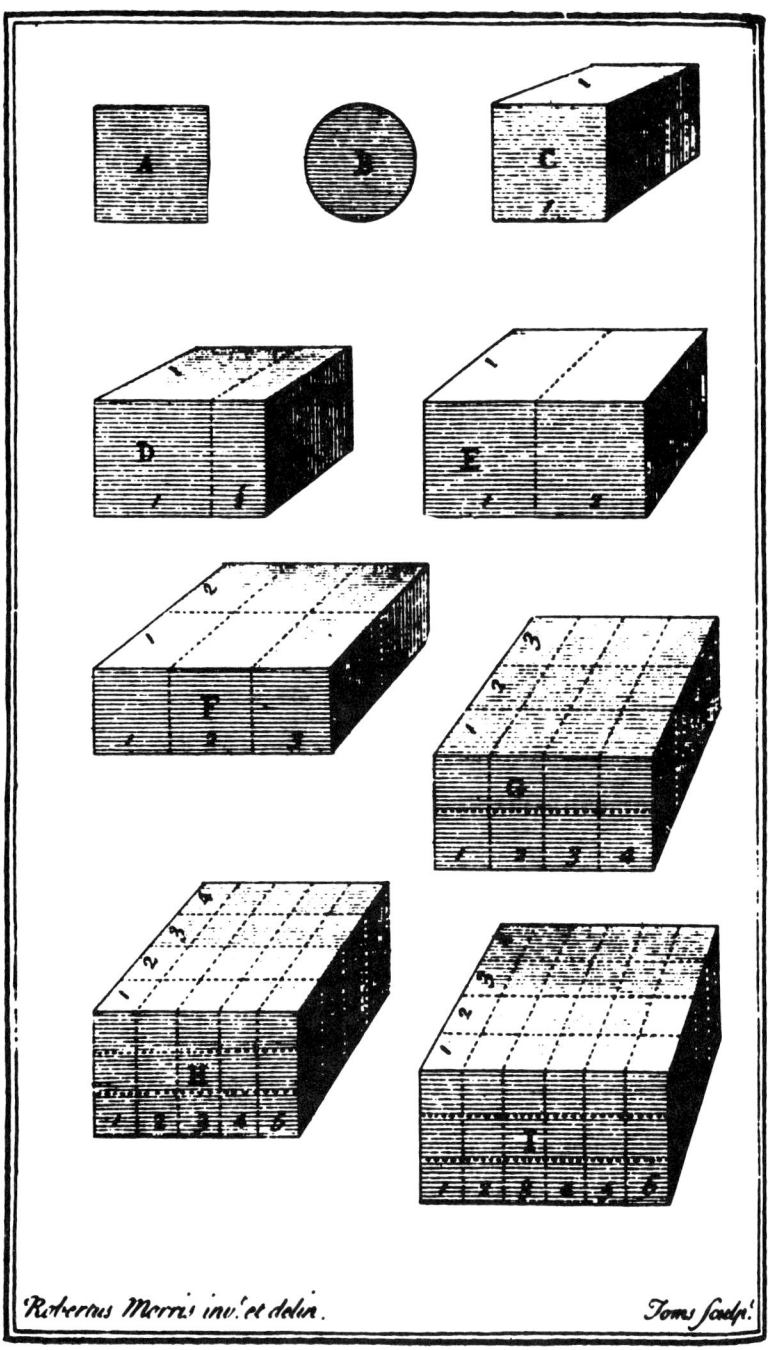

II-20.

England. In addition to Sir Christopher's letters and scientific, religious, political, and historical writings, an appendix "Of Architecture; and Observations on Antique Temples, etc.," contains commentaries on medieval and classical architecture, an account of the building of St. Paul's with a defense of the design, proposals for the City Churches, a disccussion of aesthetics and the Orders, and instructions for drawing arches and vaults. "Of Architecture" is not a book; brief, loosely organized, it is a collection of notes. But the archaeological descriptions of classical buildings and the discussions on the uses of architecture, the function and origin of the Orders and ornament, the causes of beauty, the value of geometry, and the technique of drawing, are similar to those of treatises and handbooks for the professional.

Bradley Barker

II-19.

Robert Morris (1701-1754, surveyor, architect, writer), *An Essay in Defense of Ancient Architecture, or a Parallel of the Ancient Buildings with the Modern,* London, D. Browne, 1728 (facs. ed., London, 1971).

Morris's primary contribution to architecture was as an author. His two earliest publications, *An Essay in Defense of Ancient Architecture* and *Lectures on Architecture* were the principle works on architectural theory written in support of the English Palladian movement. His *An Essay upon Harmony* (1739) was a philosophical explanation of harmony in nature and how to relate a building to its site. Morris also authored two important pattern books, *Rural Architecture* (1750) and *The Architectural Remembrancer* (1751), which supplied designs consistent with his earlier theories promoting classical proportions, symmetry and simplicity. Morris credited his architectural knowledge to his employer and kinsman, Roger Morris, to whom he dedicated Part II of his *Lectures on Architecture*. Only a few built designs have been attributed to him; building records suggest his role was usually that of a construction superintendent.

Dedicated to lovers and practitioners of ancient architecture, *An Essay in Defense of Ancient Architecture* was a plea encouraging architects to follow the design principles of proportion and harmony as used by the Greeks, the Romans, Palladio, and Inigo Jones. In tracing the history of design and the social reasons for building, Morris downgraded the architecture of the Dark Ages and the English Baroque architects. The inspiration for Morris's architectural philosophy, which supported the designs of the English Palladian architects, came not only from the ancients and Palladio, but also from Fréart de Chambray, the French author of *Parallel of the Ancient Architecture with the Modern.*

Richard Ryan

II-20.

Robert Morris, *Lectures on Architecture consisting of Rules founded upon Harmonic and Arithmetical Proportions in Building, applicable to Various Situations. Designed as an Agreeable Entertainment for Gentlemen: but more Particularly Useful to all who make Architecture, or the Polite Arts their Study,* London, J. Brindley, 1734/6 (facs. ed., London, 1971).

A series of fourteen lectures read by Morris to the Society for the Improvement of Knowledge in Arts and Sciences between 1730 and

1735, the first four lectures were a recapitulation of Morris's theories regarding the history of architecture and the advantages of using the proportional systems and Orders of the ancients, as presented in his earlier book, *An Essay in Defense of Ancient Architecture.* Lectures five through eight dealt with site selection, the Orders and the general application of Morris's nine ideal proportions; the circle, the square, the cube, the cube and one half, the double cube, 3 (width) -2(depth) -1(height), 4-3-2, 5-4-3 and 6-4-3. Morris applied his proportional rules not only to the exterior form but also to room volumes, chimneys, decorative features and window openings. The final six lectures, contained in Part II, applied proportional rules to specific sites and buildings. Many of the lectures were interspersed with poetry by Morris, lauding the wonders of harmonic proportion in nature. His belief that all rules applied to the practice of architecture should be founded on natural and harmonic proportion was acknowledged by the lines

"Yet strength and beauty fade and die away,
While just proportion never can decay."
(p. 223)

Richard Ryan

II-21.

Robert Morris (also attr. John Gwynn), *An Essay upon Harmony as it relates chiefly to Situation and Building,* London, T. Cooper, 1739 (facs. ed., London 1971).

A short essay targeted at gentlemen about to buy or build in the country. Morris discusses the elements of natural harmony that create a beautiful picture or scene and how the same elements can be used to create beautiful architecture. He supports the English Palladian idea of improving the landscape and evaluates the landscape of areas near London, recommending the appropriate classical order to use to insure a harmonious blending of the setting and the architectural elements.

Richard Ryan

II-22.

P.P.A. Bardet de Villeneuve (fl. mid-18c, captain and engineer for the King of the Two Sicilies), *Traité de l'architecture civile à l'usage des ingenieurs qui enseigne généralement tout ce-qui concerne le décoration et la distribution des édifices,* The Hague, Jean van Duren, 1740.

A synopsis of the material of the encyclopaedic *Cours d'Architecture,* this publication, like Branca's earlier *Manuale,* by simplifying the *Cours* contents, spread the academic discipline of architecture to other professional groups. This work is representative of a number of similar text books on the principles of civil architecture that were published during the second half of the eighteenth century.

Dora Wiebenson

II-23.

John Wood (1704-1754, architect), *The Origin of Building: or, The Plagiarism of the Heathen Detected,* Bath, S. and F. Farley, 1741 (facs. ed., Farnborough, 1968).

John Wood was the son of a master-builder from Bath. While his early life is obscure, it is known that he was living in London and working in Yorkshire between the dates of 1725-1727. He is best known for his inspired development of the resort town of Bath beginning in 1727. Between 1741-1750 Wood published five books on the subject of architecture including a description of the history and development of his birthplace.

The first of his publications was *The Origin of Building* in which Wood attempted to prove that the development of classical architecture was anticipated in biblical times and that the three primary orders had been divinely revealed to the Jews and exemplified in the temple in Jerusalem. The dubious thesis is a late manifestation of the attempt to remove classical architecture from pagan associations in order to justify its employment in Christian and aesthetic context. Villalpando had forwarded these ideas in 1604. There also seems to be a link between Wood's work and the principles of free masonry and mysticism.

Elise M. Quasebarth

II-24.

Charles-Etienne Briseux (1660?-1754, architect), *Traité du beau essentiel dans les arts, appliqué particulièrement à l'architecture, et démontré phisiquement et par l'expérience. Avec un traité des proportions harmoniques, et l'on fait voir que c'est de ces seules proportions que les édifices généralement approuvés, empruntent leur beauté réelle et invariable,* Paris, chez l'auteur et Chereau, 1752.

Briseux studied architecture under François Blondel, and worked in Paris. He was the architect of the Hotel de la Ferté (Paris, 1738), Hôtel d'Augny (Paris, 1750), a house for the Prince d'Isenghien at Suresnes, and the Abbey Saint-Just-en-Chaussée (Picardie). His publications include *L'Art de batir des maisons de campagne* (1743) and *Traité du beau essentiel* (1752).

In the *Traité du beau* Briseux addresses the famous Blondel-Perrault controversy about whether proportions in architecture are founded in nature or dependent upon custom and taste. Briseux's ideas reflect the teaching of Blondel rather than Perrault. Adhering to the thesis of Ouvrard's *Architecture harmonique* (1679), Briseux attempts to demonstrate that architectural proportions, like musical proportions, derive from natural harmonic relationships. Newton's demonstration that the colors of the rainbow have the same relationships as musical intervals further confirms Briseux in his conviction that Nature operates in a unitary fashion in all of its works. Hence not only are sounds and objects subject to the same laws of harmonic proportions, but these relationships are directly analogous to our own constitution. Briseux's discussion of this subject was not simply a theoretical one, but rather was intended to inspire architects to use harmonic proportions in a sensitive and creative way. To demonstrate that proportions were not a dry affair to be applied mechanically to the Orders, Briseux analyzed the proportional schemes of several famous buildings, as well as adding several of his own designs where all the parts were unified through harmonic proportions.

Richard A. Etlin

II-25.

II-25.

Marc-Antoine Laugier (1713-1769, critic, author, editor, cleric), *Essai sur l'architecture*, Paris, Duchesne, 1753 (2nd ed., 1755) (facs. ed., Farnborough, 1966).

Laugier was trained as a Jesuit priest and although he left the Order in 1756, he remained a priest until his death. His *Essai sur l'architecture* was translated into English (1755) and German (1755, 1758) as was his later book, *Observations sur l'architecture* (1765), which was given a German edition in 1768. After leaving the Jesuits, Laugier became editor of the official *Gazette de France* and between 1759-1763 served as first secretary to the French ambassador at the Academies of Angers, Marseilles, and Lyon. He was the author of a twelve-volume *Histoire de la République de Venise* (1759-1768) as well as of the *Manière de bien juger les oeuvres de peinture*, published posthumously.

The *Essai* was at the forefront of the three principal issues of the day: architectural composition, urban design, and landscape architecture. Following the example of Cordemoy's *Nouveau Traité du toute l'architecture* (2nd ed. 1714), Laugier denounced the "abuses" of Baroque architecture — broken pediments, engaged columns, pilasters, etc. — and proceeded to offer a model for future building in the memorable description of the primitive hut. At a time when Jean-Jacques Rousseau was exploring the myth of the primitive savage to determine the fundamentals of human nature and society, Laugier postulated the orgins of architecture, based on the structural and formal logic of the Greek temple, to establish the principles of architectural design. In this manner, Laugier also shifted the emphasis of architectural theory from debates about the proportions of the Orders to questions of composition through the use of pure geometrical forms. In the field of urban design, the *Essai* was one of the first eighteenth century texts on *embellissement* as it outlined a comprehensive infrastructure of streets and squares for Paris along with monumental entrances and regular but varied building facades. Finally, Laugier criticized the monotonous formality of French gardens and he called for more "natural" and "simpler" settings after the manner of the Chinese gardens as described by the French Jesuit, Attiret.

Richard A. Etlin

II-26.

Carlo Lodoli (1690-1761, Franciscan, educator, architect).
Francesco Memmo (1729-1793, diplomat, author), *Elementi d'architettura lodoliana ossia l'arte del fabbricare con solidità scientifica e con eleganza non capricciosa libri due*, Rome, 1786 (2nd ed., Zara (Zadar) 1833/4) (facs. ed., Milan, 1973).

Carlo Lodoli, Franciscan, became an influential peripatetic teacher of the younger Venetian nobility. His concern to rationalize social and political life was focused on architecture, in which he wanted the time-honoured concept of imitation replaced by that of function. By this he meant that the mechanical, structural working of the building and more particularly the internal forces within each material were to be shown. This doctrine of his was misrepresented by Francesco Algarotti (1712-1764) in his *Saggio sopra l'architettura*, 1756, (in circulation in ms. earlier) as being the total rejection of all ornament. Piranesi was probably familiar with this edition when he wrote *Della Magnificenza ed Architettura de' Romani* (1761).

Andrea Memmo, the author of the *Elementi* was at the time of its publication the Venetian ambassador to the Holy See. He had previously been ambassador to the Sublime Porte and Governor (Provveditore) of Padua; he was to become a Procurator of St. Mark, one of the highest offices of the Venetian Republic, and an unsuccessful candidate in the last election of a Doge in March 1789. Memmo's account was written to correct Algarotti's which he had first prompted to claim priority for Lodoli over Laugier. The full text of the book was published after Memmo's death by his daughter, Countess Lucia Mocenigo. Since no writings by Lodoli have survived, this and a later publication of verses and fables by Memmo dal fú Fra Carlo de'Conti Lodoli (*Apologhi immaginati, e sol estemporanamente esposti . . . Bassano, 1787*) must be regarded as the most faithful record of his thinking.

Joseph Rykwert

II-27.

Jacques-François Blondel (1705-1774, architect, teacher), *Discours sur la necessité de l'étude de l'architecture, dans lequel on essaye de prouver, combien il est important pour le progrès des Arts, que les Hommes en place en acquièrent les connoissances élémentaires; que les Artistes en approfondissent la théorie; & que les Artisans s'appliquent aux développemens du ressort de leur profession*, Paris, Jombert, 1754 (2nd ed., 1771) (facs. ed., Geneva, 1973).

Originally published as a pamphlet, this book was taken from a lecture delivered by Blondel at his Ecole des Arts (1747). It gives an insight into the leading architecture school of Paris at this time and into the contemporary architectural community. In addition to describing the curriculum of the school and the principles on which it was founded (1743), Blondel provided information on other schools, academies, libraries as well as lists of buildings and their architects, with accompanying remarks. At the end of this work is a list of books, ancient and modern, which the author considered indispensable to the students of architecture.

Steven Frear

II-28.

Christian Rieger (1714-1780, Jesuit, mathematician, educator), *Universae architecturae civilis elementa*, Vienna, Prague, Trieste, Ioannis Thomae Trattner, 1756 (Span. trans., *Elementos de toda arquitectura civil*, Madrid, 1763).

Rieger's book, which contains information on all aspects of civil architecture, follows the example of Daviler's *Cours*, although only the Spanish edition contains information on stereotomy. This book may have been the major reference work on civil architecture in central Europe in the last half of the eighteenth century.

Dora Wiebenson

II-29.

Isaac Ware (c. 1707-1766, architect), *A Complete Body of Architecture*, London, T. Osborn and J. Shipton, 1756 (2nd ed., 1767).

Ware, apprenticed to Thomas Ripley 1721-28, was possibly aided in his education and travels to Italy by Lord Burlington. Certainly a member of Burlington's circle, Ware served for over thirty years as a

II-30.

senior officer of the Works, in positions such as Clerk of Works at Windsor and Greenwich. Other than the *Complete Body,* Ware's publications include *Designs of Inigo Jones and Others* (c. 1735), a translation of Palladio's *Four Books of Architecture,* dedicated to Burlington (1756), an edition of Brook Taylor's *Methods of Perspective* (1766) and a translation of Sirigatti's *Practice of Perspective* (1766).

The *Complete Body* is a massive and comprehensive statement of Georgian architectural theory and practice. Published after Burlington's death (1753), Ware relaxes his Palladianism to include in his book's encyclopedic format references to the French publications of Daviler, Tiercelet, and Briseux. Portions of Laugier's *Essai* are incorporated into the work. Because the "discoveries and rules" in architecture were "scattered in various books" Ware proposed to "collect all that is useful in the work of others, at whatever time they have been written, or in whatsoever language," bringing them up to date with the addition of recent discoveries and improvements, making the work "serve as a library . . . to the gentlemen and the builder." It is primarily oriented to the country house clientele. Summerson evaluates Ware's book as "reflecting very fairly the solid, thoughtful competence of its author's executed works."

Elizabeth Lambeth

II-30.

Sir William Chambers (1723-1796, architect), *A Treatise on Civil Architecture, in which the Principles of that Art are laid down, and illustrated by a great number of plates, accurately designed, and elegantly engraved by the best Hands,* London, J. Haberkorn, and R. Dodsley, 1759 (rev. eds., 1768, 1791, 1825, etc.) (facs. 1791 ed., New York, 1968).

Chambers, son of a Scottish merchant, was born in Sweden, educated in England, and served in the Swedish East India Company (1739-49) which took him to the Far East. He left this career to study architecture in Paris at J.F. Blondel's Ecole des Arts (1749) where he met the future leaders of French architecture of the 1760's and 1770's. He then spent five years in Italy, primarily in Rome. After returning to England in 1755 he became architectural tutor to the Prince of Wales (later George III). In 1761 he was appointed by the Crown, with Robert Adam, as joint architect of the Office of the Works and in 1782 became the first Surveyor-General of the Works. One of the founding members of the Royal Academy, he exhibited there (1769-1777), and at the Society of Artists (1761-68). Besides numerous country houses, his work includes Kew Palace, Surrey (1757-1762), the remodelling of Buckingham House, and Somerset House (1776-1786).His other publications are: *Designs of Chinese Buildings, Furniture, Dresses, etc.* (1757) and *Plans, Elevations, Sections, and Perspective Views of the Gardens and Buildings at Kew in Surrey* (1763).

The *Treatise* is the first volume of a projected two-volume work. It is concerned with the Orders. The second volume was to have included construction and the economic aspects of architecture. Chambers' aim in his *Treatise* was to provide a course of instruction on the five Orders and their embellishments. He set out to "collect in one volume what is now dispersed in a great many and to select from mountains of promiscuous materials, a Series of Sound precepts and good Designs." Whereas Ware was encyclopedic and relied on printed sources, Chambers was selective and insisted on direct observation, practical experience and use of analytical judgment.

His precedents include the work of Vignola, François Blondel, Leclerc, Perrault, and Daviler. Chambers utilized J.F. Blondel's empirical method of comparing written accounts to executed buildings, accepting nothing as preordained or sacred, to abstract what he considered to be sound precepts and good designs. His wide range of experience not only gives authority to his conclusions and a personal flavor to the work, but served to broaden the horizons of English students. He wished to cultivate taste and increase pleasure not only by providing information, but by encouraging the development of critical judgment.

Elizabeth Lambeth

II-31.

Bernardo Antonio Vittone (1702-1770, architect, writer), *Istruzioni elementari per indirizzo de'giovani allo studio dell'architettura civile,* Lugano, Agnelli, 1760 (2v.).
Istruzione diverse concernenti l'ufficio dell'architettura civile, Lugano, Agnelli, 1766 (2v.).

Vittone was from Turin. His early buildings, before he went to Rome in 1731, already show the influences of Guarini and Juvarra. From 1731 to 1733 he studied at the Accademia di San Luca, Rome, where he received an academic training. There he copied drawings of Carlo Fontana and his followers. In May, 1732, he won the Concorso Clementino; later the same year he was elected to the Accademia di San Luca. He began *Istruzioni elementari* while a young man in Rome. In 1733 Vittone returned to Turin; in 1737, at the request of the Theatines, he brought out Guarini's *Architettura civile.* Vittone received few royal commissions, and he is best known for his central-plan, triple-dome churches in the Piedmont. During the past twenty years Vittone and his architecture have been rediscovered by an international group of scholars.

Vittone was a prolific writer and draftsman; only his two long, didactic treatises and some of his drawings have been published. *Istruzione elementari* (622 p.) is divided in to three books: (1) geometry, algebra, methods of measurement; (2) decoration; (3) perspective and blazons. The atlas volume contains 102 illustrations of his modular grid system of measurement, the orders, capitals, architectural features, etc. Many of the designs are by Borra; Belmondo was the principal engraver. *Istruzione diverse,* a supplement to the preceding work, is also in three books: (1) measurement, distribution; (2) ornament; (3) forms of modern theaters and a brief treatise, *Istruzione armoniche,* by Giovanni Galletto. The atlas volume (111 figures) has illustrations by Quarini, and is engraved by Quarini, Bianchi, and Ripa. These illustrations are of better quality; further, they show Vittone's own architecture.

Vittone's treatises are in the Vitruvian tradition, for he was steeped in Renaissance theory, in particular that of Alberti. And, in his rational approach to the rules, he followed Guarini, Perrault, and other seventeenth-century theorists. Scholars do not agree as to whether Vittone was influenced by Enlightenment thought.

Etta Arntzen

II-32.

Giovanni Battista Piranesi (1720-1778, polemicist, architect, antiquarian, publisher).

While universally recognised as a topographical engraver of genius, Piranesi was originally trained as an architect and engineer in his native Venice. Moving to Rome in 1740, he became involved in the avant garde architectural world of the French Academy and was also to exert considerable influence on a succession of visiting British architects, including Robert Adam, William Chambers and George Dance the Younger. Piranesi's speculative use of archaeological research as a source of inspiration for modern designers was the central theme of his extensive writings over thirty years. During this time he became deeply involved in the Graeco-Roman controversy as the chief protagonist of the Roman achievement against Laugier and Winckelmann.

Piranesi, properly famous for his dramatic illustrations of Roman subjects real and imaginative, ancient and modern, was also an enthusiastic polemicist. He championed the supremacy of Roman architecture in an age when Greek buildings were increasingly appreciated, battling with great vigor and laying about him without quarter. He mixes impressive knowledge with far-fetched, sometimes ridiculous material without blushing, and it is easy to couple some of his written work with those of his prints that theatrically exaggerate dimensions and scale. But in an age when the means of identifying and dating ancient buildings were just emerging, he amassed a body of knowledge probably unsurpassed until our own day. His daily, direct contact with the monuments is recorded in his more sober ideas and prints, and these are worth more consideration than they have been given in the past. His book learning was erratic, but he understood the means and objectives of the architects of imperial Rome about as well as we do. Making use of his vast legacy of printed words and images requires careful separation of fact from fancy, but that process is now underway.

Piranesi's influence has been great. He produced a familiar vision of ancient Rome that is still efficacious, partly because of the great beauty of the lifetime impressions of his prints. But he was also a true archaeologist, measuring, studying, and recording his buildings. He evolved new ways of describing buildings by graphic means, and ceaselessly prepared plates showing huge amounts of architectural detail that few could have controlled. When this side of his work is isolated from the more purely imaginary, and is combined with the solid stretches of his writing, a considerable architectural historian emerges, and an influential if sometimes wayward theorist. He anticipated most of the present-day assessment of the nature of Roman imperial architecture, and his energetic defense of his theories and notions is significant for our understanding of the reasons for its long-lived influence.

[William L. MacDonald]

Della Magnificenza ed Architettura de' Romani, Rome, 1761.

In this his first polemical treatise, Piranesi adopted an austerely rationalistic view of antiquity, based on the Etruscan origins of Roman civilization, as a rejoinder to Le Roy's *Les Plus Beaux Monuments de la Grece* of 1758. While Piranesi's excessively erudite text reveals signs of scholarly help, his ingenious visual attacks in the plates on Le Roy (and, by implication, on Laugier) are unmistakably his own. The production of this lavish work owed much to the enthusiastic patronage and financial support of the Venetian Pope Clement XIII, to whom it was dedicated. Piranesi was thereby able to include several impressive fold-out plates to accommodate the copious evidence of the Romans' decorative invention, often strangely conflicting with the rigorist standpoint adopted in the text.

Osservazioni di Gio.Battista Piranesi sopra la lettre de M. Mariette . . . e Parere su l'Architettura, con una Prefazione ad un nuovo Trattato della Introduzione del Progresso delle Belle Arti in Europa ne' Tempi Antichi, Rome, 1765 (facs. ed., Rome, 1972).

In 1764 an article by the French critic Jean-Pierre Mariette appeared in the *Gazette Littéraire de l'Europe* attacking the defence of Rome in *Della Magnificenza.* Piranesi's rejoinder a year later took the form of a publication involving three parts. The *Osservazioni* refuted the main arguments of the Frenchman sentence by sentence but the *Parere su l'Architettura* which followed is one of Piranesi's most original and significant works. It establishes a theoretical basis for his baroque inclination towards complexity as opposed to the Attic simplicity of his opponents. In a brief but decisive exchange between two architects, Protopiro represents the 'progressive' designer committed to Laugier's functionalist theories and Didascolo voices Piranesi's criticism of such an attitude from the standpoint of creative licence. Etched plates feature a series of extremely eclectic architectural compositions, mixing Greek and Egyptian as well as Etruscan and Roman motifs. Although the final part of the composite publication is ambitiously entitled *Trattato della Introduzione e del Progresso delle Belle Arti in Europa ne' Tempi Antichi,* in it Piranesi is simply content to restate his theories regarding the superior originality of Italy compared with that of Greece.

Diverse maniere d'adornare i cammini ed ogni altra parte degli edifizi desunte dall' architettura Egizia, Etrusca, e Greca con un Ragionamento Apologetico in defesa dell' Architettura Egizia, et Toscana, opera del Cavaliere Giambattista Piranesi Architetto, Rome, Salomoni, 1769.

During the 1760's Piranesi's polemical ardour was gradually absorbed by his protean activities as a designer under the patronage of Clement XIII and other members of the Rezzonico family. His imaginative application of antique elements to modern needs was expressed in an unrealised project for a sumptuous tribune for the Lateran from 1763 onwards and in his sole executed architectural commission, the reconstruction of S.Maria in Aventina between 1764 and 1766. Meanwhile his contemporary experiments in interior and decorative design were eventually assembled in a sequence of plates and published, together with a substantial essay, in 1769. This final theoretical work, the *Diverse Maniere,* was intended to illustrate the new aesthetic principles of the *Parere* in action and was dedicated to Piranesi's chief supporter Cardinal Giambattista Rezzonico. The prefatory essay, with parallel texts in Italian, French and English, was addressed to an international audience of patrons and designers, and represents Piranesi's most considered defence of his system of design. Despite a reiteration of his belief in the inventive destiny of the Etruscans, narrow issues of scholastic debate are abandoned for an impassioned defence of imaginative eclecticism. A considerable part of the essay is devoted to the Egyptian Style, involving a remarkably advanced discussion of stylistic abstraction. The prime subject of the treatise, however, is the chimneypiece as a uniquely modern architectural feature, and among the sixty-one examples illustrated Piranesi introduces thirteen in the novel Egyptian Taste. The remaining etchings include over 100 separate items of furniture and decorative design in the same idiosyncratic mode, ranging from commodes, clocks and sconces to sedan chairs and coaches. Some of these, along with at least three chimneypieces, had already been executed by 1769 and Piranesi was to extend this imaginative process to the restoration of classical antiquities during the following decade. By then the impact of the designs of the *Diverse Maniere* was already beginning to influence the course of European Neoclassicism.

John Wilton-Ely

II-33.

James Stuart (1713-1788, architect, decorator, painter) and Nicholas Revett (1720-1804, architect), *The Antiquities of Athens*, London, Haberkorn, 1762-1830 (5v.) (facs. ed., New York, 1968).

Stuart and Revett were the first architect-archaelogists to undertake the bringing out of a publication concerned with the accurate measurements of the monuments of classical Greece. The prospecti for the *Antiquities*, in circulation for more than a decade before publication commenced, inspired many of the contemporaneous expeditions and the resulting publications of ancient architecture from areas in the Levant, including Palmyra, Balbek, Paestum and Spalato. The main examples chosen for the first volume of the *Antiquities* — the Tower of the Winds and the Monument to Lysicrates — illustrate, however, not the "true" system of proportions believed to have been practised by the Greeks, the discovery of which was the object of the travels and publications, but two Hellenistic examples of very anti-classical monuments in which the Orders are interpreted as ornamental rather than as embodying either basic principles of construction or of proportions. The examples were at first models for garden ornaments rather than for monumental architecture.

Dora Wiebenson

II-34.

Ermenegildo Pini (1739-1825, scientist and philosopher), *Dell'architettura, dialogi de Ermenegildo Pini, C.R.B.*, Milan, Marelliana, 1770.

Pini is best known for his books on natural history and geology. He also wrote on metaphysics, theology, mathematics, and architecture. He was a Barnabite, a member of the Clerics Regular of St. Paul, Milan; and he taught chemistry and mineralogy at the Barnabite College of S. Alessandro. He was also architect of the Neoclassical interior of S. Giuseppe, Seregno. The complete project for the church, including the plan and facade, is illustrated in five plates of *Dell'architettura*.

Dell'architettura consists of two Socratic dialogues by students of mathematics in Milan and Longone. The first dialogue is concerned with the cupola and the central-plan church; the second with fortifications. The students exchange ideas on the mathematical calculations of domes, arches, and vaults. Borromini is praised for his technical genius; his followers, in particular the French, are condemned. A Cartesian, Pini opposed the sensationalist philosophy of Locke and eighteenth century Milanese writers, e.g. Beccaria, Verri, and Parini. The discussants agree that simple, geometric forms are intrinsically beautiful; the architect can find prototypes in the classical repertory. The second dialogue, on fortifications, is most valuable for its study of the work of the Italian engineer, Francesco Marchi (*Architettura militare*, 1599). Vauban is accused of plagiarizing Marchi.

Etta Arntzen

II-35.

Antonio Visentini (1688-1782, painter, engraver), *Osservazioni di Antonio Visentini, architetto veneto, che servono di continuazione al trattato di Teofilo Gallaccini sopra gli errori degli architetti*, Venice, Pasquali, 1771.

Visentini specialized in architectural views. His patron was Joseph Smith, British counsul in Venice, and he was the architect of the Palazzetto Giusta, Smith's palace in Venice, as well as the Smith villa in Mogliano. From 1772 to 1778 Visentini taught perspective at the Accademia di Belle Arti.

Visentini's *Osservazioni* is a continuation of Gallaccini's *Trattato sopra gli errori degli architetti*, published for the first time in 1767 by Giambattista Pasquali and his partner, Joseph Smith. Visentini's stated purpose is didactic, i.e. to show young students how not to stray from the true path; his ultimate aim was to promote the resurgence of the best ancient architecture. Rather than give rules, he looked and judged, using the critical method characteristic of writers of the Enlightenment. His observations are profusely illustrated with his own engravings; the sixty-seven figures show the errors, defects, and deformities of features of

II-33.

specific buildings, for the most part in Rome and Venice. These crimes against good sense are to be seen in the Pantheon, the Porta Pia, the architecture of Borromini, etc. The errors are similar to those listed by Gallaccini. They include, for example, broken pediments, balustrades above cornices, arches hanging in the air, incorrect superimposition of the Orders, and the placing of solids over voids. He despised the treatises and architecture of Bernardo Vittone, his contemporary, and copied some of Vittone's illustrations in order to point out specific errors.

Visentini's ideas fit into the general picture of Venetian neoclassicism in the latter part of the eighteenth century. He was in the intellectual orbit of Andrea Memmo, expositor of Lodoli. Like Memmo, Visentini was concerned with the appearance of structural honesty; like Memmo, he looked to ancient and Renaissance models.

Etta Arntzen

II-36.

Jacques-François Blondel (1705-1774, architect, architectural theorist, educator), *Cours d'architecture, ou traité de la décoration, distribution et construction des bâtiments*, Paris, Desaint, 1771-1777 (9v.).

Blondel, even more than his namesake of the seventeenth century, who also wrote a *Cours d'architecture*, should be considered as a theorist rather than a designer — though his well-mannered buildings on the Place d'Armes at Metz still survive to attest to his architectural abilities. He was the greatest teacher of architecture of the eighteenth century; including amongst his pupils not only a number of the most distinguished of French architects, but also architects from Germany and Russia and, from England, no less a man than Sir William Chambers. His entire doctrine is embodied in the *Cours d'architecture*.

He began as something of a rebel, attempting in 1742 to open an Ecole des Arts in opposition to the school of the Academy. The following year he succeeded, but by 1750 the pupils of the Ecole des Ponts et Chausées were being sent to him for instruction and in 1762 he was made professor of architecture at the Royal Academy of Architecture. His teachings were indeed academic in the best sense of that term; commonsensical and rooted in the Orders, the first part of his *Cours* being devoted to "Decoration"; the second part to "Distribution" or planning, the third to "Construction." But he was no doctinaire reactionary. His taste changed in successive years and he allowed his beliefs to be influenced by those of his younger contemporaries. He was, moreover, tolerant. Though he admired best the works of François Mansart — and also of Claude Perrault — he could see the merit of the work of Borromini (if not of his followers) and could even take in Gothic architecture, which he saw to be a proper expresion of French Catholicism. And he taught his pupils to design not only noble monuments, but also utilitarian structures. He was not, however, prepared to take in all exoticism and novelty. He disliked the taste for large scale forms that evolved in the later years of the eighteenth century, and did not approve too direct an imitation from the antique. He upheld moderation in all things. Likewise he did not share the obsessive interests of J.G. Soufflot and his circle in problems of construction, and the last three volumes of the *Cours d'Architecture*, dealing with these, were fittingly finished off — indeed largely written — by his disciple Pierre Patte (1723-1814), whose enthusiasm and range of knowledge far exceed Blondel's. Together they produced a handbook of architecture that was used throughout France, and much of Europe, until the early years of the nineteenth century — when it was superceded by the works of J.N.L. Durand and J.B. Rondelet.

Robin Middleton

II-37.

Francesco Maria Preti (1701-1774, architect, mathematician, musician), *Elementi di architettura del signor Francesco Maria Preti,* Venice, Gatti, 1780.

Preti was from an aristocratic family of Castelfranco Veneto (Treviso). He was educated in the Collegio Arici, Brescia. While a young man Preti studied Palladio by comparing the master's architecture with the theoretical precepts in *Quattro libri dell'architettura*. He then became an influential member of an intellectual circle of mathematicians, architects, and theorists centered in Castelfranco: including Count Jacopo Riccati and his sons Giordano, Vincenzo, Francesco; and Count Giovanni Rizzetti, physicist, architect, and author of *Elementi d'architettura per erigerla in scienza* (Venice, 1744). Preti followed their ideas on musical proportion in the designs of his buildings: the Cathedral of Castelfranco, the theater of the Academy in Castelfranco (illustrated in *Elementi di architettura*); Villa Pisani, Stra; and several palaces and villas in Treviso and its region. His architecture can be characterized as classicizing and neo-Palladian. Preti was a prolific draftsman; a large collection of his drawings is housed in the Biblioteca Capitolare, Treviso.

Elementi de architettura, edited by Count Giordano Riccati, was published six years after the author's death. The short text of 52 pages consists of selected passages from Preti's unfinished treatise. The book is illustrated with four plates and a plan of the theater in Castelfranco. The material on the Orders, architectural details, plans, construction, etc. is quite conventional; the most significant passages of the treatise are concerned with the harmonic mean, for Preti the only valid method of determining the height of a room. Here he summarized the ideas of Giovanni Rizzetti, who believed that musical consonance embodied scientific truth. Preti's opponent in this matter was Tommaso Temanza — Venetian architect, engineer and author of a well-documented life of Palladio.

Etta Arntzen

II-38.

Jacques-François Blondel, *L'Homme du monde éclairé par les arts,* Paris, Monroy, 1774 (2v.) (facs. ed., Geneva, 1973).

Nicolas Le Camus de Mézières (1721-1789), architect of the Halle aux Blé in Paris and author of two treatises on architecture, entered the literary arena in 1784 with a pastoral novel *Aabba; ou, le triomphe de l'innocence.* There is nothing in it of architecture. He was no doubt stirred by the posthumous publication of Jacques-François Blondel (1705-1774), the most respected teacher of architecture in Europe, professor of architecture at the Royal Academy of Architecture from 1762 on, and the author of the famous *Cours d'Architecture* (1771-1777). In *L'Homme du monde* Blondel adapted the form and style (and much of the content) of the established eighteenth century romance to didactic ends. Emulating such works as Rousseau's *Julie, ou la nouvelle Héloise* (1761) in which passions and events are recorded in an exchange of letters, Blondel offered a correspondence between the Comte de Saleran, a connoisseur, and the Comtesse de Vaujeu and their circle — in particular the Marquise de Galeas — stiff with innuendo and intrigue, and also a duel, but interspersed in addition with tracts of instruction on architecture (in its three parts, "decoration," "distribution," and "construction") and also on sculpture and painting (in its three schools, Italian, French and Flemish). The Comtesse de Vaujeu is left in no doubt as to what she might admire, and she learns well enough, presuming all too soon to instruct the Comte de Saleran himself. His early conquests are priggishly recounted as conquests of taste (teaching a young girl to judge of her hostess's house), and his own didactic tracts are clearly intended to demonstrate and reinforce his worth, while cooling his passions, which they all too effectively do. He is seduced in the end by the untutored Marquise de Galeas, who savours the more her long-planned triumph by refusing his hand. Saleran is left to the solaces of the Fine Arts.

Blondel's text was edited and perhaps written in part by that lively critic and artist C.N. Cochin, but even he failed to make any less awkward the conjunction of amorous adventure and academic discourse attempted. The book cannot have been too widely read; certainly it was not much remarked by contemporaries, though it is just possible that its very ineptitude served as a spur to Choderlos de Laclos' *Les Liaisons dangereuses* (1782). Historians of eighteenth century architecture have returned to it often for the opinion provided on the works of M.A. Laugier, C.N. Ledoux and Jacques Gondoin.

Robin Middleton

II-39.

Nicolas Le Camus de Mézières (1721-1792, architect), *Le Génie de l'architecture ou l'analogie de cet art avec nos sensations,* Paris, chez l'auteur et chez B. Marin, 1780 (facs. ed., Geneva, 1972).

Le Camus de Mézières was an "architecte-expert bourgeois" for over forty years (1751-1792). His major work was the Halle au Blé (1762-1769), much appreciated as an important addition to the markets of Paris and celebrated for its round form and its double helical stairs. His publications include: *Recueil de différentes plans concernant la nouvelle halle aux grains* (1768); *Le Génie de l'architecture . . .* (1780); *Le Guide de ceux qui veulent bâtir* (1781, 2nd ed. 1786); *Traité de la force des bois* (1782); *Description de Chantilly et des jardins.*

Le Camus de Mézière's *Le Génie de l'architecture* was a pivotal document in the evolution of the French Neoclassical theory of "caractère." Germain Boffrand (*Livre d'architecture*, 1754) and Jacques-François Blondel (*Cours d'architecture*, 1771-1777) had argued that every building should have an appropriate architectural expression or "character" and that this character was to be derived primarily through massing as opposed to the decorative use of the Orders. Inspired by theater decoration and, more importantly, by the new picturesque landscape gardens in France, Le Camus de Mézières shifted the emphasis of "caractère" from the purpose of identifying a building to evoking a suitable emotion. The text explores how this could be achieved by composing architectural forms under the effect of light and shadow. In the two decades after the appearance of *Le Génie,* Etienne-Louis Boullée would apply these prescriptions to the design of numerous projects for public buildings as he formulated his complementary cities for the living and the dead.

Richard A. Etlin

II-40.

Francesco Milizia (1725-1798, writer, amateur, architectural theoretician), *Principj di architettura civile,* Finale, Jacopo de' Rossi, 1781 (Vols. 1-3); 1800 (Vol. 4, Atlas).

Milizia was the only son of a nobleman in Oria, Otranto. He studied literature in Padua, logic and metaphysics at the University of Naples. In 1761 he settled permanently in Rome. Although his autobiography tells us nothing about his life in Rome, his letters to Temanza and Sangiovanni in the Veneto are filled with news about politics, foreign visitors, books, new buildings, and current art events. Milizia was a professional writer with encyclopedic interests — he wrote on medicine, mathematics, natural history, astronomy, political economy, architecture, aesthetics, and the theatre. Except for his books on architecture and the theater, these writings are abridgements or modified translations of the works of other authors, for the most part French and English. All were directed to the general reader. His best, most-quotable, architectural criticism is in his lives of architects (*Vite,* 1768; *Memorie,* 1781); *Roma delle belle arti di disegno* (1787); and in his treatise on civil architecture, *Principj.* An enthusiastic disciple of the critical spirit of the age, he wrote with the polemics of a utopian reformer; his comments were original, lively, and frequently mordant.

Principj di architettura civile was first published in a luxury edition of three quarto volumes without plates. There are several other editions: 2d. ed., Bassano, 1785; 4th vol. of 1st ed., 1800 (plates engraved by Giovanni Battista Cipriani, who worked with the author in Rome); reprint eds., with the plates, Bassano, 1804, 1813, 1825; Milan ed., with critical commentary and corrections by Antonio Antonlini, 1817; other Milanese eds., 1832, 1837; last ed., Bassano, 1875, with notes by Luigi Masseri.

Milizia classified his text according to the Galiani outline of Vitruvius, but with the Vitruvian order reversed. The first volume of *Principj* is concerned with beauty and taste, the second with commodity, the third with building materials and techniques. There is, in the treatise, no rational theoretical system. Milizia scorned abstract notions of beauty; he ridiculed the idea that musical proportion provided the key; any one system of measuring the orders was for him fantasy. Nor did he follow, without contradiction, the functionalist ideas of Lodoli and the modern *rigoristi*; and he disliked unquestioned obeisance to antiquity. But if he gave no hard and fast rules, he did keep faith with certain broad aesthetic standards, for the most part literary in origin. These were principles firmly grounded in the belief in a law of nature, the lessons of history (source of self knowledge), and the guidelines of decorum. And he had classical taste.

Milizia was an "electic" — in Diderot's sense of the term — for he paraphrased, abstracted, plagiarized, and combined many sources to make up his textbooks for students of architecture. He took ideas from here and there and cited very few of his sources. His mentors include Vitruvius (the Perrault and Galiani editions), ancient sources of literary criticism and ethics, several Renaissance authors, in particular Alberti and Vasari, and the eighteenth-century writings of Algarotti, Cordemoy, Laugier, Frézier, D'Alembert, Diderot, Montesquieu, and other contributors to the *Encyclopédie,* J.F. Blondel, Hume, Chambers, and other British authors.

Principj deserves a place in the mainstream of architectural theory. It provides the historian with insight into the specific nature of those transformations of thought which occurred during the latter part of the eighteenth century.

Etta Arntzen

II-41.

Jean-Louis Viel de Saint-Maux (fl. 1762-1786, painter, architect, lawyer, theoretician), *Lettres sur l'architecture des anciens et celle des modernes, dans lesquels se trouve développé le génie symbolique qui presida aux monumens de l'antiquité,* Paris, 1779-1784 (2nd ed., 1787) (facs. ed., Geneva, 1974).

Jean-Louis Viel de Saint-Maux was a painter, architect, and lawyer at Parlement. He is often confused with his brother, Charles-François Viel, architect of the Hôpital Général in Paris. From 1762 onward, Viel de Saint-Maux was associated with the Académie Royale des Beaux-Arts et Architecture Navale de Marseille. The first two of his *Lettres* were published separately in 1779 and 1780 in Brussels and then integrated into the complete work which appeared in Paris in 1787.

In his letters, Viel de Saint-Maux interpreted the architecture of early peoples and primitive societies as symbolic structures which celebrated the Supreme Being while explaining the workings of the Universe. These letters seemed to have had a considerable influence on the projects with cosmological symbolism designed in the last years of the eighteenth century. Perhaps the closest analogy is to Gay's prize wining Cenotaph to Newton (1800), which is replete with the type of numerical symbolism which formed the basis of so many of Viel de Saint-Maux's examples. The seventh and final letter ends with a scathing attack on contemporary architects who would level so much of Paris to build their squares and align their street facades. To these *niveleurs,* Viel de Saint-Maux sarcastically suggested that all the houses of Paris be constructed on rollers. Then, whenever an architect wished to create a new perspective, the buildings could easily be shifted about.

Richard A. Etlin

III. The Elements of Architecture

A. The Orders

III-A-1.

Diego de Sagredo (fl. 1520's, cleric, architect), *Medidas del Romano: necessarias alos oficiales que quieren seguir las formaciones delas Basas, Colunas, Capiteles, y otras piecas delos edificios antiguos,* Toledo, Remon de Petras, 1526 (facs. ed., Valencia, 1976).

Diego de Sagredo held ecclesiastical appointments at Burgos and Toledo in the second and third decades of the sixteenth century. He was aware of the Roman ruins in Spain, e.g. at Merida, and at some time between 1517 and 1522 was in Italy, where he studied the ancient ruins and brought back drawings including Composite capitals he saw at Rome and (probably) at Verona. He was appointed chaplain to the Queen Mother and became the architectural adviser of Alfonso de Fonseca, Cardinal archbishop of Toledo, to whom he dedicated *Medidas del Romano.*

Sagredo cites the treatises of Alberti and Pomponius Gauricus as well as Vitruvius and fourteen other classical authors including Pythagoras and Pliny. The persistent fiction that Sagredo merely wrote an epitome of Vitruvius goes back to the fifth Spanish edition (Toledo, 1549) entitled: *Medidas del Romano o Vitruuio.*

Though much simpler than Serlio's *Regole generali* (1537), Sagredo's treatise anticipates it as a vernacular primer of the Orders. Sagredo pays greater attention to ornament than Serlio but adopts a similar practical orientation, further stressed by his use of a dialogue form of exposition. Unclassical features such as segmental pediments, and baluster and candelabrum columns, are given some prominence by Sagredo but whether or not to use them he leaves entirely to the craftsman's discretion.

A French translation entitled *Raison d'architecture* appeared at Paris c. 1537; and the book was reprinted five times in Spanish (at Lisbon and Toledo) and five times in French between 1539 and 1564. At least one copy of the French version, in the edition of 1542, early reached England (Bodley's Library).

Medidas del Romano was the first independent treatise on the Orders in any language, and was only anticipated in the number and quality of its woodcut architectural illustrations by Fra Giocondo's Vitruvius of 1511 and the Como translation of 1521. Sagredo was also the first to make a clear distinction between the professions of *architeto* and *oficiale mecanico* (craftsman) — without showing any disrespect for the latter.

John B. Bury

III-A-2.

Sebastiano Serlio, *Regole generali di architetura sopra le cinque maniere de gli edifici, cio è thoscano, dorico, ionico, corinthio et composito, con gli essempi dell'antiquita, che, per la magior parte concordano con la dottrina di Vitruvio,* Venice, Francesco Marcolini, 1537.

Dedicated to Ercole II, Duke of Ferrara, and titled *Regole generali,* Book IV of Serlio's *Trattato* is intended to demonstrate to the largest possible public the theory of correct proportions for the five Orders of ancient architecture: Tuscan, Doric, Ionic, Corinthian, and Composite. Serlio's sources are mainly his experience as an architect, the *De architec-*

III-A-2.

III-A-4.

tura of Vitruvius, the archaeological studies of his master Peruzzi, and perhaps also a treatise in manuscript form on the Orders (now lost) by an unknown Italian, of which a version copied toward 1520-1530 is conserved in the Bibliothèque Nationale in Paris. The oldest publication on the Orders, Book IV had an immense success as is attested by the numerous editions from 1540, by the translations (Flemish, 1539; French, 1542; German, 1542; Spanish, 1552; Latin, 1569; English 1611), and by an extensive posterity of treatises consecrated to the same subject.

Vladimir Juřen
Dora Wiebenson, translation

III-A-3.

Hans Blum (1520/27 - c.1570, carpenter, woodworker), *Quinque columnarum exacta descriptio atque deliniatio, cum symmetrica earum distributione . . . Utilis est hic liber pictoribus, sculptoribus*, Zurich, Christophorum Froscoverum, 1550 (facs. ed., Farnborough, 1967).

All that is known of Hans Blum's life and career is described by E. Von May. Blum's slim volume on the Orders is the only reason for his name to be remembered. Judging from its numerous reprints, it was, without doubt, the most popular graphic demonstration of the Orders and their proportions in Northern Europe up to the last quarter of the seventeenth century.

The first edition had its short descriptive notices on each Order in Latin. German editions of the book were published at Zurich in 1555, 1558, 1567, 1579, 1596, 1627, 1660, 1662, 1668 and 1672, at Amsterdam in 1612, 1623 and 1647 and Colgne in 1644. Two French editions appeared at Lyon in 1562 and 1648. A Dutch edition appeared at Amsterdam in 1619, and French and Dutch editions in 1623 and 1641. One Flemish edition is known, published at Antwerp in 1572. English language editions were printed in London in 1608, 1620, 1635, 1660, 1668, 1669, 1670, 1674, 1676, 1678 and 1690. Blum's book, which is based on the general recommendations of Serlio, is neither antiquarian nor intellectual, but a technical draftsman's guide on how each Order may be drawn and proportioned. The illustrations are woodcuts.

David Thomson

III-A-4.

Giacomo Barozzi da Vignola (1507-1573, painter, architect), *Regola delli cinque ordini d'architettura di M. Iacomo Barozzi da Vignola*, [Rome, 1562] (facs. ed., Vignola, 1974).

Vignola began his career as a painter and architectural draftsman, and, primarily in the service of the Farnese family, rose in the second half of the sixteenth century to become one of the most renowned architects in Italy. His commissions include the palace of the Villa Giulia and S. Andrea in Rome (1551-55), the Farnese palaces in Caprarola (begun 1556) and Piacenza (1559-68, unfinished), and two churches in Rome, S. Anna dei Palafrenieri (begun 1565) and Il Gesu (begun 1568). In addition to the *Regola*, he also wrote a manual on perspective, *Le due regole della prospettiva practica*, edited posthumously by Ignazio Danti in 1583.

The *Regola delli cinque ordini* describes a method for correct proportion in the Orders. Vignola, whose ideas developed from the five-part canon of the High Renaissance as delineated by Serlio in his Book IV, on the

Orders (1537), was the first to conceive of a coherent system of proportion which encompassed all the elements of the Orders. To arrive at this new conception, it became necessary to reject the Renaissance belief in objective laws of proportion, which artists had hoped to rediscover through the study of ancient buildings and of Vitruvius. Instead, Vignola subordinated his contradictory measurements of individual elements to a purely pragmatic and ultimately subjective rule of mathematics: "Se qualche membro non havera ubidito alle proportioni dei numeri . . . questo l'havero accomodato nella mia regola." He established a constant relationship between pedestal, column, and entablature for all the Orders (4:12:3), and defined all of the individual dimensions of an Order's components in relation to the radius of its respective column ("module"). This allowed the reader to adapt any Order to a given height by making a simple algebraic calculation. Though originally intended as a technical manual, the *Regola* found its greatest audience among dilettantes already immediately after its publication. Vignola's large, impressive illustrations thus became more important that his doctrine, and made the *Regola* the ideal pattern book for the formation of the Orders, and the most published tract of classical architecture.

The first (undated) edition was published by the author and appeared in 1562. It contained 32 folio-sized engravings: a title-page with a portrait of the author and allegorical figures (designed by Federico Zuccari); two pages of text with the copyright (II), dedication and foreword (III); and 29 plates with short explanatory captions: the Tuscan Order (IV-VIII), Doric Order (IX-XIV), Ionic Order (XV-XX), Corinthian Order (XXI-XXVI), Composite Order (XXVII-XXIX), figural capitals and an Attic base (XXX), construction of the entasis and a spiral column (XXXI), a Palace cornice (XXXII). An expanded edition adding five unpaginated plates illustrating works by Vignola — a chimney from the Farnese Palace in Rome, two portals each from Caprarola and the Cancelleria — can still be connected with Vignola himself; all further additions and changes, however, are apocryphal. Unauthorized versions already appeared in the author's lifetime; there are innumerable later editions, versions, and translations in eight languages.

Christof Thoenes
Nicola Courtright, translation

III-A-5.

Hugues Sambin (1520-1601, sculptor, architect, cabinet maker, surveyor), *Oeuvre de la diversité des Termes, dont on use en Architecture, reduict en ordre*, Lyon, Jean Durant, 1572.

A student of Michelangelo, Sambin was born in Dijon where much of his work was done. He directed a school of talented provincial architects in Burgundy, placing a strong emphasis on rich sculptural surface treatment. His concern with ornament is evident in his buildings, for example: the Maison Milsand, 1561; and the Petit Château at Tanlay, 1568. He also built the Palais de Justice at Besançon. His mannerist style was influential throughout France, and particularly in Paris.

Oeuvre de la diversité des Termes consists of 36 plates of columnar figures depicting a range and variety of sculptural invention and fantasy. The designs culminate in a crescendo of massed forms of satyrs, goats and putti intermingled with heavy fruit and flower garlands and neoclassical motifs of masks, ram heads, acanthus leaves, lion's heads, birds, and finally is sublimated to the Three Graces. This work, as a presentation of creative interpretations of the Orders, is comparable to those of Boillot and Dietterlin. These inventions helped open the way to a process of fragmentation of columns which reached its extreme in the eighteenth century Hispanic *estípite*. In recent times Sambin's terminal figures have proved a barometer of changing taste. For Reginald Blomfield (1911) they were: "designs of stupefying hideousness;" for Anthony Blunt (1953): "brilliant and fanciful engravings."

Martin C. Perdue
John B. Bury

III-A-6.

Hans Vredeman De Vries (1526-1606, architect, painter, engraver, decorator), *Architectura Oder Bauung der Antiquen auss dem Vitruvius, woellches sein funff Collummen Orden, daer auss mann alle Landts gebreuch vonn Bauuen zu accomodiere dienstlich fur alle Baumag stern Maurrer, Stainmetzlen, Sthreineren, Bildtshneichren, und alle Liebhadbernn der Architecturen anndag gebracht durch Johannes Vredeman vriesae Inventor*, Antwerp, Geerhardt de Jode, 1577-1581 (facs. ed., Hildesheim, 1973).

Vredeman De Vries was born in Leeuwarden, the capital of Friesland, and was active in Mechlin and in Antwerp, where he is recorded in 1549 working on the triumphal arch for the Entry of Charles V and Philip II. Returning to Freisland, he studied with Pieter Coecke. From 1563/64 to 1570, Vredeman was established at Antwerp, but left with the Spanish occupation and went to Aachen where he resided with Lucas and Maarten Valkenborgh. Though primarily based in Antwerp where he designed a palace for the Prince of Orange and the fortifications of the city, and collaborated on the construction of the city hall, he also worked in Wolfenbuttel, Brunswick, Danzig, and in Prague in the service of Emperor Rudolf II. Vredeman studied the treatises of Vitruvius and Serlio and the ornamental work of Du Cerceau. Since few paintings, architectural works, or temporary décor remain, he is known largely through his published work — the engravings of ornaments, constructional elements, architectural views, books on perspective and décor including cartouches, vases, and gardens. His oeuvre did much to disseminate the Northern mode — strapwork, interlaced bands, organic motifs — throughout central and southern Europe and, in the seventeenth century, in England. Vredeman was surely the leader among contemporary architectural printmakers; his perspective views were well known to later architectural painters.

An elaborate frontispiece introduces the large folio of the five Orders. The book's organization is consistent: for example, five types of Tuscan are given and uses are demonstrated on succeeding plates; these include banded columns, and their deployment on bridges. Throughout one notes the presence of the local ambient — the great concern with shipbuilding, and the reflections of these Orders and Renaissance details in the local architecture. Seventeen plates of ornament follow the Orders; these are invented by Vredeman and engraved by Coecke, and include pediments, columns, gables, portals with pediments, bases, entablatures, and a few inscriptions. Much of this "manneristic" oeuvre is characterized by strapwork and grotesques and is reflected in the engravings of Wentzel Jamnitzer and Pieter Coecke.

Naomi Miller

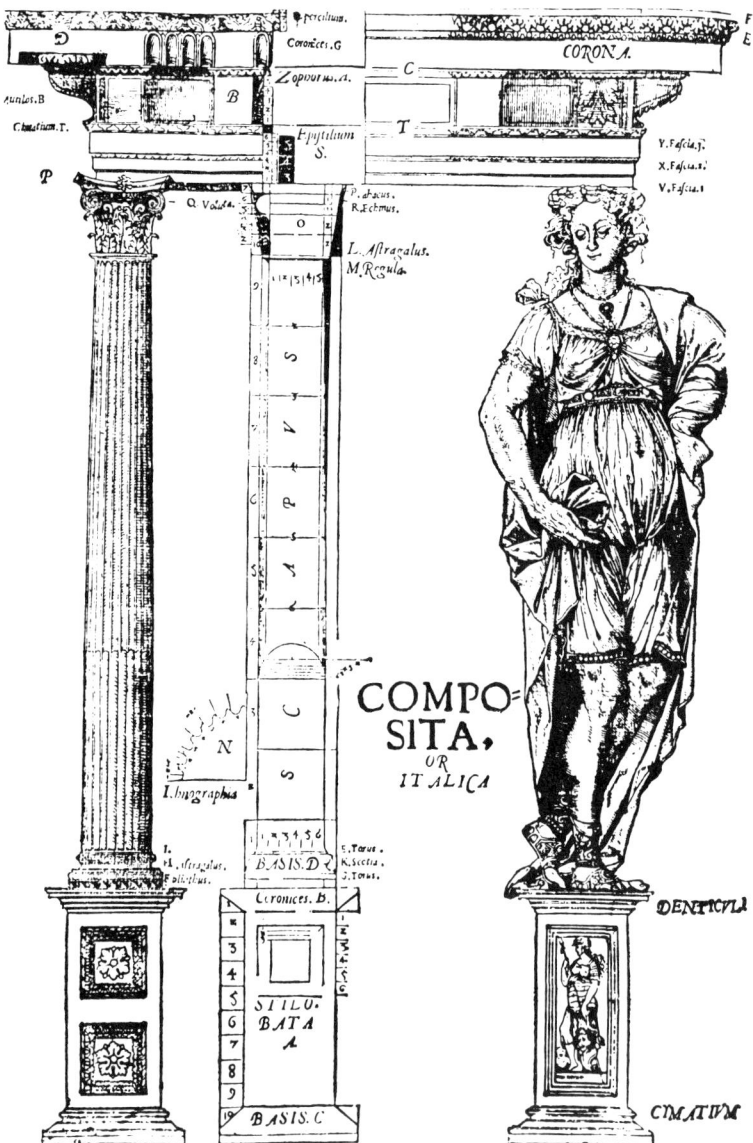

III-A-7.

III-A-7.

John Shute (?-1563, painter and architect), *The First and Chief Groundes of Architecture*, London, Thomas Marshe, 1563 (facs. ed., London, 1964).

The chief source of information about Shute is the preface to his book where he informs the reader that he travelled to Italy in 1550 under the patronage of the Duke of Northumberland to study building. Shute refers to himself as 'painter and architect'; the few surviving documents concerning his property in London describe him only in the former profession, as did the inscription on his tomb in the church of St. Edmund, King and Martyr, destroyed in the fire of 1666.

The First and Chief Groundes was the first illustrated work on architecture produced in England and the first to describe the Orders in the native language. Shute acknowledges his debts to Vitruvius, Philander's commentary and Serlio, and he hints that the book is the first part of a larger study of architecture. The book passed through four editions before 1587 (though few examples of any of these survive today) but the only direct evidence of its use is found in the copying of ornament on a pilaster at Kirby Hall, Northamptonshire (probably from the building campaign of 1570-75). The short, intentionally purist approach to classical architecture remains a crucial document for the architectural interests of the Protestant group of courtiers in power at the court of Edward VI.

Maurice Howard

III-A-8.

Jean Bullant (c. 1520/5-1578, architect), *Reigle generalle d'architecture des cinq manieres de colonnes*, Ecouen, Iehan Bullant, 1568 (2nd ed., Paris, 1619).

Probably in Rome about 1540-1545, Bullant's career as an architect is centered around his service first for the Constable Montmorency, for whom he worked at Ecouen, Frère-en-Tardenois and Chantilly, and then for the Queen Mother, Catherine de'Medicis, for whom he designed the fantastic project for the enlargement of Chenonceau.

In addition to the *Reigle generalle*, Bullant published the *Petit Traicte de Geómetrie et d'horlographie* (1564). The *Reigle* is based on his observation of Roman ruins as well as on the scholarly studies of ancient texts on architecture being undertaken, particularly in Rome during the years of his stay there.

Dora Wiebenson

III-A-9.

Wendel Grapp, called Dietterlin (1550-1599, painter, engraver, architectural theorist), *Architectura von Ausztheilung, Symmetria und Proportion der Funff Seulen, und aller darauss volgender Kunst Arbeit*, Nurnberg, Pauluss Furst, 1598 (facs. ed., New York, 1968).

Dietterlin was a designer of large decorative wall and ceiling murals; the most important of these works was the ceiling mural in the ceremonial hall of the Stuttgart "Lusthaus," which he painted in 1590-1591 for the Count Ludwig of Wurtenburg. In the last decade of his life he also completed the work on his principal work, the *Architectura*.

The first book on the Orders was printed in 1593 in Stuttgart, with a later Latin edition. It contained, in addition to a small text, forty plates with architectural themes (there was also a Latin publication of this book).

The second book on gates and entrances was printed in 1594 in Strassburg with a later Latin and French edition. It contained two leaves of text and fifty-eight plates with architectural themes. The second edition of the *Architectura* was published in 1598 in Nurnberg, when the two books were enlarged and reorganized. Divided in five books, it contained titleplates and two hundred and nine etched plates dealing with the five Orders of columns (Tuscan, Doric, Ionic, Corinthian, Composite).

Every Order was described with a short text placed before the following scheme on a plate: next to the construction diagram of the column stood its type, then an anthropomorphical column, where the nature of the respective Order was illustrated (a farmer with the Tuscan, a warrior with the Doric, etc.), and concluded with an ornamental column, based on the Order. On the preceding plates are ornamental column shafts, capitals, entablatures, etc., followed by examples of their application to interrelated building elements: windows, chimneys, doors, portals, fountains, epitaphs are designed in the highest fantasy in the character of that Order. Along with the sequence of the Orders (Tuscan, Doric, Ionic, etc.) Dietterlin composed a history of architecture: from the architecture of the first people, through the Biblical architecture after the flood, to the present times, with a deceptive composite allegory at the finish of the work.

Dietterlin's fantasy *Architectura* was based on Vitruvian principles and represented the further development of the ideas of Serlio, Blum and Vredeman de Vries. Vitruvius's theory of the nature of columns was expanded and systematized by Serlio, Blum had revised the formal construction of the column Orders and Vredeman de Vries had developed, through the ornamentation of the columns, entablatures, etc., the possibility of the difference of the nature of the columns and their effect upon the entire building. Dietterlin's *Architectura* represents the climax and the conclusion of speculative classical theory in Germany. The *Architectura* is a vast graphic work of art, there is little direct influence on built architecture.

Dietterlin's signature to the *Architectura* has been preserved in Academy of Art in Dresden.

Volker Hoffmann
Barbara Powers, translation

III-A-10.

Julien Mauclerc (1543-c. 1607), *Le Premier Livre d'Architecture de Julien Mauclerc, Gentilhomme Poitevin . . . Traictant tant l'ordre Tuscanique, Doricque, Ionique, Corinthe, que Composite*, La Rochelle, Hierosme Haultin, 1600.

Mauclerc published no other book but this work which describes and illustrates the Orders. The title page of the very rare first edition of 1600 tells us that he intended to publish numerous other works on architecture dealing with temples, country houses and fortresses with descriptions of all their details, as well as a treatise on hydraulics. None of these were published, nor are any of them known to have survived in manuscript. Mauclerc's recorded interests extended to botany and to tropical birds.

Mauclerc's is one of the most beautiful books on the orders with fine large copperplate engravings by René Boivin, to which additions were

III-A-9.

made for the more common edition published by Pierre Daret in 1648. The proportions of the Orders are taken from Hans Blum's book, to which Mauclerc adds plates to show in greater detail the proportion and decoration of the smallest components. Only three editions of this book are known of 1600, 1648 published at Paris, and an English edition published by Robert Pricke at London in 1669.

David Thomson

III-A-11.

Ottavio Revesi Bruti (c. 1575-c. 1640, gentleman and amateur of civil and military architecture), *Archisesto Per formar con facilità li Cinqve Ordini d'Architettvra; Con altri particolari intorno la medesima Professione. Del Signor Ottavio Revesi Brvti Gentilhuomo Vicentino*, Vicenza, Domenico Amadio, 1627.

Revesi Bruti may be regarded as one of those knowledgeable *dilettanti* to whom Palladio refers in the Proemio of the *Quattro Libri*. Among other designs he gave for buildings in his native town were those of monumental gates (1600, 1608), the facade for the bishop's palace (1627), and a fortified perimeter with 17 bastions (1630). In 1637 he advised on the stabilisation of the cathedral vault.

The *archisesto* was an instrument which enabled an architectural draughtsman easily to read off the relative proportions of the principal members of each of the five Orders, and the proportions of apertures and colonnades appropriate to each Order, as well as the fluting of column shafts, and shaping of volutes and consoles — instead of having to work them out by a laborious series of arithmetical sums. Interestingly, a double bulb baluster (notorious for its lack of antique precedent) is included at the end of the book. In the introduction (fol. a4 verso) the reader is told where to go, in Padua, to buy an *archisesto*.

A variant issue of the book includes among other changes a different Ionic portal (p. 49).

Brunet mentions a French translation by "M. Godde"; and an English translation by Thomas Malie was published in London in 1737. Later in the 18th century Milizia suggested that Revesi Bruti's invention was serviceable not only for architecture but also for geometry, arithmetic and music. Cicognara (1821) more realistically concluded that the instrument had been a failure because its employment was very time-consuming and it did not in compensation offer greater precision than obtained by other methods.

John B. Bury

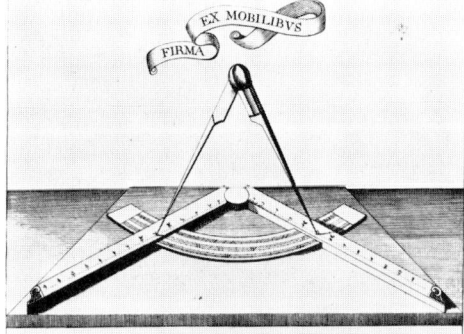

III-A-11.

III-A-12.

Alexandre Francine, or Alessandro Francini (c. 1570-1648, hydraulic engineer, architect), *Livre d'architecture contenant plusieurs portiques de differentes inventions, sur les cinq ordres de colomnes. Par Alexandre Francine Florentin, ingenieur ordinaire du Roy. Dedié a Sa Maieste*, Paris, Melchior Tavernier, 1631 (2nd ed., 1640; Eng. trans., Pricke, London, 1669) (facs. ed., Farnborough, 1966).

Born in Florence, Francine was well known in Italy for his hydraulic engineering and fountain design. Marie de' Medici took him to France where he was presented to the court of Henri IV as a capable engineer. Later appointed royal engineer to Louis XIII, he was entrusted with the development of the grounds of Ste. Germaine-en-Laye and Fountainbleau, where he built elaborate fountains and encrusted grottoes adorned with shell work and statuary. He remained in France until his death in 1648.

Francine's *Livre d'architecture* consists of 40 plates, including the frontispiece, of designs for gateways, small triumphal arches, and grandiose doorways, accompanied by brief notes. Although grouped according to the five Orders, the designs are dominated by proto-Baroque ornamentation; large cartouches framed by statuary and sculptured pediments surmount heavy swags and urns above columns displaying all manner of rustication. Throughout, one can see Francine's intention to illustrate the variety of designs and elaborations which one could develop upon the theme of the five Orders.

Martin C. Perdue

III-A-12.

III-A-13.

Andrea Palladio, *Traicté des cinq ordres d'architecture desquels se sont seruy les anciens*, Paris, Langlois, 1645 (ed. P. Le Muet).

Palladio's Book I of his *Quattro Libri* includes his version of the Orders as well as basic building information. It was translated into French by Pierre Le Muet in 1645, and reprinted three times in French, as well as being translated into English from the French by George Richards as *The First Book of Architecture, by Andrea Palladio* in 1663, with six later editions to 1729, thus even overlapping, in its continued popularity, the Burlington-inspired Palladian editions of the early eighteenth century.

Dora Wiebenson

III-A-14.

Roland Fréart de Chambray (1606-1676, diplomat connoisseur), *Parallèle de l'architecture antique et de la moderne, avec un recueil des dix principaux autheurs qui ont écrit des cinq ordres, scavoir: Palladio et Scamozzi, Serlio et Vignola, D. Barbaro et Cataneo, L.B. Alberti et Viola, Bullant et de Lorme, comparez entre eux,* Paris, E. Martin, 1650.

Fréart de Chambray was one of three brothers from a noble family of Le Mans who belonged to the new breed of seventeenth-century connoisseurs participating in the formation of artistic taste. The others were the collector Jean Fréart, and Paul Fréart de Chanteloup, best known for his *Journal du voyage du cavalier Bernin en France*. On Roland's first trip to Italy 1630-1635, he established contacts with French classical painters in Rome and studied ancient architecture. During the second trip, 1640, he pursuaded Poussin to return to France, secured copies of antiquities for the Crown, and initiated work on the *Parallèle*. Returning to Le Mans in 1640, he devoted his energies to a series of publications: a translation of Palladio, *Les Quatres livres d'architecture* (1650); a translation of Leonardo, the *Traitté de la peinture* edited by Cassiano del Pozzo (1651); the immensely influential *Idée de la perfection de la peinture* (1662); and *La Perspective d'Euclide* (1663).

The *Parallèle*, addressed to an audience of architects and educated *amateurs*, comprised a series of visual comparisons with explanatory texts dealing with the Orders as employed by ancient and Renaissance architects. In condemning recent designers for the liberties taken in the use of the Orders, and in recommending ancient architecture as the sole source of architectural principles — indeed of the very laws of nature — Fréart opened the famous architectural part of the Quarrel between the Ancients and Moderns. For Fréart, the Greeks alone had produced a perfect architecture which could serve as a touchstone for the present. He found the three Greek Orders so beautiful that even the two Roman Orders left him cold. His unyielding didacticism, which followed the theoretical goals of the newly founded Academy, was later challenged by Perrault. But the general theory of the rational character of beauty was of great importance; it was echoed in a different form a century later in Laugier's *Essai sur l'architecture* (1753). At least four subsequent editions of the *Parallèle* were published in Paris (the last in 1766), and John Evelyn's translation, *A Parallel of the Ancient Architecture with the Modern*, went through five editions in London.

Robert Neuman

III-A-14.

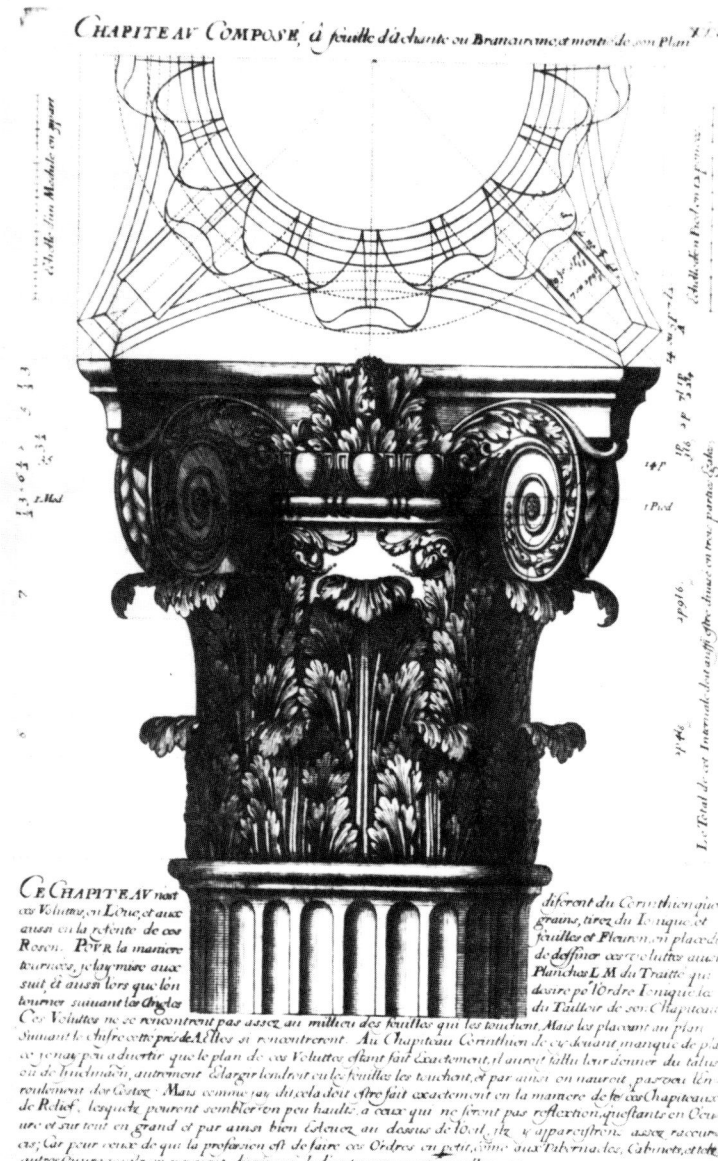

III-A-15.

Abraham Bosse (1602-1676, Huguenot, engraver), *Traité des manières de dessiner les ordres de l'architectue antique en toutes leurs parties. Avec plusieurs belles particularitez qui n'ont point parû jusques à présent, touchant les bastiments de marque,* Paris, Chez l'auteur, 1664 (2nd ed., 1688).
Des ordres de colonnes en l'architecture et plusieurs autres dependances d'icelles, Paris, 1664.

Bosse, a well known engraver, described in some 1500 engravings the daily life of French society at the reign of Louis XIII and Louis XIV. In 1645 he published the *Traité des manières de graver en tailledouce,* a famous technical handbook which had many translations and editions in the eighteenth ccentury. From 1648 to 1660 Bosse taught perspective and its "dependances" in the new Academy of Painting and Sculpture. From 1643 Bosse published several books about the theory of perspective by Girard Desargues (1593-1661). Adapting the geometrical perspective method of Desargues to fine arts Bosse wrote many treatises on perspective and art theory including the theory and practice of architecture, among them *Représentations géometrales, Traité des manières de dessiner les ordres de l'architecture antique,* and *Des ordres de colonnes en l'architecture.* Bosse was the first art theorist in France to develop a systematic art doctrine. His defense of this rational foundation of fine arts as demonstrated in Desargues' geometric perspective method caused Bosse to be involved in a quarrel with some members of the Academy and led to his exclusion in 1661.

The *Traité des manières de dessiner les ordres de l'architecture antique* included the *Représentations géometrales.* Together with the work *Des ordres de colonnes en l'architecture* these books belong to a category of more technical treatises, in which Bosse applies the geometrical perspective method of the geometrician Desargues to fine arts, here to the special problems of architectural design.

The frontispiece of the *Traité* shows an allegorical representation of Reason or Architecture manifesting a classical theory of architecture which anticipates the doctrine of the Academy of Architecture founded in 1671. In addition to summing up Vitruvius's and Palladio's ideas of antique Orders Bosse's *Traité* includes some examples of modern architectural design, among them the plans of two staircases built after the design of Desargues.

Characteristic for Bosse's geometric conception of architecture also explained in his treatise *Des ordres de colonnes en l'architecture* is a demand for flat fronts excluding a multitude of "avant-corps" and "arrière-corps" with the argumentation that the sides are not seen by the spectator. Referring to a theory of vision similar to the so-called "sehkugel" of Dürer, Bosse also treats of the problem of optical corrections and notes for instance that figures placed on a higher level must have a greater size than figures placed on a lower level.

Walter Kambartel

III-A-16.

Vincenzo Scamozzi, *A Brief and Plain Description of the Five Orders of Columns of Architecture*, London, 1669 (ed. R. Pricke, from the 1640 Dutch ed.).

Scamozzi's Book VI on the Orders, taken from his *Idea*, was published in 1640 in Dutch, and from this version the much-reprinted English edition of Robert Pricke was taken. One edition of Book VI was translated from the original Italian into French by Charles Daviler in 1685. Like Palladio's Book I, this abbreviated version of Scamozzi's *Idea* responded to a need for handbooks on solutions to the designing of the Orders as they had been developed by the major architectural theorists of the sixteenth century.

Dora Wiebenson

III-A-17.

Robert Pricke (fl. 1669-1698, engraver, publisher), *The Ornaments of Architecture*, London, for Robert Pricke, 1674 (facs. ed., Farnborough, 1967). *The Architects Storehouse*, London, for Robert Pricke, 1674 (facs. ed., Farnborough, 1967).

Pricke kept a shop for maps and prints in London. Here he published some important architectural works, mostly translated from the French, and illustrated with engravings by himself. Among the authors he published were Mauclerc, Francini, Le Muet and Dubreuil. While he did publish a few of his own works, his importance lies in the link he established between French and British designers.

The Ornaments of Architecture contains fifty copperplate prints of architectural details and some designs for coaches. These Baroque designs were collected from the works of "several eminent masters."

The Architects Storehouse contains door and ceiling designs and a brief treatment of the Orders at the end of the book.

Elise M. Quasebarth

III-A-18.

Simon Bosboom (1614-1670, architect, chief mason of the city of Amsterdam), *Cort onderwys van de Vyf Colommen*, Amsterdam, I. Danckerts, [1680?].

This book is the best known example of the Dutch handbooks on the Orders which were produced mainly during the last half of the seventeenth century. The authors of these books illustrated and described the systems of the Orders of the major sixteenth century Italian architects, chiefly Scamozzi, and occasionally developed comparisons of these systems. The books were in fact manuals from which builders and workmen were able to reproduce literally the best modern versions of classical ornament for their buildings. Among the other publications of this type are Joost Vermaarsch's *Eerste deel der Bouw-kunst* (Leiden, 1664) and Georg-Caspar Erasmus's *Seulen-buch* (Nurnberg, 1688).

Dora Wiebenson

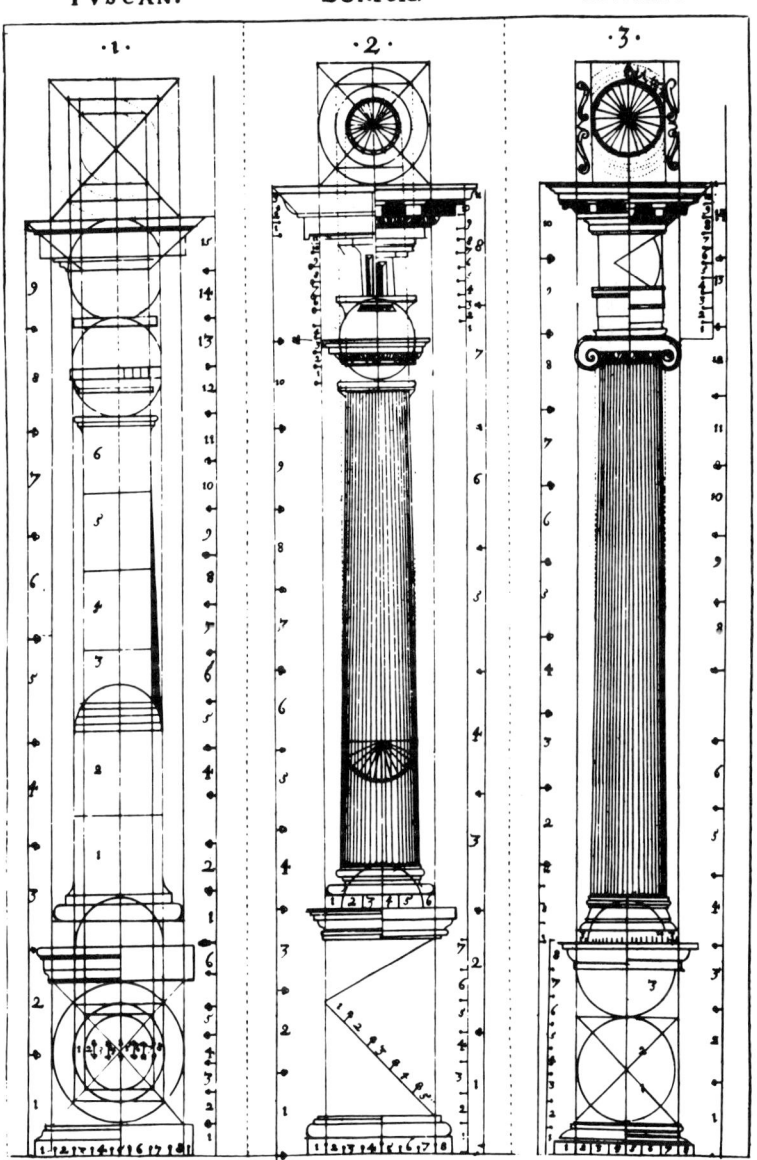

III-A-17.

III-A-19.

Claude Perrault, *Ordonnance des cinq especes de colonnes selon la méthode des anciens,* Paris, Jean Baptiste Coignard, 1683 (Eng. transl., London, 1708).

One of the most important architectural treatises of the seventeenth century, this book firmly established Perrault as the leader and guide of eighteenth century architects. Its influence was furthered by the English translation of John James. The text is in two parts: the first is concerned with the common basis of all Orders; the second with the characteristics of each Order. Unlike François Blondel, the Director of the Academy of Architecture, Perrault does not strictly obey Vitruvian tenets. Rather than adhere to the absolute authority of the ancients, Perrault maintained that the architect must be guided by his own taste. In his dedication to Colbert, he states his aim to be useful, in other words to clarify "the confusion that Modern Authors have left the major part of what concerns the five Orders." Perrault hopes that his book "may give to the rules of the Orders of architecture the precision, the perfection and the facility of remembering them (the proportions) which they lack." Wolfgang Herrmann concludes that the treatise is at one with the Establishment: rather than moving towards greater artistic freedom, "the limits within which the Orders can move are narrowed, and with the Orders, necessarily the scope of the total architectural composition. Uniformity, order, and the middle way — these were Perrault's tenets."

Naomi Miller

III-A-20.

Jean LeBlond (c. 1635-1709, painter), *Deux exemples des cinq ordres de l'architecture antique, et des quatres plus excelens autheurs qui en ont traitte scavoir Palladio, Scamozzi, Serlio, et Vignole,* Paris, Chez 'autheur, 1683.

LeBlond was admitted to the Royal Academy in 1681. He painted both religious and secular works, as well as executing numerous published engravings. These include a series of altarpieces bound with Jean Marot's *Recueil des plusieurs portes,* a collection of Chinese costumes published by Jollain, and sixteen engravings of gates and railings titled *Grille de Versailles,* published by the artist. LeBlond's original publication includes a two page dedication to the *Premier peintre du Roi,* Charles LeBrun, which stresses the importance of the relationship between painting and architecture.

The year after LeBlond died his comparison of the architectural orders under the title *Paralelle des cinq ordres d'architecture tiré des exemples antiques les plus excelens et des quatre principaux auteurs modernes que en ont écrit scavoir Paladio, Scamozzi, Serlio et Vignole* (Paris, 1710), was published by Jean Mariette, who called LeBlond a mediocre painter. Mariette's interest in publishing this work was probably due to the influence of LeBlond's son, Jean-Baptiste Alexandre LeBlond (1679-1719), a well known architect greatly admired by Mariette, who is sometimes erroneously credited as the author. Although Mariette published another edition of the *Paralelle des cinq ordres . . .* in 1716, LeBlond's brief treatise was greatly overshadowed in influence and importance by lengthy and well known comparisons of the five Orders written by François Blondel and Claude Perrault, both published approximately at the same time as the original treatise by LeBlond.

Kathleen Russo

III-A-19.

III-A-21.

Johann Indau (1651-1690, architect, cabinetmaker), *Wienerische Architectur-, Kunst- und Saülenbuch*, Vienna, Johann Jacob Kürner, 1686 (later eds., 1713, 1722).

Indau, first mentioned in Vienna in 1682, travelled in Italy and Germany and in 1686 became royal cabinetmaker. His only known work is the Mercy Altar at Mariazeller Pilgrimage Church, illustrated (no.18) in *Saülenbuches*. A typical book on the Orders, this work served as a teaching handbook. Locally it was considered as complementary to W.W. Praemer's *Theorie und Praxis der Architektur* and *Werk von der Architektur* by Fursten Karl Eusebius of Liechtenstein. Indau's book, concerned mostly with the design and composition of the Orders, was a mixture of contemporary and classical ideas. Two other books are by Indau: *Neue Romanische Zichrathen, inventiert u. gemacht durch den kunstberuhmten Johann Indau* (Augsburg, before 1685) and *Neue invenzione di Rabischi, e Fogliani Romani di Giovanni Indau ebanista di camera* (Vienna, 1685).

Elizabeth Lambert

III-A-22.

William Halfpenny, alias Michael Hoare (?-1775, architect, author), *Practical Architecture; or, A Sure Guide to the True Working According to the Rules of that Science, representing the Five Orders with their Several Doors and Windows*, London, Bowles, n.d. (later eds., 1724, 1730, 1736, 1748, 1751) (facs. ed., New York, 1968).

Halfpenny's early career is clouded in obscurity. He first appears as a practising architect in 1729 as the author of an unexecuted design for a church at Leeds. His recorded architectural works are not numerous but he did construct a few buildings in Hillsborough, Ireland and Bristol. Halfpenny was the first architectural writer to translate Palladio into feet and inches.

Practical Architecture is a small handbook written with a view to being useful to "those who are engaged in ye noble art of building." Halfpenny provides proportional tables juxtaposed with illustrations of the Orders.

Elise M. Quasebarth

III-A-23.

William Halfpenny, *Magnum in Parvo, or the Marrow of Architecture*, London, Bowles, 1722 (2nd ed., 1728) (facs. ed., New York, 1968).

Magnum in Parvo was intended for the student of architecture: "... so plain and easy [is it] that a young gentleman tho' an utter stranger to ye art, may apprehend the whole, by seeing only one example wrought in a method entirely new." The first chapter is devoted to the description of a drawing board; the remaining twelve treat the method of drawing the five Orders, "according to the proportions laid down by Palladio." In format and principle Halfpenny relied on Venturus Mandley's *Mellificium Mensionis: of the Marrow of Measuring* (1682) which was in its fourth edition when Halfpenny's work was published.

Elise M. Quasebarth

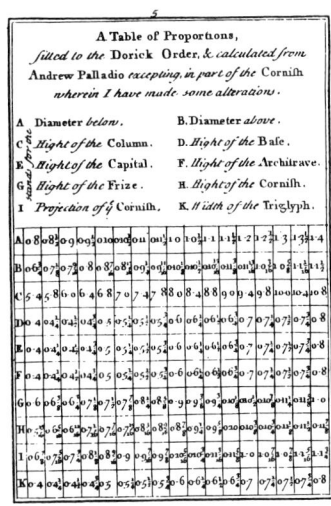
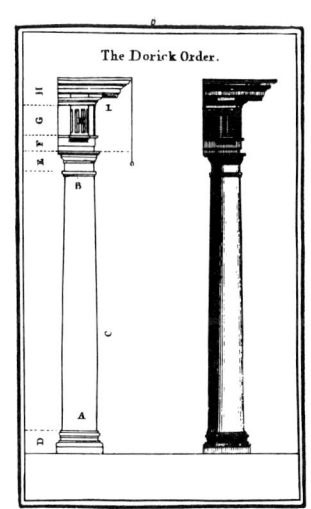

III-A-22.

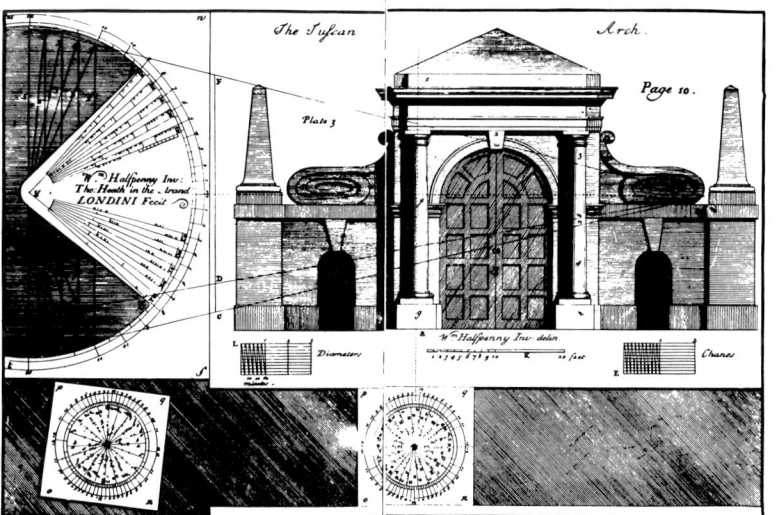

III-A-23.

III-A-24.

Batty Langley (1696-1751, landscape gardener, author, teacher, architect), *The Builder's Chestbook: or a Compleat Key to the Five Orders of Columns in Architecture*. London, J. Wilcox, 1727, 1739 (reprinted as *The Builder's Vade Mecum*. Dublin, 1729, 1735) (facs. ed., Farnborough, 1971).

Batty Langley, the son of a gardener, was born in Twickenham. Little is known of his early years. Evidently he received some instruction in his father's trade, for, in 1722, he designed a 'Quadruple Spiral' labyrinth at Twickenham Park. By 1727, he had established an office in London and was advertising that he could design and construct 'Grottos, Cascades, Caves, and Gardens in General.' He published several books on landscape gardening in the 1720's, and worked on the Serpentine Brook at Castle Howard. Although he is not known to have had any background in the building trades, he published over twenty architectural books, and, with his brother Thomas, ran a school that offered instruction to artisans in architecture and related disciplines. In 1734 he entered a design in the competition for the Mansion House. But he built little and none of his work survives.

Langley's architectural books are primarily manuals for builders and artisans. After the Great London Fire, through the mid-eighteenth century, London experienced a considerable economic expansion. This, and the effects of the fire, stimulated an expansion of building activity. The architectural profession was undeveloped at this time and most of the building was carried out by artisan contractors. It was to this group that Langley's books were directed.

While the artisans and builders constituted a lucrative market for Langley's books, his prolific production may have been partly motivated by his association with the Fraternal Order of Masons. Established in England in 1717, the Masonic Order was dedicated to a fraternal ideal. This ideal was embodied in the concept of self-improvement and advancement through education and fraternal assistance. Langley's books constitute a compendium of information from a wide variety of architectural books useful to craftsmen with aspirations of becoming independent builder-contractors.

The Builder's Chestbook is an elementary manual of instruction in the history and uses of the Orders in building. Fundamental problems of proportion, intercolumniation, and ornament, are introduced, terms of architecture and the building trades are defined, and instructions offered in drawing, estimation of materials, and methods of construction. Instruction is presented in a format of problems and solutions between master and student, a Masonic device. The language of the text, appropriate to the craftsman, is simple and direct.

Bradley Barker

III-A-25.

Pierre Nativelle (fl. 1st quarter 18c, architect), *Nouveau traité d'architecture, contenant les cinq ordres suivant les quatre auteurs les plus approuvez: Vignole, Palladio, Philibert de Lorme et Scamozzi*, Paris, Gregoire Dupuis, 1729 (2v.).

These rare folio volumes may contain the most beautiful illustrations of the Orders of any treatise on this subject. Little more than the name of their author is known.

Dora Wiebenson

III-A-26.

James Gibbs (1682-1754, architect), *Rules for Drawing the Several Parts of Architecture, in a more exact and easy Manner than has been heretofore practised, by which all Fractions, in dividing the principal Members and their Parts, are avoided*, London, R. Innys and R. Manby, 1732 (later eds., 1738, 1753) (facs. ed., Farnborough, 1968).

Gibbs was the most thoroughly professional architect of his generation in Britain. A Scot, he went to Rome in 1703 to study for the priesthood, but was soon diverted into architecture and became the pupil of Carlo Fontana. On his arrival in London in 1709 he was taken up by the elderly Wren, who recommended him for a surveyorship to the Commission for building Fifty New Churches in London. The church of St-Mary-le-Strand, designed in his capacity as surveyor to the Commission, shows equally the influence of the Italian Baroque and of Wren. As a Scot and a Tory he found his career blighted by the political shift which took place on the accession of the Hanoverians, but nevertheless built up a big private practice, mainly of house commissions but including the church of St. Martin's-in-the-Fields and the Radcliffe Library, Oxford.

His *Rules for Drawing* which provided a simple method of dividing Orders into parts without fractions, was effective in transmitting Gibbs' somewhat schematic vision of classical architecture throughout Britain and North America. His clear outline engravings and simplified system of proportioning the Orders brought classical design within the reach of every joiner and mason who cared to follow his patterns. Gibbs obtained a fourteen-year copyright on the book, and between them his publications earned him nearly 2000 pounds.

John Newman

III-A-27.

Batty Langley, *Ancient Masonry*, London, The author, 1734-1736 (2v.)

This book elaborates on the format of basic instruction in arithmetic, geometry, trigonometry, the Orders, and methods and materials of construction, and, in 494 plates of designs taken from the engraved works of well known architects from all over Europe, as well as from England, offered the artisan-builder a broad vocabulary of design. The "legendary history of geometry" in *Ancient Masonry* is a masonic text. This is the *dernier mot* among pattern books, and although hardly portable, it would become invaluable as a reference encyclopaedia.

Bradley Barker

III-A-28.

Alessandro Pompei (1705-1772, architect, painter, writer), *Li cinque ordini d'architettura civile*, Verona, Jacopo Vallarsi, 1735.

Li cinque ordini is a comparative study of the Orders including chapters on Vitruvius, San Michele, Alberti, Palladio, Serlio and Vignola. Part I is a general treatment of the Orders; Part II provides biographical sketches of the architects and Part III contains the comparative illustrations. Pompei provides San Michele's Orders as a foil for the architectural details of the other architects, indicating a distinct preference for San Michele's work.

Elise M. Quasebarth

III-A-29.

Batty Langley, *Ancient Architecture, Restored and Improved by a Great Variety of Grand and Useful Designs, entirely new in the Gothic Mode...* London, Batty and Thomas Langley, 1741 (repub. 1747 as *Gothic Architecture*) (facs. 1747 ed., Farnborough, 1967).

Langley's only original work, this book attempts to formalize Gothic architecture into systematic Orders. Although somewhat derivative of William Kent's neo-Gothic style, *Ancient Architecture* and *Gothic Architecture* were important early works in opposition to the Palladian taste. Langley's Gothic Orders are clumsy and inaccurate, but they are an original attempt to encompass the Gothic in a comprehensive formal system. The books place Langley in company with Félibien who had attempted something similar. Moreover, the books are the first attempt to associate the Gothic with the English national character.

Bradley Barker

III-A-30.

Batty Langley, *The Builder's Director, or Bench-Mate: Being a Pocket-Treasury of the Grecian, Roman and Gothic Orders of Architecture, made easy to the Meanest Capacity by near 500 Examples,* London, Piers and Wentz, 1747 (later eds., 1751, 1761, 1763, 1767) (facs. 1751 ed., New York, 1970).

The full title is self-descriptive. This was a much-used handbook.

Dora Wiebenson

III-A-31.

Stephen Riou (1720-1780, architect and architectural writer), *The Grecian Orders of Architecture. Delineated and Explained from the Antiquities of Athens.* London; J. Dixwell, for the author, 1768.

The son of a London merchant of Huguenot origin, Riou served in Flanders during the war of 1741 as a Captain in the second troop of Horse Grenadier Guards. He retired on pension and attended the University of Geneva where, in 1743, he wrote a treatise (in French) on civil architecture based on the works of Vignola, Daviler and others. A second treatise, *Itineral Remarks from Italy to the Archipelago and Constantinople by Sea and thence by land thro' Rome to Bulgaria, Servia, Hungary to Vienna in the years 1753 & 1754 with Designs,* documents his travels as a guide for a Mr. Barton. During this trip he met and spent some time with Stuart and Revett, who were on their way to Athens, in Smyrna. After returning to England, he wrote *Short Principles for the Architecture of Stone Bridges,* 1760, and *The Grecian Orders* which he dedicated to James Stuart. Although there are no known buildings by Riou, he did many designs for royal palaces, Palladian buildings, etc.; he exhibited drawings at the Free Society of Artists, and competed for the Royal Exchange at Dublin in 1769.

The Grecian Orders is a scholarly discussion of the Grecian Orders as executed (and brought to light by Stuart and Revett) in comparison with the theoretical proportional systems of Palladio, Scamozzi and Vignola. Riou also reconsiders Vitruvius in relation to the Grecian discoveries and includes a checklist of Vitruvian manuscripts and printed editions.

In addition there are essays on town planning with a proposal for the redevelopment of London, plus a section of designs for buildings by Riou.

Martin C. Perdue

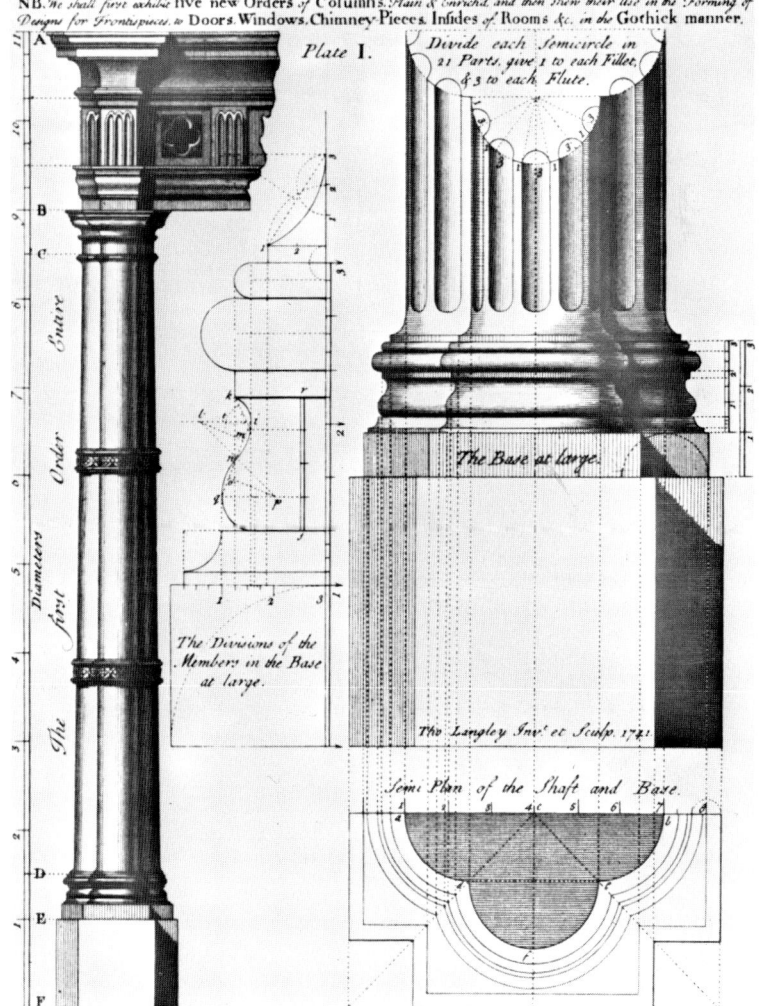

III-A-29.

B. Geometry and Perspective

III-B-1.

Jean Pèlerin, called Viator (1435/40-1524), *De artificiali p(er)spectiva*, Toul, Petrus Jacobi, 23 June 1505 (crit. ed., Brion-Guerry, Paris, 1965).

An astonishing book, whichever way one comes to it. The first product of a new provincial press, and the first printed book to treat perspective in relation to art rather than optics (Alberti, Leonardo, et al., were still in manuscript only), and already the result is perfection. Open it at random, and a fully-fledged piece of perspective in landscape or group of people will all but leap at you from the immaculate page. Even so, the book is neither aggressive nor dogmatic. It simply presents three-point perspective as the most obvious and enjoyable of pastimes, in so economical a way that the visual aspect of the work has not dated at all — it remains fresh and valid and quite as startling as it must have been to its first readers. Through it all, quietly and casually, Pèlerin throws up a concept that was as revolutionary as his visual approach: that the eye is not a fixed point, and that consequently the *linea diametralis*, or line of vision, is *mobile. Pace*, Alberti.

Jean Pèlerin was born at Maillezais in Vendée sometime before 1445. He travelled through France in the 1490s: a church at Angers, the bridges of Brioude and St. Esprit, the rock of Ste. Baume, Notre Dame of Paris and the Sainte Chapelle are the subject of his illustrations, as are his own bedroom and the courtyard of his house, and the cathedral of Toul in Lorraine where he settled as canon after his journey. His chosen Latin name of Viator (traveller), used also for his commentary on Job, is probably a pun on his name (pilgrim). The capitular archives at Toul invariably refer to him as Pèlerin, even in Latin documents.

Pèlerin himself enlarged and altered his work twice before his death which occurred sometime before February 1524. *De artificiali p(er)spectiva. Viator. Secundo* appeared from the same press 12 March 1509. It does not use the original woodblocks (this has never been explained) but close copies of most of them plus new plates including the famous Promenade. In this version each plate is explained in a distych. The plates are no longer printed on one side of the paper only. *De artificiali p(er)spec.va. Viator. Ter.o* is the even more terse title of the last edition, same press again, 7 September 1521. The title page of this edition pays verse tribute to some of the leading artists of the day, many of them known personally to the author.

Gregor Reisch took the 'Introductio architecturae et perspectivae' in his popular *Margarita Philosophica* (1508, 1512, 1515, 1535, 1583) from Viator, and Georg Glockendon's *Von der Kunst Perspectivae* (Nurnberg, 1509, 1540) is nothing but a quickly pirated version of *Viator Secundus*. In 1626 and 1635 Mathurin Jousse published *La perspective positive de Viator* — 'reduite du grand en petit' adding the 1635 title page. A facsimile edition of the 1509 with a "notice historique et bibliographique" by Anatole de Montaiglon appeared in 1860 and was itself reprinted in 1978. Sumptuous (and pretentious) editions of both the 1505 and the 1509, the plates newly cut in wood, were announced in Paris around the same time. Each was to have a foreword by Liane Brion-Guerry, who had earlier written the definitive study of the author and his three editions (*Jean Pèlerin Viator*, Paris, 1962). See also William M. Ivins, *On the Rationalization of Sight* (New York, Metropolitan Museum of Art, *Papers* 8), 1938.

Paul Breman

III-B-2.

Johann II of Pfalz-Simmern, *Eyn schön nützlich buchlin und underweisung der kunst des Messens, mit dem Zirkel, Richtscheidt oder Linial*, Simmern, Hieronymus Rodler, 24 July 1531 (facs. ed., Graz, 1973).

    Duke John installed a private press in his Simmern residence and on it produced a remarkable series of eight first editions translated or illustrated by his own hand. An expert woodcutter (he is known to have made wooden sculptures for a neighboring convent) and a fair draughtsman and painter (pupil of Conrad Faber who gained fame as Schöffer's illustrator of Livy and Caesar), the Duke was also a man of letters. His court was bilingual in French, and he himself made the first German versions of French classics such as *Le roman de Fierabras le Géant*. Duke John, in a word, was the perfect Renaissance prince.

    He knew and admired Dürer's recent works on perspective and proportion, but he had already absorbed the Italian influence to a far greater extent than the master whose heavy-handed 'Northern' seriousness he disliked. The present treatise is a revolt against specialist dogmatism, written in an easy vernacular and illustrated with a simple elegance and deftness that points towards the French school. Most of the full-page views were drawn from life in the grounds, halls and corridors of the castle and the title-page presumably shows the workshop there, with a self-portrait of Duke John at work.

    Only the very first woodcuts used on the press, those in Rüxner's *Thurnier-Buch*, are signed: HH, for Herzog Hans, or Hans von Hunsrück, the Duke's vernacular name. The same signature occurs once more, in Sebastian Münster's *Cosmography* which includes a cut of Simmern and mentions the press. Münster acknowledges his Hunsrück material to have been contributed by Duke John. Hieronymus Rodler, who supervised the press and to whom the present work continues to be wrongly attributed (his own preface clearly mentions another anonymous author) was the Duke's secretary. The book was reprinted under his name in 1546 by Cyr. Jakob at Frankfurt, to whom passed most of the Simmern press material. See Elsbeth Bonnemann, *Die Presse des Hier. Rodler* (1938).

Paul Breman

III-B-3.

Jean Cousin (1501-1590, painter, sculptor, engraver), *Livre de perspective*, Paris, Jean le Royer, 1560 (facs. ed., Unterscheidheim, 1974).

    Cousin was a successful Renaissance artist, equally skilled as painter, miniaturist, draughtsman, engraver, sculptor, designer of stained glass and architect, and leaving a substantial body of work in each of these professions.

    His work on perspective was probably inspired by the appearance in 1557 of Loys Meigret's translation of Dürer, but its frontispiece is adapted from Viator. Totally geometrical in approach, it concentrates on architectural subjects such as columns, buildings, a staircase and ruins: no trick subjects, and only one of the stereometric objects so beloved of the mannerists and other counter-reformers. There was only one edition of the work, in complete contrast to Cousin's *Livre de Pourtraicture* which by the beginning of the nineteenth century had gone through 24 printings. The most rewarding study of the man and his work is still Ambroise Firmin-Didot, *Etude sur Jean Cousin* (Paris, 1872).

Paul Breman

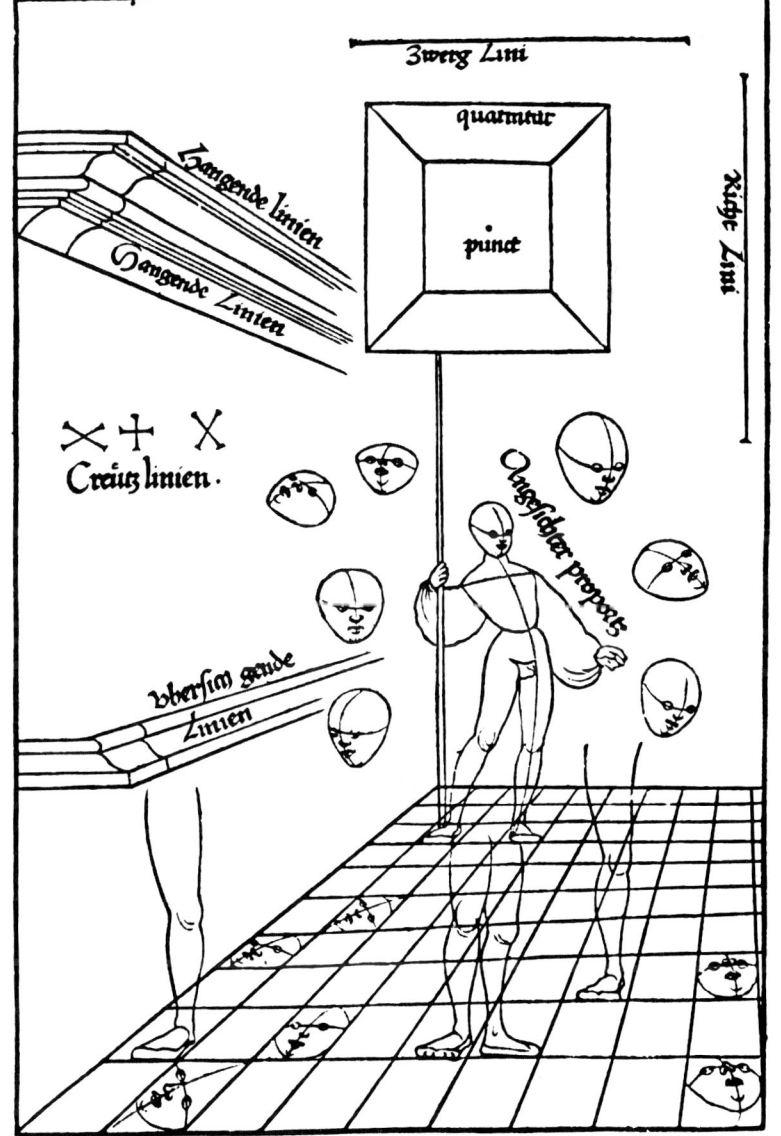

III-B-2.

III-B-4.

Jacopo Barozzi da Vignola, *Le due regole della prospettiva pratica di M. Iacomo Barozzi da Vignola con i comentarij del R.P.M. Egnatio Danti.* Rome, 1583 (facs. ed., Vignola, 1974).

Vignola mastered the precepts of perspective construction as a painter and intarsia designer in Bologna during the early 1530s. Turning to architecture, he soon developed strong theoretical concerns through Vitruvian studies with the Accademia della Virtu, concerns reflected in his building in Rome, Caprarola, Bologna and elsewhere and in the *Regola delli cinque ordini d'architettura* of 1562. Writing on perspective late in life, Vignola was unable to see his treatise through the press before he died (1573). The manuscript passed to his son, Giacinto, who in 1580 entrusted its publication to the Dominican mathematician and cartographer Egnazio Danti (1536-1586).

The *Due regole* is the most comprehensive, systematic and authoritative exposition of one-point and two-point perspective construction methods published in the sixteenth century. Vignola's lean text, consisting of only a series of succinct definitions, theorems and demonstrations, was richly annotated with comments by Danti, who added the engraved illustrations. Danti also included a biography of Vignola, the earliest in print. The treatise was intended for a diverse readership — painters, scenographers and mathematicians as well as architects — and while it did not enjoy the immense popularity of Vignola's book on the Orders, it was republished at least eight times in the course of the seventeenth century.

Richard J. Tuttle

III-B-5.

Ioan de Arphe y Villafane (1535-1603, silversmith, sculptor), *De Varia Commensuracion para la Escultura, y Arquitectura,* Seville, Andrea Pescioni y Ivan de Leon, 1585 (comprising *Libro primero de las figuras Geometricas, Libro segvndo de la proporcion del cuerpo humano, Libro tercero de las formas de los Animales y Aues,* and *Libro quarto de Architectura, y piecas de Iglesia*) (with later editions).

Juan de Arfe was the son and grandson of famous silversmiths, and was responsible, among other magnificent pieces, for the largest and most impressive single example of the Renaissance silversmith's art, namely the *custodia,* or processional monstrance, of Seville Cathedral (1580-1587). He was unwilling however to accept membership of the Burgos guild of silversmiths (*plateros*); because, he said, his true professions were those of "escultor de oro e plata, e architecto," and, besides, he was an "hidalgo e persona principal . . . e de los más eminentos hombres de Espana en su arte."

In *De varia commensuracion,* his medallion portrait and personal cipher under a coat of arms bear witness to his strong sense of personal dignity and status. The purpose of the book, he says in the address to the reader, is limited to "what can teach art in sculpture and architecture," i.e. it is essentially a didactic manual — directed specifically to instrument makers (Book I: sundials), sculptors (Books II & III: human figures, animals) and architects and silversmiths (Book IV: the Orders, ecclesiastical vessels).

Book IV titulo I provides a masterly brief summary of the five Orders, based on Serlio but with the strong Plateresque slant, and the interest in "permissible" ornament, which was appropriate for the architecture of silversmiths, and also for that of small buildings, as Palladio explains in his *Quattro Libri* (IV, 15).

John B. Bury

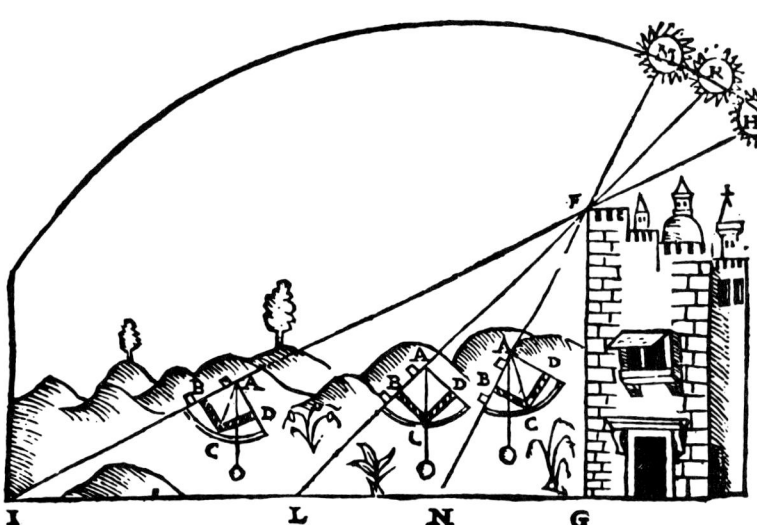

III-B-6.

III-B-6.

Cosimo Bartoli, *Del modo di misurare le distantie, le superficie, i corpi, le piante, le provincie, le prospettiue, & tutte le altre cose terrene,* Venice, Francesco Franceschi, 1564 (with later eds.) (facs. ed., Portland, Oregon, 1972).

Bartoli was one of the first members of the *Accademia degli Umidi*. He edited Alberti, translated Oronce Finé, and published a commentary on difficult passages in Dante. His reading was altogether surprisingly wide: the list of sources at the beginning of the *Modo di Misurare* includes not only Finé and Alberti but also Dürer, Gemma Frisius, Peuerbach and Appianus — not the most common references South of the Alps.

The book on mensuration is generally reckoned to be the best sixteenth century treatise on practical geometry, and it certainly is the most handsome. It gives particularly good accounts of early surveying instruments, including the construction of a compass. The illustration of an astrolabe derives from Juan de Rojas (*Commentarium in astrolabium,* Paris, 1550) who is duly acknowledged as Giovan Roia. A separate chapter is devoted to square and cube roots, with a table of square roots up to 662. There were further editions in 1589 and 1614.

Paul Breman

III-B-7.

Daniele Barbaro, *La practica della perspettiva di Monsignor Daniele Barbaro eletto patriarca d'Aquileia, opera molto utile a pittori, a scultori, & ad architetti*, Venice, Camillo & Rutilio Borgominieri, 1568 (facs. ed., Bologna, 1977-8).

In his commentary on the three scenic modes as presented in Vitruvius's *De architectura* (V, viii), Barbaro expanded the ancient author's laconic descriptions and outlined his own plans for a full book on "la prospettiva pratica." Asserting that little had been published on the subject and reproving his contemporaries for their supposed neglect of the practical intricacies of perspective, he himself undertook to correct the situation through his treatise.

The preface to *La pratica della perspettiva* recapitulates the same argument; here, however, Barbaro does acknowledge the work of his Renaissance predecessors. He cites and uses the studies of Piero della Francesca, and he recognizes the "ingenious and subtle" investigations of Albrecht Dürer and the less acute work of Serlio. Although critical of all three, Barbaro nonetheless makes extensive use of the examples of their work — indeed, to the point of outright plagiarism. He is also critical of contemporary painters who, while "otherwise celebrated and famous, are content with a very simple practice, failing in their pictures to demonstrate an understanding of perspective worthy of much praise, and offering no real principles in their writings." No names are mentioned, although the earlier of two manuscript drafts of the book (Venice, Biblioteca Nazionale Marciana) singles out for praise one living artist, Jacopo Sansovino, "famous not only as sculptor and architect, but a most subtle master of perspective."

Basically a practical manual, *La pratica della perspettiva* offers a series of lessons in projective geometry and includes as well chapters on architectural ornament and the Orders, the scenic modes, human proportions — in which Barbaro borrows from Dürer's *Vier Bucher von menschlicher Proportion*, including the illustrations — universal clocks, and mechanical aids to the *camera oscura*. Barbaro's treatise was reissued in 1569, its title slightly revised as *opera molto profittevole a pittori, scultori, et architetti*.

David Rosand

III-B-8.

Wenzel Jamitzer (1508-1585, engraver, jeweler), *Perspectiva corporum regularium*, Nurnberg, Gotlicher Hulff, 1568 (2nd ed., Amsterdam, 1618) (Fr. transl., Paris, 1964; facs. ed., Graz, 1973).

In this work of noteable interest and originality — above all, for the splendid engravings made in collaboration with Jost Ammen — Jamitzer, a jeweler, presents perspective illustrations of the five platonic polyhedrons and their many complex variations. A product of the most refined German Mannerism, this type of perspective illustration, focusing on the object rather than the space in which it is contained, would serve as a pattern for marquetry and related decorative arts.

Dora Wiebenson

III-B-8.

III-B-9.

Martini Bassi (1542-1591, architect), *Dispareri in materia d'architettura, et perspettiva. Con pareri di eccellenti, et famosi architetti, che li risoluono*, Brescia, Francesco & Pietro Maria Marchetti, 1572 (2nd ed., Milan, 1771) (facs. ed., Bologna, 1977-8).

Bassi, a native Milanese architect, objected strongly to plans drawn up by fashionable Pelligrino Tibaldi for the unfinished cathedral. In his attempts to get the work stopped Bassi enlisted the help of some of the greatest practitioners and theoreticians of the age. In his book he includes letters from Palladio, Vignola, Vasari and Bertano as well as his own earlier correspondence with the magistrats and the superintendent of the fabric.

The book centers on the projected Annunciation group and Bassi's treatment of the vexed question of the perspective of sculptural ensembles. His first four plates are devoted to this, but like other writers of his time (notably Serlio) he still falls far short of an adequate theoretical solution. On this part of the work see Fiorillo, *Kleine Schriften* (1893), 1:288 ff. and Erwin Panofsky, *Die Perspektive als symbolische Form*, pp. 325 ff. For more general notes on the cathedral controversy see J.S. Ackerman, "Ars sine scientia nihil est," pp. 84-111. Fowler cat. 40. Harvard (Italian) 46. The work was reprinted in 1771 by F.M. Ferrari, who added a useful Life of the author.

Paul Breman

III-B-10.

Jacques Androuet du Cerceau the Elder, *Leçons de perspective positive*, Paris, Mamert Patisson, 1576 (2nd ed., 1676) (facs. ed., Paris, 1978).

The small folio of twelve pages and sixty plates etched by Du Cerceau, comprising lessons in perspective with accompanying diagrams exploits traditional perspective problems. The plates include views of buildings, designs for courtyards and loggias, and a fountain taken from Du Cerceau's *Livre d'architecture*, especially from the third book. L.W. Fowler *(The Fowler Architectural Collection)* has noted the book's "considerable charm because of the arrangement of the diagrams on the plates and the introduction of characteristic slim figures: all in crisp, clean lines."

Naomi Miller

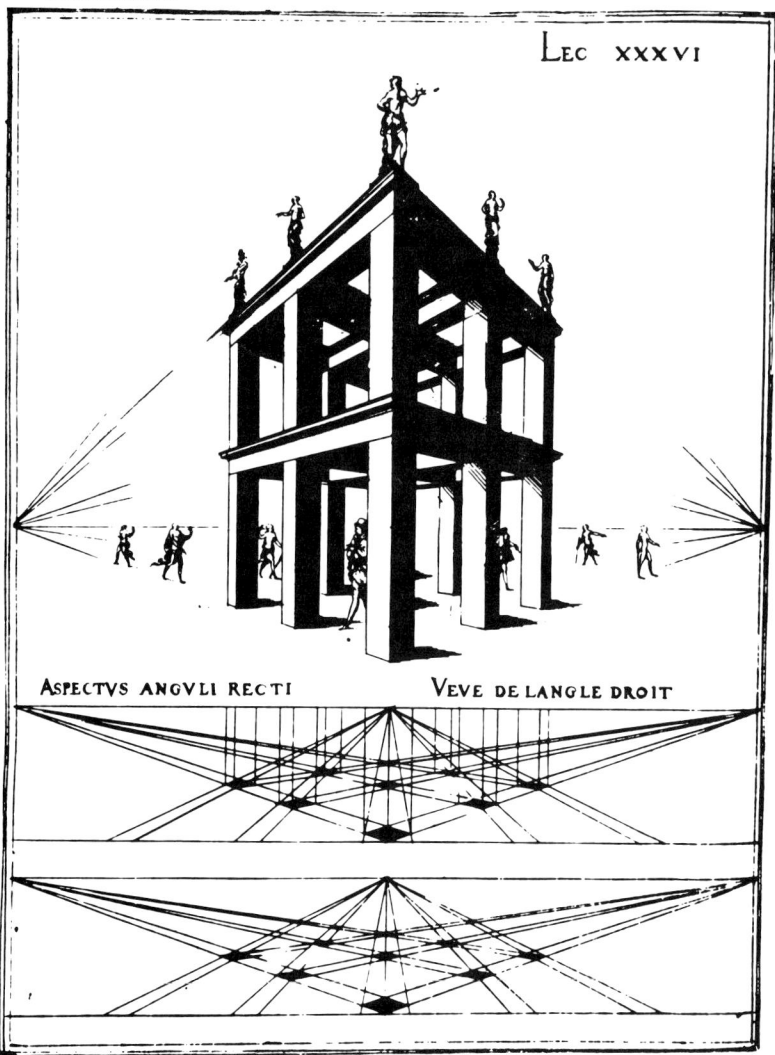

III-B-11.

Lorenzo Sirigatti (?-1596/7), *La pratica di prospettiva,* Venice, Girolamo Franceschi, 28 October 1596 (Eng. ed., I. Ware, London, 1756).

Sirigatti takes his reader through twelve plates of carefully explained 'basics' and then through a succession of arches, vaults, capitals, doors and facades to intricate representations of the violin and the lute. The second book (which has no text) shows applications of the various techniques to buildings and their parts and to a really spectacular variety of open and closed polyhedra. Baltrusaitis, in his stimulating chapter on the objects in Holbein's Ambassadors painting of 1533 (*Anamorphoses,* 1955, pages 58-70) ignores Sirigatti's treatment of the crucial lute, yet Sirigatti's plate 42 is the direct source of De Caus (1612) and Accolti (1625). Earlier in his same book, Baltrusaitis cites plate 43 as an advanced example of 'accelerated' perspective: 'la scene entière est inclinée. Les comédiens ne se trouvent plus dans la réalité.'

Sirigatti's treatise was appreciated equally for its good looks and its good sense. Perspective, to the painters and architects of the Renaissance, was one of the most highly valued of all the sciences, and Sirigatti can rightfully claim a place among the most important writers on the subject. His work was much in vogue again during the eighteenth century when it was admired as easily intelligible and intensely practical. Isaac Ware translated volume one into English in 1756. The beautiful title design had already found English admirers when it was adapted for Mauclerc's *New Treatise of Architecture* in 1699.

Paul Breman

III-B-12.

Guidobaldo del Monte (1546-1607, mathematician), *Perspectivae libri sex,* Pesaro, Hieronymus Concordia, 1600.

This is the only edition of one of the most important contributions to both theoretical and applied perspective, little known now because the book has become very rare.

Guido Ubaldo del Monte, pupil of Commandino, friend of Galileo and Tartaglia, was one of the foremost mathematicians of his time. His books on the calendar and on mechanics, issued also by Concordia in the author's native Pesaro, were classics from the moment they appeared. This book on perspective first established the vanishing point, a concept without which we now find all mention of perspective almost unintelligible but one which in Ubaldo's time was just an esoteric notion of pure mathematics, not at all appreciated by the 'practical' perspectivists.

The sixth part of Ubaldo's work, "De Scenis," ranks in the literature of theatre perspective alongside Serlio, Sabbatini (who was his pupil) and Carini-Motta. Schlosser affirms (page 413) that 'Il difficile problema del rilievo prospettico . . . trovo . . . la sue definitiva soluzione scientifica nel libro del grande matematico G. del Monte.' Thomas Malton (Appendix, pages 80-84) has a fulsome essay in praise of Del Monte whom he pays the unusual compliment of ranking right alongside his revered Brook Taylor, another mathematician, and the only writer to make full use of the idea of vanishing points in his own two treatises on perspective (1715 and 1719).

Paul Breman

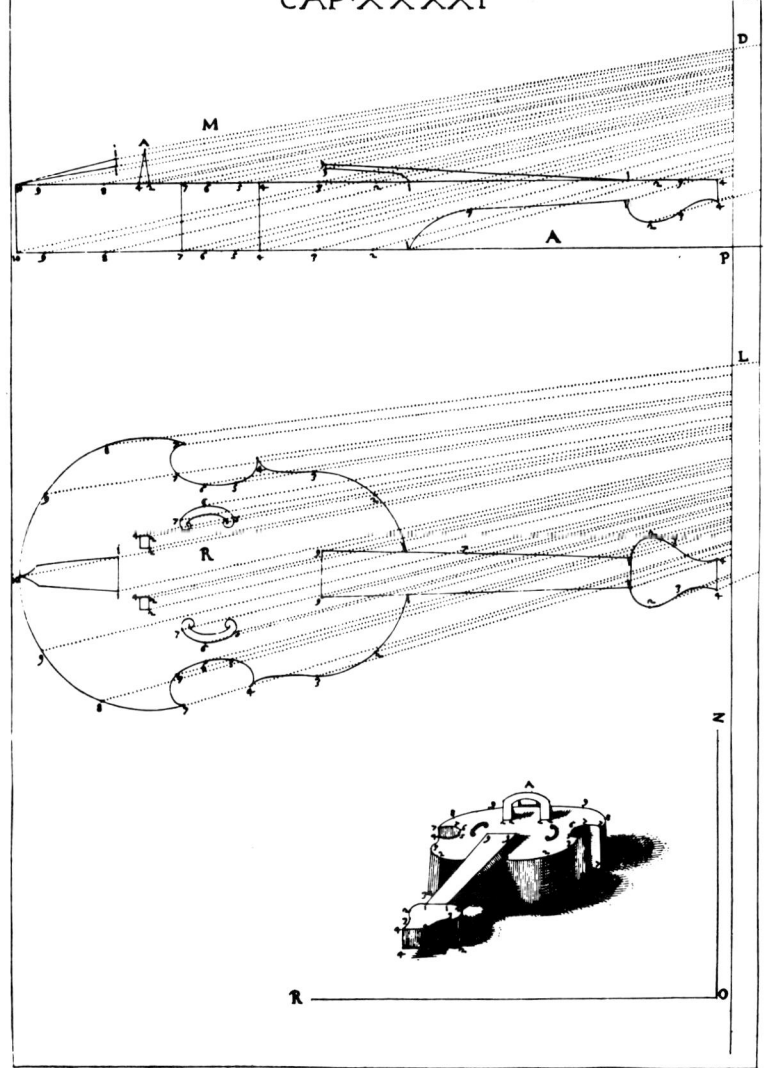

III-B-11.

III-B-13.

Hans Vredeman de Vries, *Perspectiva, id est celeberrima ars inspicientis aut transpicientis oculorum aciei, in pariete, tabula aut tela depicta*, The Hague, Leyden, 1604-1605 (facs. ed., New York, 1968).

De Vries's first essay on perspective, *Artis perspectivae formulae* (Antwerp, 1568), culminated in this major treatise which is strongly influenced by Dürer's work on perspective. De Vries oriented his treatise toward practical use by painters, engravers, sculptors, ironworkers, architects, masons, cabinetmakers, and carpenters. The work was a standard reference for these practitioners, and it was often republished and revised.

Dora Wiebenson

III-B-14.

Hendrik Hondius, *Onderwysinge in de perspective conste*, The Hague, Hondius, 1622.
Institutio artis perspectivae, The Hague, Hondius, 1622.
Instruction en la science de perspective, The Hague, Hondius, 1625.
Grondige onderrichtinge in de optica, oft perspective konst, Amsterdam, 1640 (also The Hague, 1647 and later)

The elder De Hondt, born 1573 in the southern Netherlands but gone north with the reformed States' war of independence against Catholic Spain, was a pupil of Vredeman de Vries whose influence is as evident in De Hondt's work as it was in that of Samuel Marolois a decade earlier. Hondius had engraved and published Vredeman's work on perspective in 1604, and Marolois in 1615. The relationships between the three works is unusually close.

There are, however, some interesting and very practical aspects to De Hondt's work which set it far apart from that of his fantasizing master. His selection of objects, which includes a fine representation of a press, is evidence of a different spirit, but more important are plates 30 and 31 showing the plan and perspective view of "het nieuwen Hof van den Doorl. Prince van Oranjen te 's Graven-hage." These are the only record of the reputedly superb garden which Jacob de Gheyn made for Maurice of Nassau in the bassecour of the Buitenhof in The Hague. Many other plates from Hondius' book were used for Joseph Moxon's *Practical Perspective*, London 1670.

Paul Breman

III-B-15.

Pietro Accolti (1578-1627), *Lo inganno de gl'ochi, prospettiva pratica*, Florence, Pietro Cecconcelli, 1625 (facs. ed., Portland, Oregon, 1972).

Accolti describes himself as "gentiluomo fiorentino, e della Toscana Accademia del Disegno" and his treatise is addressed primarily to draftsmen and painters. He is thorough in his treatment of light, shadow and reflection but does not yet differentiate between differing sources of light. He seems to have a good working knowledge of optics and treats at length of the camera obscura. The usual array of stereometric objects is presented solely as visual parlour tricks.

The real value of the book (which was never reprinted) lies in the "Discorso sul disegno" on pages 144-152. This is the first appearance in print of any part of Leonardo da Vinci's essay on painting, hitherto believed lost. It was not until five years later that Cassiano dal Pozzo, secretary to one of the Barberini cardinals, gained access to a full manuscript.

Paul Breman

III-B-16.

I.L. de Vaulezard (active 1st half 17c., mathematician), *Perspective cilindrique et conique; ou traicté des apparences veuës par le moyen des miroirs cilindrique et conique*, Paris, J. Jacquin, 1630.
Abrégé ou raccourcy de la Perspective par l'imitation, dans lequel est traicte du moyen de changer une Perspective en une autre semblable, ayant la distnce et hauteur de l'oeil comme aussi les distances ou enforcement des objects plus grands ou moindres que leurs semblables en la prémier, Paris, Chez l'Autheur, 1631 (2nd ed., 1643).

Vaulezard was considered by Niceron to be 'the greatest analist and scholarly man on geometry, optics, and their dependencies that we have today.' His works are particularly important to the history of perspective in the seventeenth century not only because they mark the beginning of a long French predominance on the subject, but also because the second edition of *Abrégé ou raccourcy...* (and its title variation) states clearly a strong opposition to Desargues, the major contemporary scholar of perspective. Vaulezard's works must therefore be considered to initiate the violent controversy that took place in the following years about the work of Desargues and his most important follower, Abraham Bosse.

While Vaulezard's first book is didactic, being compiled to meet the desires of his students, it develops theoretical and practical aspects of images in perspective reflected by cylindrical and conical mirrors, as an introduction for the development of the study of anamorphosis. The second book is an outline of linear perspective developed according to rigorous mathematical principles. In this work is described the "perspective compass" which increases the dimensions of figures; however, it is no more than the compass to determine proportions already described by Galileo in 1606.

Elizabeth Lambeth

III-B-17.

Girard Desargues (1591-1661, geometer), *Example d'une des manières universelles*, Paris, the author, 1636.

The most controversial figure in perspective literature, object of virulent attacks and abuse, Desargues was born at Lyon, moved to Paris in 1626 where as a geometer esteemed by Richelieu he also became a much respected friend of Descartes. The last ten years of his life were spent in his family's native Condrieu where he had always owned and then actively tended the vineyards which even now produce the Rhone district's most famous white wine.

His thoughts on perspective and the related matter of stone cutting (conic sections) were printed in rather cryptic private pamphlets between 1636 and 1644. Hard to understand and uncompromisingly Cartesian, they were either condemned (Jacques Curabelle, *Examen des oeuvres du Sr Desargues*, Paris 1644) or adapted in a more popular form without

any acknowledgement (Dubreuil). Only through the staunch defense by his pupil Abraham Bosse did Desargues' work on perspective gain any honourable recognition in his own time. His debt to Viator has been ably demonstrated by Brion-Guerry (*Viator,* Paris 1962) but in his own turn Desargues can be said to have founded projective geometry, making it possible for Monge, building out from this groundwork, to establish descriptive geometry.

René Taton has collected Desargues' scattered work in *L'oeuvre mathematique de G. Desargues. Textes publiés et commentés avec une introduction bibliographique et historique.* Paris, 1951.

Paul Breman

III-B-18.

Jean François Niceron (1613-1646, mathematician, painter), *La perspective curieuse, ou magie artificielle des effets merveilleux de l'optique . . . la catoptrique . . . la dioptique,* Paris, Pierre Bilain, 1638.

Niceron, of the order of Minims, enjoyed a considerable reputation both as a mathematician and as a painter. He decorated convents of his order in Rome (where he taught) and in Paris with frescoes which unfortunately no longer survive.

His book is chiefly concerned with 'special effects,' especially anamorphoses of different kinds. Niceron gives the rules for constructing anamorphic compositions and discusses several works in the genre by other artists. The much enlarged second edition of his work was published, in Latin, by Langlois of Paris in 1646 under the title *Thaumaturgus opticus.* The author died in August of that year, before the book came off the press. The new edition includes what may well be a portrait of Niceron at work on a large anamorphic St. John on Patmos. Later editions are combined with a work on optics from the hand of Niceron's old teacher Mersenne, another Minim. Langlois' widow published this version in 1651 and 1663.

Paul Breman

III-B-19.

Jean Dubreuil (1602-1670, Jesuit), *La perspective practique . . . par un Parisien, Religieux de la Compagnie de Iesus,* Paris, Melchior Tavernier & François Langlois, 1642 (with later eds.).

The rare first edition of what is quite probably the most influential book on perspective ever published expressly for the use of a lay audience. Raffed together with greater cunning than scruple from a number of sketchily acknowledged sources, this book aroused the kind of public squabbles that ensure wide publicity and instant success. Chief victims were Aleaume (never named), whose original plates were plundered before ever his book saw the light (the four-page privilege of the 1643 edition provides many details of this story) and Desargues.

All the same, the book obviously filled a shrewdly-judged gap. As an easily understandable manual for non-professionals it enjoyed considerably more than a *succès de scandale.* As the "Jesuit perspective" it saw many English editions, in two different translations by the publisher Robert Pricke (1672) and the encyclopedist Ephraim Chambers (1726). Thomas Malton (Appendix, pages 18-21) gave a fair and ultimately very

III-B-19.

critical account of the work, acknowledging that it was the one book which had made him want to study perspective in the first place.

A second edition in 1651 was augmented with a section on military works. Meanwhile, two further volumes had appeared (1647 and 1649) which were of an entirely different (if equally borrowing) nature. The third volume, especially, is devoted entirely to the rather outdated conceits of Renaissance 'op art,' with emphasis on stage design: in his youth, Dubreuil had taken part in performances at the Collegio Romano, and his ideas accurately reflect the practice of the Jesuit school theatre movement which had been so influential at that time.

Paul Breman

III-B-20.

Abraham Bosse, *Manière universelle de Mr Desargues pour pratiquer la perspective par petit-pied, comme le géometral,* Paris, the author, 1648.
Moyen universel de pratiquer la perspective sur les tableaux, ou surfaces irregulières, Paris, the author, 1653 (with a 'supplement' in 1669).

Abraham Bosse, able trade engraver born at Tours but active in Paris, reprinted Desargues' *Example* of 1636 and added several elaborations of a purely geometrical nature, among them the statement and proof of what is now known as Desargues' theorem of perspective triangles, the theoretical foundation of relief perspective which had eluded earlier writers such as Bassi.

The second work elaborates on the intricacies of anamorphic construction on vaults and ceilings. Dubreuil's unauthorized and unacknowledged use of Desargues' ideas had been the occasion of a particularly virulent and public quarrel, and this defense of the original work eventually cost Bosse his post at the Académie Royale of Colbert and Le Brun. His own *Traité des pratiques géométrales et perspectives* of 1665 was issued after his dismissal, as a defiant summary of the course he had been teaching for fifteen years.

Through the Dutch translations of these two works (*Algemeene manier, Algemeen middel,* both Amsterdam 1664) Desargues' ideas became one of the first European texts on geometry known and used in Japan — see George Sarton in *Isis 41* (1950). See also A. Blum, *Abraham Bosse* (1924).

Paul Breman

III-B-21.

Abraham Bosse, *Représentations géometrales de plusieures parties des bastiments faites par les reigles de l'architecture antique et de qui les mesures sont réduittes en piedz, poulces et lignes, afin de s'accomoder a la maniere de mesurer la plus en uzage parmy le commun des ouvriers,* Paris, the author, 1659.

The *Représentations geometrales* is conceived as a handbook for stonemasons and gives a popular version of Desargues' perspective theory and of its application to regular designs for the carving of complicated curved stonework. A German translation of this handbook was published at Nurnberg in 1767.

Walter Kambartel

III-B-22.

Sébastien Leclerc, *Pratique de la geometrie sur le papier et sur le terrain,* Paris, Thomas Jolly, 1669 (Eng. trans. R. Pricke, *Magnum in Parvo, or The Practice of Geometry,* London, 1667).

Leclerc published two treatises on geometry, the *Pratique de la géométrie* of 1669 (often referred to as *La Petite géométrie*) and the slightly larger *Traité de géométrie,* 1690 (*La Grande géométrie*). Both provide instructions for drawing geometrical figures beginning with the simplest shapes and working toward more complicated problems. In general the earlier book is the more theoretical while the later is more attuned to the practical uses of geometry in building construction, surveying, and so forth. The books were of great importance to draftsmen, architects, engineers, and amateurs because the reader could easily study the subject without recourse to formal training. In addition, Leclerc put all of his artistic abilities at the service of the illustrations (105 in the *Pratique,* not all used in each edition; 18 plates for the *Traité*) which on account of their inventiveness became collector's items. The *Pratique* was reprinted in eight editions up to 1754, and revised in several nineteenth-century French versions. The first English edition appeared in 1670 under the title *Magnum in Parvo,* followed by several eighteenth-century editions under various titles. A German translation appeared in 1758 as the *Abhandlung von der theoretischen und practischen geometrie.*

Robert Neuman

III-B-21.

III-B-23.

Sébastien Leclerc, *Discours touchant le point de veüe, dans lequel il est prouvé que les choses qu'on voit distinctement ne sont veües que d'on oeil*, Paris, Thomas Jolly, 1679.

Leclerc's little book, the *Discours touchant le point de veüe*, was one of the first French investigations into the nature of sight. The text, with some thirty-one illustrations in wood and copper, was aimed at an audience of artists and connoisseurs interested in problems of optics. Its purpose was to defend current theories of perspective against accusations that their use in painting had been based on false premises. The arguments were later expanded in Leclerc's *Système de la vision fondé sur de nouveaux principes* (1712).

Robert Neuman

III-B-24.

Giulio Troili (c. 1613-1685, painter), *Paradossi per pratticare la prospettiva, senza saperla, fiori, per facilitare l'intelligenza, frutti, per non operare alla cieca*, Bologna, heirs of Peri, 1672.

Troili, a pupil of the quadratura painter Michelangelo Colonna, became scene painter for the Farnese theatre at Parma. Ferdinando Bibiena saw his work there (probably after the artist's death) and absorbed its influence. This original edition of Troili's exceptionally handsome book on perspective is one of the real milestones in the history of theatrical scenery: it describes the conscious use of visual deception, the creation of greater 'depth' by means of oblique positioning of the wings, as common practice twenty years before Pozzo.

Gordon Craig was the first modern man of the theatre to draw attention to Troili's work, just as his son Edward Craig would retrieve Carini-Motta from oblivion half a century later. Hélène Leclerc summed up the significance of Troili and his position as a forerunner of Pozzo in her immensely readable *Les Origines italiennes de l'Architecture Théatrale Moderne* (pages 181-184): "Plus modestes et moins originaux que le traité du grand Pozzo, les Paradossi ont d'autant plus de signification historique pour l'évolution du décor en perspective. Ils constituent, à notre connaissance, la première démonstration de la scène à coulisses moderne, non pas du point de vue mécanique, mais étudiée sous l'angle du décor en perspective qui se présente désormais avec la forme de simples châssis, dépourvus du retour d'équerre qui les caractérisait au temps de Sabbatini."

The augmented second edition of Troili's work (Bologna, 1683) was also its last. It consisted of the original two parts plus a third called "Paradossi overo fiori, e frutti di prospettiva prattica parte terza." This new part opens with a section of random notes on perspective problems, including Troili's translation of Christoph Scheiner's essay on parallelograms from his *Pantographice* of 1631. It also devotes some attention to shadows, but its main subject is the correct delineation of all aspects of military architecture, based on Guarini.

Paul Breman

III-B-24.

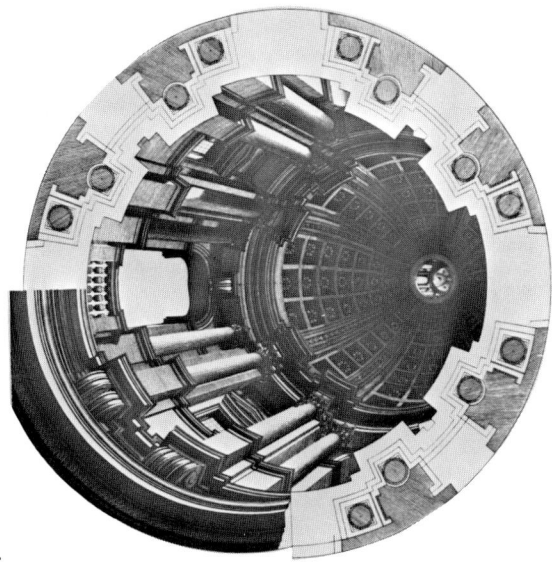

III-B-25.

III-B-25.
Andrea Pozzo (1642-1709, architect, painter), *Perspectiva pictorum et architectorum Andreae Putei e societate Jesu*, Rome, Joannis Jacobi Komarek Bohemi, 1693-1700 (2v.) (facs. ed. New York, 1971).

Pozzo was a self-taught architect, learning his craft from sixteenth-century Italian treatises. Nonetheless, his early training and continued practice as a painter determined his attitude toward architecture and, consequently, the contents of the treatise. In keeping with the developments of the Late Baroque in Rome, Pozzo's approach was scenographic. However, he went a step further than his contemporaries, declaring that architecture proceeded from painting and the requisite skill of a painter — perspective. "Chi e buon pittore, e buon prospettico, dunque sarà buon architetto."

The treatise is almost entirely practical and therefore is for the most part original. Not satisfied merely to elucidate the principles of perspective, Pozzo demonstrated step-by-step procedures for its application in varying situations, ranging from single objects, to stage settings, to *quadratura* ceilings. Although obviously of benefit to painters, the treatise was primarily directed to architects. Pozzo made no qualitative distinction between real and fictional architecture or permanent and provisional structures. From his point of view, therefore, the mastery of perspective was a necessary tool of the architect. In many respects Pozzo's treatise was a summation of Baroque aims. For him, perspective was the means by which the ultimate illusion could be produced, that is, the creation of a spatial continuum in which the real and the imaginery were completely merged. The treatise was extremely popular and had considerable impact. By 1708 it had been translated into German, French, Flemish, Spanish, and English and new editions appeared throughout the eighteenth century. As a result, his perspective studies, as well as his architectural designs, continued to serve as sources of inspiration.

Cathie C. Kelly

III-B-26.
Bernard Lamy (1640-1715, cleric, theologian, mathematician), *Traité de perspective, ou sont contenus les fondemens de la peinture,* Paris, Anisson, 26 February 1701.

Lamy was a great popularizer of the mechanical and mathematical sciences. A cleric, he also wrote on rather unusual subjects in Christian theology. One of his pet projects was the description and reconstruction of the Temple of Jerusalem — a favorite pastime of the later seventeenth and much of the eighteenth century. Lamy says that it was because of this that he took up the study of perspective.

As the title indicates, his treatise is emphatically pictorial. This is particularly evident in the careful (and useful) differentiation between shadows cast by artificial light and those caused by the sun. Another interesting feature of Lamy's approach is his attempt to illustrate the rules of linear perspective as the three dimensional phenomenon they really are, by means of two planes intersecting at right angles — a device used also by the ill-fated Aleaume (see entry on Dubreuil). An Amsterdam 1734 edition of Lamy's book had the plates engraved instead of cut on wood. As *Perspective made easie* the work had appeared in London in 1710, but a little known English version by 'an Officer of His Majesties Ordnance' (A. Forbes) had long preceded this, in 1702.

Paul Breman

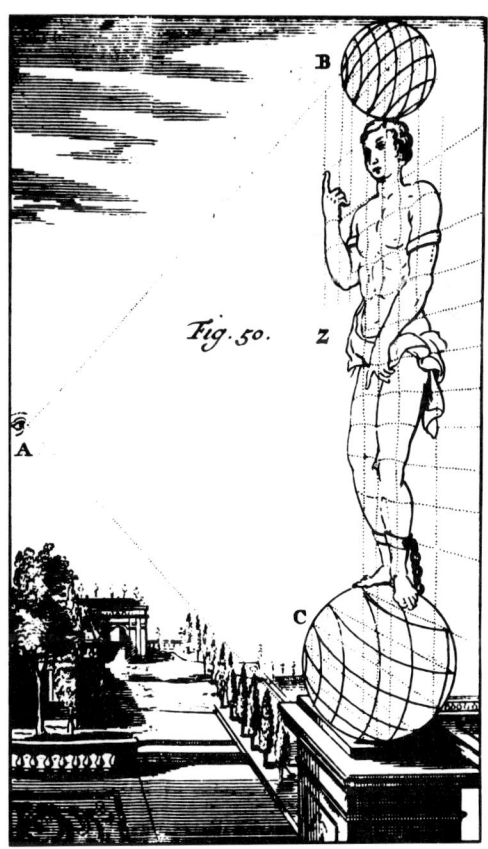

III-B-26.

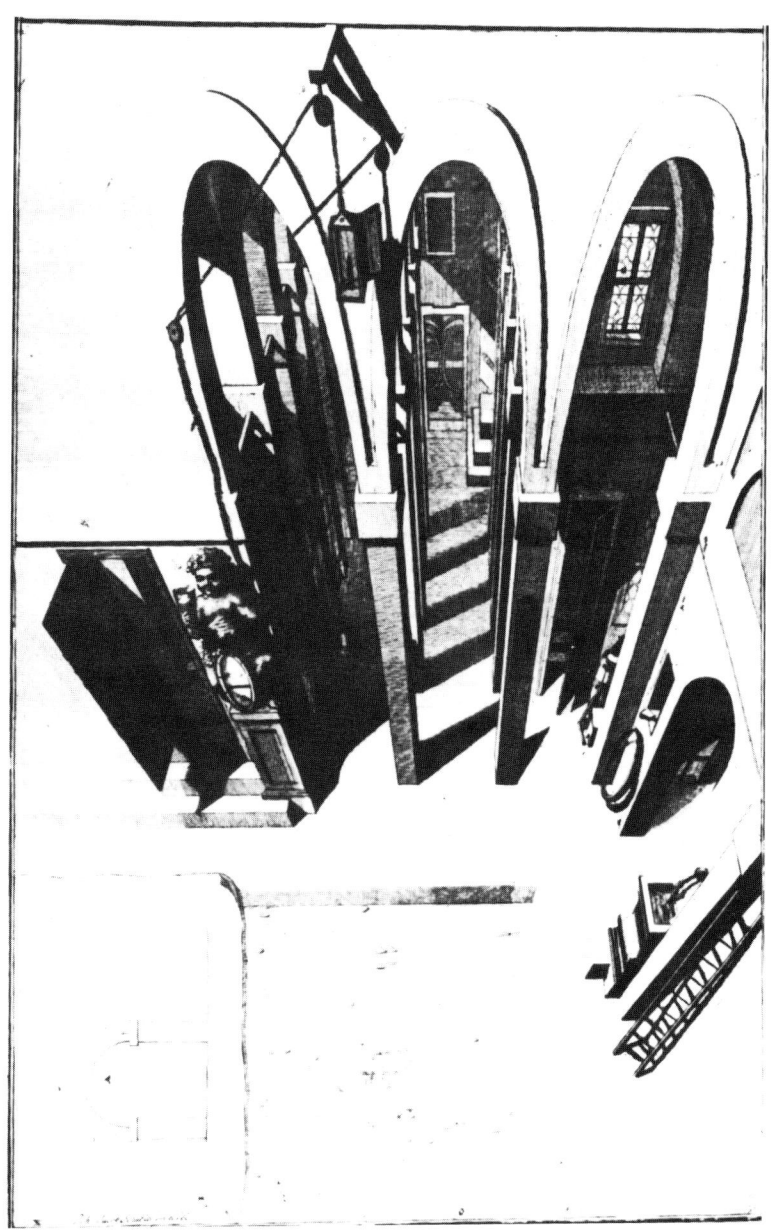

III-B-28.

III-B-27.

Brook Taylor (1685-1731, geometer, mathematician), *Linear Perspective: or, a New Method of Representing justly All Manner of Objects as They Appear to the Eye in all Situations*, London, R. Knaplock, 1715.
New Principles of Linear Perspective, London, R. Knaplock, 1719.

Taylor became a member of the Royal Society in 1712 and his fame as a geometer and mathematician was second to none. His work on logarithms and his quarrels with Bernouilli were equally famous. His two treatises on perspective are the first original works on the subject in English — in fact, they are the first original works in any language for a very long time.

Taylor stated flatly that, if most works on perspective were longwinded and boring, it was because their authors were better draughtsmen than geometers, their examples pretty but unsound. The really short and easy way to good practice was not to copy other people's fancies but to obtain a thorough understanding of the few principles involved. Taylor's own books were mercifully short, and although they failed to excite contemporary artists, later English writers such as Joshua Kirby and Thomas Malton drew heavily on them. Italian and French versions appeared in 1755 and 1757.

Paul Breman

III-B-28.

Jean Courtonne (1671-1739, architect), *Traité de la perspective pratique, avec des remarques sur l'architecture, suivis de quelques édifices considérables mis en perspective, and de l'invention de l'auteur*, Paris, Jacques Vincent, 1725.

Courtonne taught at the Paris Academy of Architecture for the last ten years of his life and from there exercised a great influence on the younger architects. This, his only book, can claim a double importance: it is not only an exceptionally good manual on perspective devised expressly for architects by an architect, but it also provides the only published record of that architect's most important buildings, the hôtels Matignon and Noirmontier (both still extant, the latter as the official residence of the Prime Minister).

The plates devoted to the author's own buildings appear here for the first time, but they already bear the numbers assigned them for Jombert's collection *Architecture Moderne*, usually attributed to Briseux but in reality compiled by several architects of whom Courtonne was one. The frontispiece, too, is a plate designed by Courtonne for the same publication. Hautecoeur, *Histoire de l'architecture classique en France*, said 'Courtonne fut un des artistes les plus complets de son temps: il possède une science accomplie des plans, des proportions, du décor'.

Paul Breman

III-B-29.

William Halfpenny, *Perspective Made Easy*, London, John Oswald, 1731.

Halfpenny presented this publication as an instructional manual for the student. In the same manner that he described a drafting board in *Magnum in Parvo* (1722) Halfpenny describes here a "scenographical protractor" by which to execute perspectives. He illustrates not only simple geometrical forms in perspective, but also chairs, bridges, gardens and houses, and specific examples were taken from Bristol and Bath. Each plate faces an explanatory text.

Elise M. Quasebarth

III-B-30.

Ferdinando Galli Bibiena, *Istruzioni a'giovani studenti di pittura, e architettura nell'Accademia Clementina dell'Istituto delle Scienze*, Bologna, Lelio della Volpe, 1732.

    Like the *Direzioni a giovani studenti*, this text was destined to instruct architectural and painting students of the Institute. It differs from the *Direzioni* and the original text only in its introduction of "operazione 69" and the accompanying illustration of a *veduta per angolo* with a ground plan that permits the reader to reconstruct the placement of the set pieces and wings. Subsequent editions of the book were published in Bologna in 1745, 1764, 1777 and in Venice in 1769.

Diane M. Kelder

III-B-31.

Edme-Sébastien Jeaurat (1725-1803, mathematician, astronomer), *Traité de perspective à l'usage des artistes ou l'on démontre géométriquement toutes les pratiques de cette science*, Paris, J. Chardon for Ch. Ant. Jombert, 1750.

    Jeaurat held the chair of mathematics at the military academy and was also active as an astronomer. His ideas on perspective derive mostly from the teaching of Sébastien Leclerc and his very precise and detailed illustrations were ably designed by Soubeyran in a clear and easily digestible style which owes much to the master without every being slavish. The book received immediate acclaim (*Journal des Scavans*, 1751, p. 157) but was never reprinted.

    In our days the book is better known as a superb example of the period's book production thanks, in no small degree, to the enchanting rococo vignettes on architectural subjects which fill out many of its pages with unusually decorative compositions. Most of these are by Babel.

Paul Breman

III-B-32.

Johann Heinrich Lambert (1728-1777, scientist), *La perspective affranchie de l'embaras du plan géometral*, Zurich, Heidegger, 1759 (2nd ed., Zurich, 1774) (crit. ed., M. Steck, Berlin, 1943).

    Lambert, a self-taught Alsatian, was one of the most original scientists of the age of reason, especially in the related fields of optics, photometry and perspective. His equal-area conical projection would revolutionize cartography.

    The present work gives fairly concise instructions for central and parallel projections. It was actually written in French (not an altogether uncommon thing for an Alsatian author) and the simultaneous German version (*Die freye Perspektive*) was a translation. The work had grown out of Latin notes made in Lambert's *Monatsbuch* from November 1756 on. The second edition contained an additional section of "Anmerkungen und Zusätze" which included 32 pages on the history of perspective.

Paul Breman

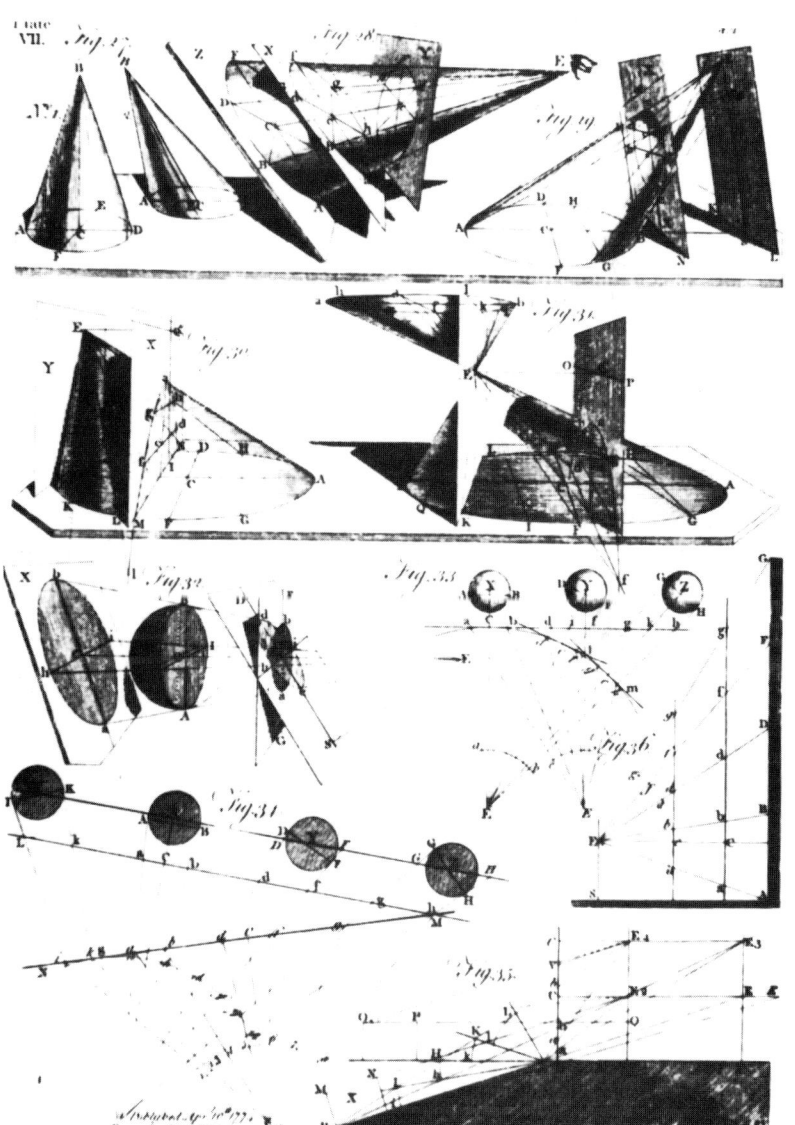

III-B-33.

III-B-33.

Thomas Malton (1726-1801, draftsman, writer), *A Compleat Treatise on Perspective, in Theory and Practice; on the True Principles of Dr. Brook Taylor. Made Clear, in Theory, by Various Moveable Schemes, and Diagrams,* London, the author, 1776;
An appendix, or second part, to the compleat treatise, London, the author, 1783.

Malton, originally an upholsterer, earned his living mostly as an architectural draftsman. He also wrote on geometry, and seems to have given lectures on perspective first at his house in Soho, London, and after about 1785 in Dublin. His sons Thomas junior and James gained fame as topographical artists.

Although Malton's book is expressly based on the mathematical principles of Brook Taylor, his treatment (especially the use of moveable overflaps) was sufficiently picturesque to appeal to the day's painters and architects. Apparently only some 300 copies of the original edition escaped a fire at the printers. A second edition followed in 1778, with a list of subscribers including Gainsborough and Reynolds. The Appendix, announced from the start but much delayed by financial difficulties, contains a very valuable "brief history of perspective, from the earliest and most authentic accounts of it, down to the eighteenth century."

Paul Breman

III-B-34.

Gaspard Monge (1746-1818), *Géométrie descriptive,* Paris, Baudouin, an VII (1798-1799) (later eds., Paris 1802, 1811, 1814, 1820, 1827, 1838, 1847; and Eng., Germ., Russian transls.) (crit. ed., Brisson, Paris, 1922).

Monge, the whizz-kid who taught physics at 14, founder of the polytechnic type of school, lifelong friend of Berthollet with whom he accompanied Napoleon on the voyage of plunder into Egypt, had early in the Revolution been stampeded into accepting the ministry of naval affairs. He put his considerable energy behind the Comité de Salut Public and its preparations for war (at that time still said to threaten from outside). Monge's *Description de l'art de fabriquer les canons* (1794) is one of the earliest basic handbooks for the arms race.

The *Géométrie descriptive* is another of his pioneering works. It was conceived as an aid in military engineering, closely linked to his book on the manufacture of ordnance as well as to the new concept of polytechnic education, and it provided an entirely new approach to design and manufacture. In Monge's method an object is represented by its plan and elevation, obtained by parallel projections to a (horizontal or vertical) plane by rays perpendicular to that plane (orthographic projection). Without Monge's geometry "the wholesale spawning of machinery in the nineteenth century would probably have been impossible. Descriptive geometry is the root of all mechanical drawing and graphical methods that help to make mechanical engineering a fact" (Bell, *Men of Mathematics,* 183). See also René Taton, *L'Oeuvre scientifique de Monge* (1951), which includes a bibliography.

Paul Breman

C. Technology

III-C-1.

Philibert Delorme, *Nouvelles inventions pour bien bastir et à petit fraiz*, Paris, 1561.

    This is Delorme's first architectural publication, begun while he was superintendent of buildings to Henry II and finished after the King's death in 1559. It was first published as a separate specialized treatise, and then incorporated into his treatise on architecture. *Nouvelles inventions* is a technical and practical treatise on the economical and simple construction of timber roofs, vaults and ceilings. It is the ancestor of all later manuals on carpentry construction.

Dora Wiebenson

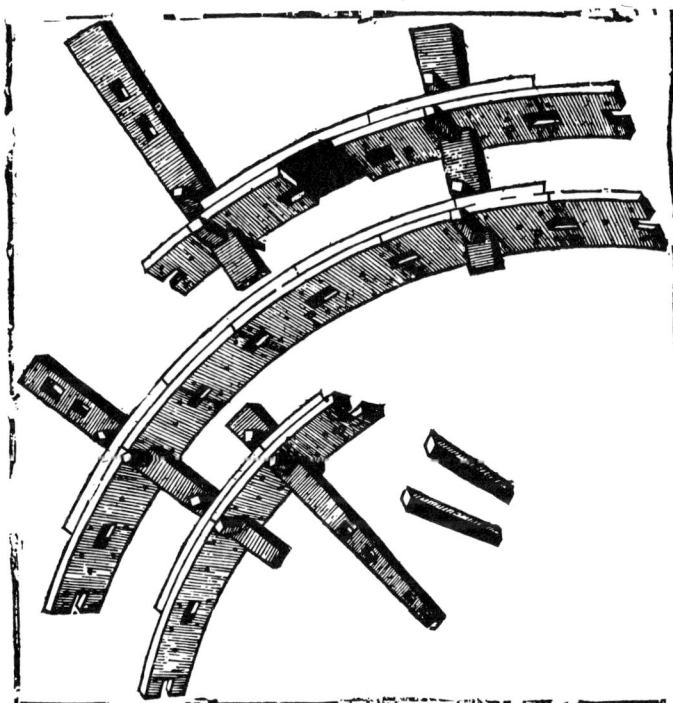

III-C-1.

III-C-2.

Jean Chéreau (fl. 2nd half 16c, master mason), *Livre d'architecture* (ms. 2280, Bibliothèque Municipale, Gdansk).

    Chéreau was born in Joigny (Yonne) and was active around this city in the last half of the sixteenth century. His book, written for publication between 1567 and 1574, is a compilation of several treatises, notably those of Serlio and Delorme. The most interesting section (fo 102v to 119) is concerned with stereotomy. It is mainly inspired by Delorme, but enriched by some unpublished models.

Jean-Marie Pérouse de Montclos
Dora Wiebenson, translation

III-C-3.

Alonso de Vandelvira (active 1584-1626, architect), *Libro de tracas de cortes de piedras* (ms. Biblioteca de la Escuela de Arquitectura, Madrid) (facs. ed., Geneviève Barbè-Coquelin de Lisle, *Tratado de arquitectura*, Albacete, 1977).

    Despite the title of the 1977 edition, the *Libro* of Vandelvira, written between 1575 and 1580, is not a treatise on architecture, but a treatise dedicated entirely to *montea* and especially to stereotomy. Vandelvira's stereotomy is close to that of Delorme, but it is extended to a greater number of examples. The direct influence of Delorme on Vandelvira is improbable; the similarities between the work of the two authors is principally due to their similar inheritance of the stereotomic tradition of Romanesque Languedoc, but Vandelvira was able to learn from Frenchmen in his region of the modern solutions discovered by Delorme. His master was Andres de Vandelvira, his father, whose Andalousian works he cites as stereotomic models with filial respect. Almost all the other references of Alonso are of works in Andalousia which he built himself. Vandelvira's treatise has an exceptional importance. By its richness it is perfectly representative of the fecundity of Spanish architecture in the sixteenth century; there is nothing equivalent in French theory before the seventeenth century. It is authentic: the treatise of Vandelvira is a pure product of the masonic tradition transmitted by apprenticeship.

Jean-Marie Pérouse de Montclos
Dora Wiebenson, translation

III-C-4.

Louis Savot (c. 1579-c. 1640, physician), *L'Architecture françoise des bastimens particuliers*, Paris, S. Cramoisy, 1624 (facs. ed., Geneva, 1973).

    Savot held the positions of Physician to the King and member of the Faculty of Medicine of the University of Paris. In the first chapter of *Architecture françoise*, Savot explained that his study of physiology, "la qualité, nature, et différence des matières," and of mathematics, "la connoissance des mesures, formes, et proportions," qualified him to write on the subject of architecture. He also published a translation and analysis of a Greek text on medicinal bleeding (*Le Livre de Galien, de l'art de guérir par la saignée*, 1603) and a description of the statue of Henri IV on the Pont Neuf (*Discours sur le subject du colosse du grand roi Henri*, n.d.).

    Architecture françoise instructed the building patron about basic architectural practices so that he could intelligently plan and supervise construction of his *hôtel* or *maison*. Sections on siting, the composition of houses according to the resident's rank, and the arrangement and dimensions of rooms condensed classical theory and conventional design ideas into simple, standardized rules. Savot also introduced chapters on the costs and properties of building materials, methods of measuring construction (*toiser*), and building regulations from the Paris *Coutome*. The attention given to practical and comercial aspects of housing construction distinguished *Architecture francoise* from preceding publications. It was reprinted in 1642, and new editions by François Blondel appeared in 1673 and 1685 with additional material on the *Coutome*, survey methods, and current prices of supplies. Savot's book initiated a new type of architectural manual which proliferated in seventeenth century France. But, while *Architecture françoise* was prepared by and for the amateur, later handbooks were written by architects for their colleagues and discussed only technical information and procedures, reflecting the growing professionalism of the architect.

Hilary Ballon

III-C-5.

Mathurin Jousse (1607-?, architect, writer), *Le Théâtre de l'art de charpentier*, La Flèche, chez Georges Griveau, 1627 (facs. of 1702 ed., Paris, 1978).

Jousse worked as an architect and writer in his native town of La Flèche, France where he was affiliated with the Jesuit community. He is more widely recognized for his publications which include a manual on metalwork (*La Fidelle ouverture de l'art de serrurier . . .*, 1627), a French translation of Viator's Latin treatise *La Perspective positive* (1635), and a guide to stereotomy (*Le Secret d'architecture*, 1642).

Le Théâtre de l'art de charpentier is a guide to timber frame construction for the amateur and apprentice carpenter. A summary of the five Orders and a review of the geometric operations and equipment necessary to the practice of carpentry preceded a series of one hundred twenty-five figures with accompanying text describing methods of constructing timber walls, roofs, staircases, and a bridge. Jousse treated an encyclopedic range of examples in an uncomplicated, instructive manner. The frequent reprinting of Jousse's book indicates that it long survived as a standard guide to carpentry. In addition to copies in 1650, 1664, and 1692, Philippe de La Hire, member of the Académie Royale d'Architecture, produced a new edition in 1702 retitled *L'Art de charpenterie* (reprinted 1751), with supplementary information on tools, timber dimensions, and Paris building regulations, and new designs for bridges, a windmill, and a mansard roof (*toit brisé*).

Hilary Ballon

III-C-5.

III-C-6.

Mathurin Jousse, *Le Secret d'architecture découvrant fidèlement les traits geometriques, couppes et dérobements necessaires dans les bastimens*, La Flèche, Georges Griveau, 1642 (privilège, 1635).

The *Secret d'architecture* is the first treatise to be published which is devoted entirely to stereotomy. Mathurin Jousse was very probably a master mason; he seems to have been connected with the college of Jesuits at La Flèche, which he may have built. He could have worked with Derand, the author of *Architecture des voûtes*, who taught mathematics there. The *Secret* had an important readership among the masons, but one that was limited by the contemporary publications of the *Architecture des voûtes*.

Jean-Marie Pérouse de Montclos
Dora Wiebenson, translation

III-C-7.

Girard Desargues (1593-1661, architect), *Brouillon project d'exemples d'une manière universelle du Sieur G. D. L. touchant la practique du trait à preuve pour la coupe des pierres en architecture*, Paris, Melchoir Tavernier, 1640.

The ambition of the mathematician Desargues, famous for his study on conical sections, was to reunite in one method called the "manière universelle" geometry applied to stereotomy, to perspective and to dialing. His method prefigures the descriptive geometry of Gaspard Monge. The *Brouillon project* is a mémoire of several pages which has had only a slight influence (we know today only several examples: the library of Quimper contains the only illustrated copy). The method of Desargues, which breaks completely with the masonic tradition, was very cooly received by practitioners, who did not understand it and who accused the author of having masked by the obscurity of his language a total ineptitude for the practice of architecture. But Desargues had his disciples: Bosse, La Hire, Frézier.

Jean-Marie Pérouse de Montclos
Dora Wiebenson, translation

III-C-8.

Abraham Bosse, *La Pratique du traict à preuves de Mr Desargues, lyonnois, pour la coupe des pierres à l'architecture*, Paris, P. Des Hayes, 1643.

The engraver Bosse, a faithful disciple of Desargues, appointed himself editor of his master's work. His treatise is an application of the method which is succinctly developed in the *Brouillon project* on several types of vaults. Bosse no more convinced the masons than had Desargues.

Jean-Marie Pérouse de Montclos
Dora Wiebenson, translation

III-C-9.

Le Père François Derand (1580-1644, architect, Jesuit), *L'Architecture des voûtes*, Paris, Sebastien Cramoisy, 1643.

There is not a treatise on stereotomy that has been more widely publicized that that of Père Derand, mathematician and architect. *L'Architecture des voûtes* is listed in inventories of the libraries of French architects up to the end of the eighteenth century. The success of this work is limited neither by the publications of the treatise of De La Rue, which is clearer, nor by the treatise of Frézier, which is more comprehensive, as is testified by the new editions of 1743 and 1755. Derand is not an innovator like Desargues; he has only projected mathematical logic on the tradition transmitted by Jousse.

Jean-Marie Pérouse de Montclos
Dora Wiebenson, translation

III-C-8.

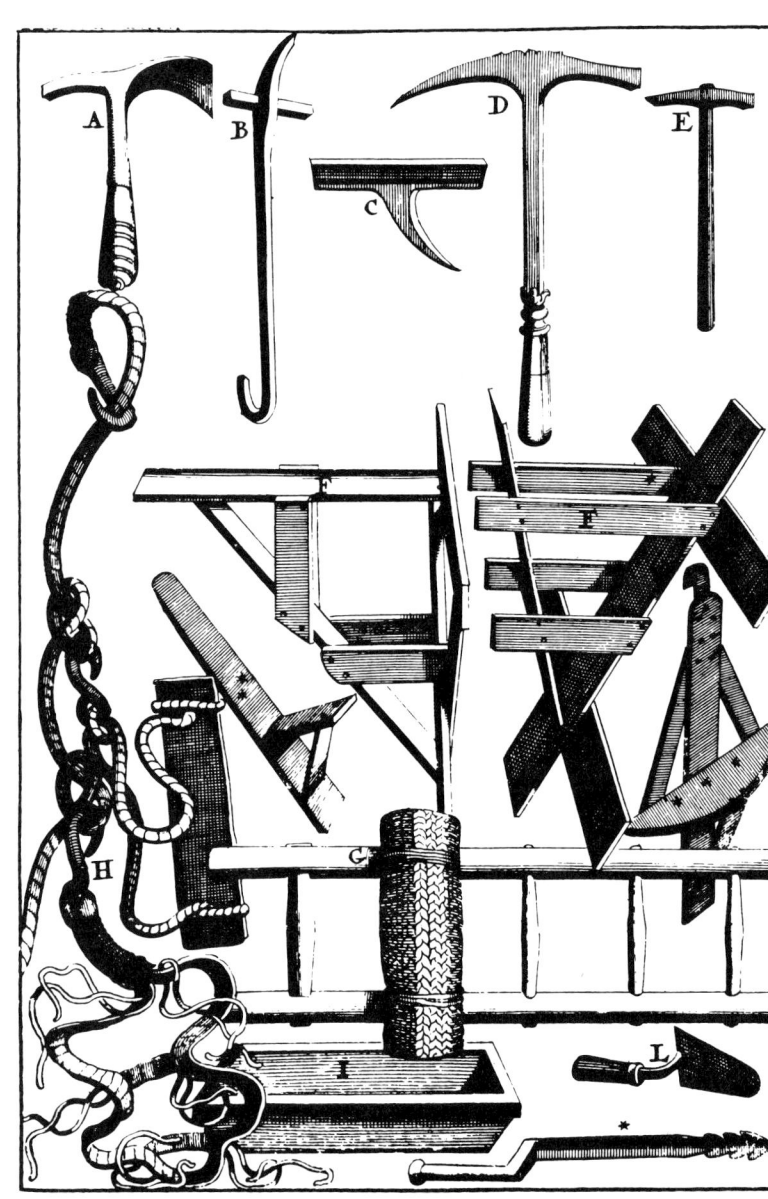

III-C-12.

III-C-10.

Juan de Torija, *Breve tratado de todo genero de bovedas asi regulares commo irregulares*, Madrid, 1660.

By its successs (new editions in 1661, 1664, 1728), this mediocre work, in which stereotomy is reduced to several elementary examples, demonstrates the decadence of stereotomy in eighteenth century Spain. In reality, the problem which distinguishes stereotomy, knowledge of the treatment of the voussoirs of massive vaults, is not even approached. Moreover, the true author of the treatise is Pedro de la Pena (?-c. 1660, architect). It is then only because of a double usurpation that Torija would pass for the author of the first treatise on stereotomy published in Spain.

Jean-Marie Pérouse de Montclos
Dora Wiebenson, translation

III-C-11.

Thomas Wilsford, *Architectonice, the Art of Building; or an Introduction to All Young Surveyors in Common Structures.* London, N. Brook, 1659 (facs. ed., Farnborough, 1969).

Wilsford is known only as the author of this early surveyor's manual. This practical handbook, obviously intended for "young surveyors," contains "estimates, valuations and contracts with the general Rates, Rules and Proportions most frequently used by Bricklayers in plaine-work" as well as proportions and dimensions of the roof, the five Orders, the "covering of a House with the materials valuations and proportions allowed by Architectors."

Elizabeth Lambeth

III-C-12.

André Félibien des Avaux (1619-1695, diplomat, historian, connoisseur, art theorist). *Des Principes de l'architecture, de la sculpture, de la peinture et des autres Arts qui en dependent. Avec un dictionnaire des Termes propres à chacun de ces Arts,* Paris, Jean Baptiste Coignard (?), 1676 and later editions (facs. ed., Farnborough, 1966).

André Félibien des Avaux spent two years (1647-1649) as a secretary at Rome where he acquainted himself with the art of antiquity and the Renaissance and with such modern French artists as Nicholas Poussin and Claude Lorrain. After his return to France Félibien was introduced to the royal Court and took several offices. Belonging to the eight Members of the Académie des Inscriptions et Belles-Lettres founded in 1663, Félibien became successively 'historiographe du Roy' (1665), "historiographe des Bâtiments du Roy" (1669) and historiographer of the arts and manufactures. In 1671 Félibien was appointed secretary to the new Academy of Architecture. Besides some translations and historiographical works like his "Description sommaire du château de Versailles" Félibien published several treatises on art theory, among them the *Entretiens sur le vies et sur les ouvrages des plus excellens peintres anciens et modernes* (1666-1668) and the *Principes,* both known as documents of the academic art doctrine in France during the reign of Louis XIV.

As historiographer of the buildings of Louis XIV, Félibien was occupied with the defining of terms of architectural theory and practice which were quite unknown to many persons of the royal Court. Félibien determined to write a dictionary in which were explained all terms concerning the theory and practice of architecture, sculpture, painting and other arts depending on them. The result, the *Principes*, included not only a dictionary of terms but also a survey of the principles of the different arts beginning with the principles of architecture. The connection of a more generally conceived treatise on art theory and practice with a dictionary of terms is typical for the new role of publications in the establishing and disseminating of information about the fine arts. The *Principes* was intended to be a handbook for a public which included all persons interested in fine arts — the author himself belonged to that group of amateurs. Being a compilation of older publications on art theory and practice — Félibien notes Claude Perrault's commented translation of Vitruvius's *Architectura* — the work of Félibien was a suitable instrument to influence and to control the communication about fine arts through academic art doctrine. On the other hand it demonstrates a trend toward the development of criticism as part of public opinion.

Walter Kambartel

III-C-13.

Joseph Moxon (1627-1700, Hydrographer to the King), *Mechanick Exercises; or, the Doctrine of Handy-Works, applied to the Art of Smithing, Joinery, Carpentry, Turning, Bricklaying, to which is added, Mechanick Dyalling*, London, the author, 1677-1680 (facs. ed., New York, 1970).

The *Mechanick Exercises* was published as a series of pamphlets on the building trades, and it contains elaborate descriptions of each trade, along with plates illustrating the tools associated with it. The work is a pragmatic, limited English version of Félibien's *Principes*, published one year earlier.

Dora Wiebenson

III-C-14.

Pierre Bullet (1639-1716, architect), *L'Architecture pratique, qui comprend le detail du toisé et du devis des ouvrages de massonerie, charpenterie, menuiserie, serrurerie, plomberie, vitrerie, ardoise, tuille, pave de grais et impression. Avec une explication de la coutume sur le Titre des servitudes et rapports qui regardent les bastiments*, Paris, chez Estienne Michallet, 1691 (facs. ed., Geneva, 1973).

Bullet, son of a master mason, attained the highest positions available to an architect during the reign of Louis XIV: member of the Académie Royale d'Architecture (from 1685) and royal architect. Bullet's career began as a student and associate of François Blondel, and as architect to the city of Paris. The expansion of the capital provided Bullet with numerous ecclesiastic and private commissions; he achieved particular renown as a designer of *hôtels*. In addition to *Architecture pratique*, his most important book, Bullet wrote three tracts: *Traité de l'usage de pantomètre* (1675), *Traité du nivellement*... (1688), and *Observations sur la nature et sur les effets de la mauvaise odeur des lieux d'aisances et cloaques*... (1696).

Architecture pratique provided information on basic building procedures for the use of contractors, architects, and other tradesmen. Topics covered are materials, methods of measuring construction and appraising costs (*tosier*), articles from the Paris building code, and the format of specifications (*devis*). Despite criticizing Savot's amateurism, Bullet conformed to the model of *Architecture francoise*, elaborating the material on

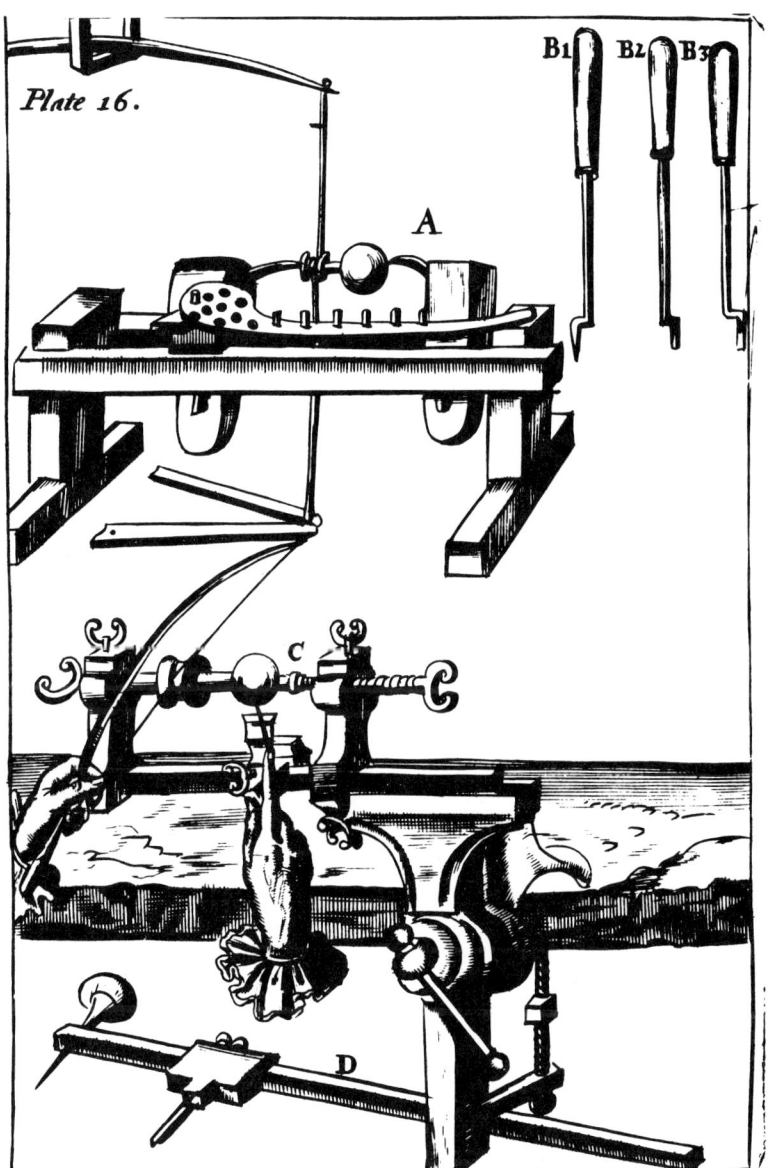

III-C-13.

contemporary professional practices for all the building trades. Bullet's guide as well as Blondel's edition of Savot reveals the Academy's interest in defining norms for the architect and other craftsmen. A standard handbook throughout the eighteenth century, *Architecture pratique* was reprinted in 1722 and new, "enlarged and corrected" editions appeared in 1755 (reprinted in 1726, 1768, 1774), 1812, 1825, and 1826, gradually losing fidelity to Bullet's original text.

Hilary Ballon

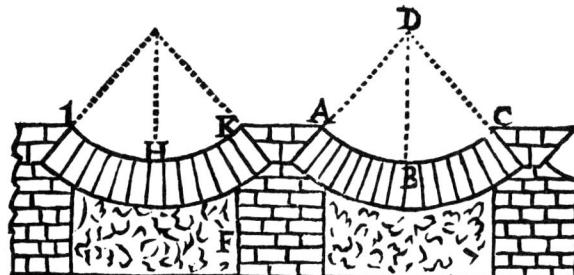

III-C-14.

III-C-15.

William Halfpenny, *The Art of Sound Building, demonstrated in Geometrical Problems*, London, Sam Aris, 1725.

This handbook, intended for the craftsman, illustrates Halfpenny's understanding of geometry. The first section concentrates on a method of drawing arches by the intersection of straight lines, an invention attributed to Halfpenny. The author also explains how to work these arches in brick and stone. Other problems addressed are the formation of groins, niches and twisted rails.

William Halfpenny, *The Builder's Pocket Companion*, London, Richard Ware, 1728 (later eds., 1731, 1747)

This book was published under Halfpenny's alias, Michael Hoare, and is dedicated to Batty and Thomas (?) Langley, two other prolific producers of architectural handbooks. In this handbook Halfpenny provides the carpenter instructions for laying lines for arches, and rules for constructing roofs. He also includes a section on the Orders.

Elise M. Quasebarth

III-C-16.

Jean-Baptiste de la Rue (fl. 1st half 18c., architect), *Traité de la coupe des pierres*, Paris, Imprimerie royale, 1728 (facs. ed., Nogent-le-Roi, 1977).

La Rue is practically unknown (in 1728 he was promoted to the second class of the Académie Royale d'Architecture; he lived in Versailles and died there in 1750): he was incontestably an architect practicing stereotomy. His work contains nothing new, it is written in the tradition of Derand; but, by the clarity of the demonstrations and the quality of the edition, his book becomes an important reference work. it was republished in 1764 and in 1858 and perhaps translated into English.

Jean-Marie Pérouse de Montclos
Dora Wiebenson, translation

III-C-17.

Antoine Desgodets, *Les Lois des Bâtiments suivant la Coutume de Paris*, Paris, 1748 (later eds., Paris, 1768, 1777, 1787; Avignon, 1802).

Les Lois des Bâtiments was published twenty years after the author's death (1728) by the architect Goupy. According to the introduction by Goupy it was to have formed the last section of Desgodets's unpublished *Cours d'Architecture*, a compilation of lectures given at the Academy of Architecture. The book contains the publication and explanation of building laws and is related to the works of Bullet and Savot.

Steven Frear

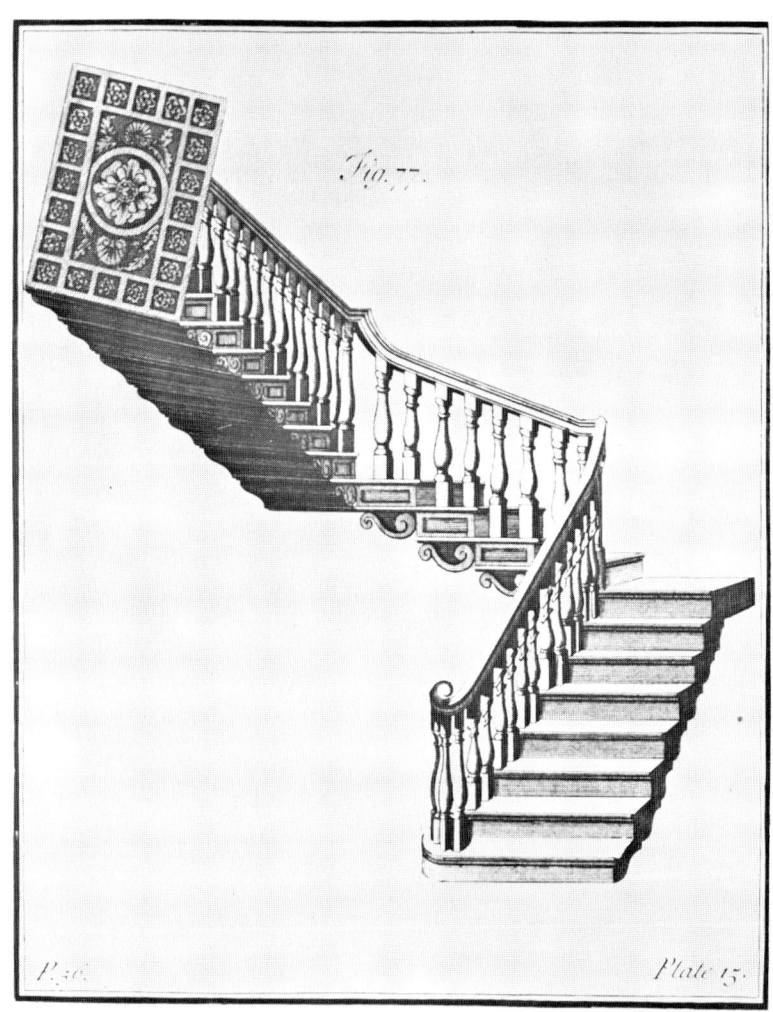

III-C-15.

III-C-18.

Francis Price (c. 1704-1753, architect, carpenter), *The British Carpenter or a Treatise on Carpentry,* London, C. Ackers, 1733 (later eds., 1735, 1753, 1759, 1765, 1768) (facs. 1753 ed., Amersham, Bucks.).

Price was Surveyor or Clerk of the Works of Salisbury Cathedral from 1737 until his death. In addition to repairs there, he did alterations and repairs at Bishop's Place, and was consulted by Ivory Talbot on the alterations made at Lacock Abbey. He was also the author of *A Series of particular and useful observations . . . upon . . . The Cathedral Church of Salisbury* (1753), 'the first serious attempt to describe and analyze the structure of a major Gothic building.'

The British Carpenter was recommended by Nicholas Hawksmoor, John James, and James Gibbs as "a very Usefull and Instructive Piece". Price compiled "the most approv'd methods of connecting timbers together . . . with the rules necessary to be observed therein"; his object was "to make the whole particularly useful." The work was intended for not only carpenters, "but at the same time (to) be of use to the ingenious theorist in Building." It needed "little or no explanation, otherwise than carefully inspecting the Plates" (Introduction). General observations include geometry, joining timbers together, framing timber roof trusses, bridges, vaults, domes, and stairs. The supplement to the fourth edition contains "Palladio's Orders of Architecture with the Ornaments of Doors and Windows." The book appeared in a number of editions and was long considered to be one of the best of its kind.

Elizabeth Lambeth

III-C-19.

William Salmon (c. 1703-1779, carpenter, joiner), *Palladio Londinensis, or the London Art of Building,* London, 1734, with many later editions (facs. ed., Farnborough, 1969).

Salmon was the successful author of a number of builder's manuals, concerned mainly with advice on estimating for work on new and old buildings. *Palladio Londinensis* achieved the most editions of any of his popular works, eight by 1773.

Dora Wiebenson

III-C-20.

Amédée-François Frézier (1682-1773, military engineer), *La théorie et la pratique de la coupe des pierres et des bois pour la construction des voûtes . . . ou traité de stéréotomie, suivi de Dissertation sur le genre de decoration apelle* (sic) *les ordres d'architecture,* Strasbourg-Paris, C.A. Jombert, 1737-1739 (later eds., Paris, 1754, 1769) (facs. ed., Nogent-le-Roi, 1980).

The summation of stereotomic knowledge is in the monumental treatise by Frézier, which was successful enough to be reprinted in two later editions. The military engineer Frézier is also the author of a *Traité des feux artifices* (1747) and of several dissertations on architecture published in the *Mercure de France.* The first volume of the *Théorie,* or a third of the work, is a course in mathematics where Frézier appears to be a disciple of Desargues, but of Desargues as theoretician of conical sections rather than of the "manière universelle." The two other volumes present a collection of stereotomic case studies, exceptional by their amplitude and by the very methodical organization, much in the spirit of the century of the *Encyclopédie.*

Jean-Marie Pérouse de Montclos
Dora Wiebenson, translation

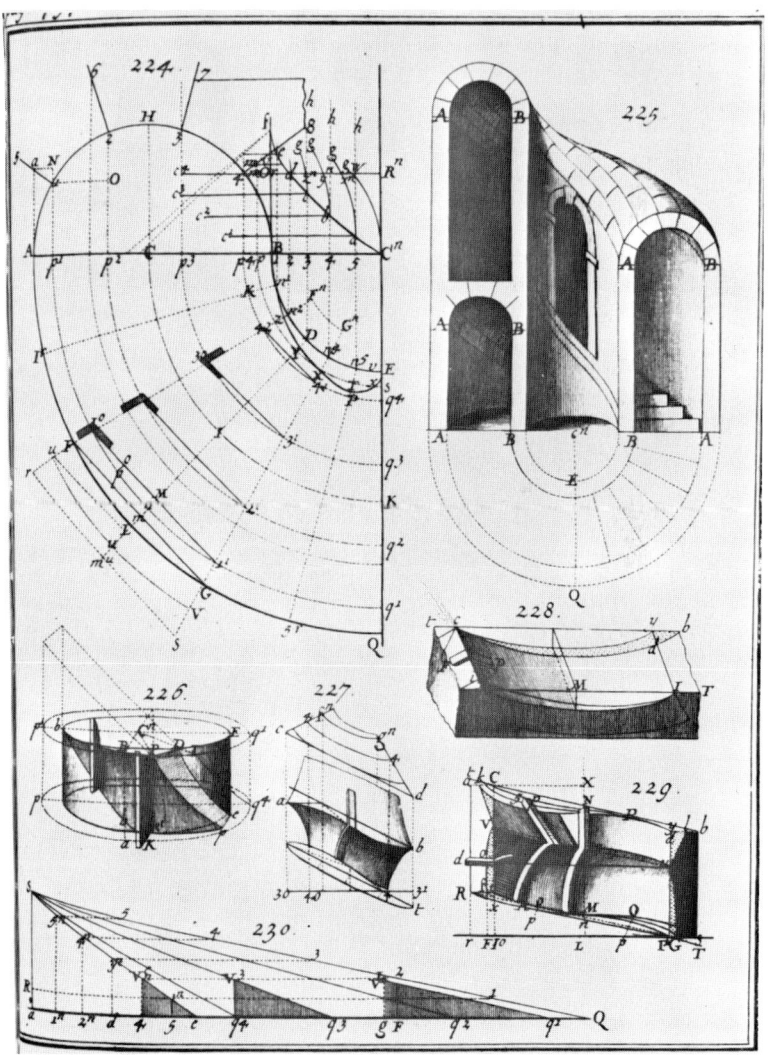

III-C-19.

III-C-21.

Amédée-François Frézier, *Eléments de stéréotomie à l'usage de l'architecture pour la coupe des pierres,* Paris, C.A. Jombert, 1760.

This mediocre work is of interest only because of its relation to the *Théorie* of 1737-1739, which is abbreviated in the *Eléments* for use in teaching. That Frézier had felt the need to produce this abbreviated work demonstrates that the *Théorie* was a work for the library and not for the field.

Jean-Marie Pérouse de Montclos
Dora Wiebenson, translation

III-C-22.

Abraham Swan (fl. 1745-1768, carpenter and joiner), *The British Architect: or the Builder's Treasury of Staircases,* London, Robert Sayer, 1745 (later eds., 1750, 1758; Philadelphia, 1775; Boston, 1794) (facs. eds., New York, 1967).

Little is available on Swan's life and career. He published a number of books of architectural designs between 1745 and 1768. In the preface to *Designs in Architecture* (1757) he stated that he had "more than thirty years application, and experience in, the Theory and Practice of Architecture." There is evidence of his work at several locations in England and some of the engravings in his books illustrate executed designs. The published elevations are basically Palladian in character, with his interiors showing the contemporary taste for the rococo. His books were popular in America; the Philadelphia edition of *The British Architect* was the first architectural book to be printed there. William Buckland is known to have owned a copy of the London 1745 edition.

Elizabeth Lambeth

III-C-23.

Menand, *L'Art d'appareil qui fait une partie essentielle de l'architecture,* Paris, 1757.

Menand, completely unknown, calls himself professor. His work is more mediocre than Frézier's *Eléments.* Stereotomy is now only a school exercise. The author does not appear convinced that it is possible to develop practical applications from it.

Jean-Marie Pérouse de Montclos
Dora Wiebenson, translation

III-C-24.

William Pain (c. 1718-?, carpenter, joiner, architect), *The Builder's Companion, and Workman's General Assistant . . .* Printed for the author and Robert Sayer, London, 1758, 1762, 1769 (facs. ed., Farnborough, 1972).

William Pain may be "the William Paine of Bellyard, Temple Bar, carpenter and builder" (Colvin) who in 1774, at the age of 56, unsuccessfully ran for the District Surveyorship in Middlesex. His son, James (ca. 1779-1877), a 'builder and surveyor' aided him in the writing of *The British Palladio.* Pain published a number of architectural handbooks and pattern books, many of which appear to be re-writings of earlier publications.

Pain's earliest work, *The Builder's Companion,* is a practical-minded collection of plates and captions illustrating how to design and execute foundations, chimneys, geometrical figures for architectural use; brick and stone arches; roof and dome framing; stairs and railings; etc. There are two chapters on the Orders and related details, such as entablatures, mouldings, mantels and a 'Venetian' window. There is also a chapter on Gothic columns, doors, windows, and mouldings. The imposition of Gothic details on classical structures suggest the influence of Langley's *Ancient Architecture.*

The Builder's Pocket-Treasure; or, Palladio delineated and explained . . . W. Owen, London, 1763 (later eds., 1766, 1783, 1785; Boston, 1794).

This is essentially a reduced version of Pain's *'Builder's Companion,'* written for the 'workman,' in a size "by which he will have his whole Trade in his Pocket, and not to be at a Loss for any Thing which may occur in the ordinary Course of his Profession." Meant to be a very practical book, Pain criticizes, in the preface, the lack of usefulness generally to be found in contemporary books and treatises. In addition to the 'how-to-do-it' plates and tables, there are several designs for Chinese and temple garden structures plus a Gothic greenhouse.

William Pain and James Pain, *Pain's British Palladio: or, The Builder's General Assistant,* London, I. and J. Taylor, 1786.

One of Pain's last works, this book is transitional, spanning the period concerned primarily with building technology to that of the early house publications. It is pragmatically oriented with introductory notes on the construction of foundations, chimneys and walls. There is also a price list of materials and labor (with pay rates for Bricklayers, Carpenters, Masons, Painters, Plumbers and Plasterers). This section is followed by a series of plates of designs for houses, including plans, elevations, sections, and framing and construction details. The designs combine Palladian massing, plans and details with Neoclassical surface treatment and Adamesque interiors.

Martin C. Perdue

III-C-25.

Nicolas Le Camus de Mézières, *Le Guide de ceux qui veulent batir, ouvrage dans lequel on donne les rensignements nécessaires pour se conduire lors de la construction, et prevenir les fraudes qui peuvent s'y glisser,* Paris, 1781-2(2v.) (2nd ed. 1786) (facs. ed., Geneva, 1972).

The product of "forty years" of experience, *Le Guide* is directed toward people who want to have a house built. Written in the form of short letters, in order to make the subject matter less dry, this book presents an account of the operations of the building industry. The author forewarns his readers of the most common types of fraud as well as explaining what to expect from an architect and from the eleven different types of craftsmen involved in constructing a dwelling. By showing how to establish a schedule for payments, Le Camus de Mézières both educates the reader about his own responsibilities and assists him to assure the orderly completion of his building.

Richard A. Etlin

III-C-26.

Jean François Monroy (stone mason, surveyor and Royal building inspector), *Traité d'architecture pratique*, published by the author, Paris, 1785 (facs. ed., Geneva, 1973).

This volume represents a break with the French tradition of scholarly architectural treatises intended for the professional. Monroy's work is concerned with contemporary building methods, prices of materials and workers' salaries. In its presentation of informational tables it is related to, if not derived from, the work of the Englishman, Wilsford's *The Scales of Commerce and Trade* (1660).

Elise M. Quasebarth

III-C-27.

Charles Séguin (builder), *Manuel d'architecture*, Paris, chez Didot, fils., 1786 (facs. ed., Geneva, 1973).

Like Monroy's work, published in the preceeding year, Seguin's volume was intended for the trades associated with building, not for the professional. As such, it is related to the earlier works of Jousse, Desargues and Derand. It is concerned with geometry and stereotomy and the format consists of a series of problems and solutions.

Elise M. Quasebarth

III-C-28.

Simonin, *Traité élémentaire de la coupe des pierres, ou Art du trait*, Paris, Joubert, 1792 (new ed., Delagardette, 1874).

Simonin, professor of mathematics, is as unknown as Menand, and his work succeeds no better. It was however translated into Spanish (*Tratado elemental de los Cortes de Ganteria*, Madrid, 1795) an example of the belated diffusion of French theory, while in France even recourse to stereotomy is in fact condemned in theory from the years 1750-1770.

Jean-Marie Pérouse de Montclos
Dora Wiebenson, translation

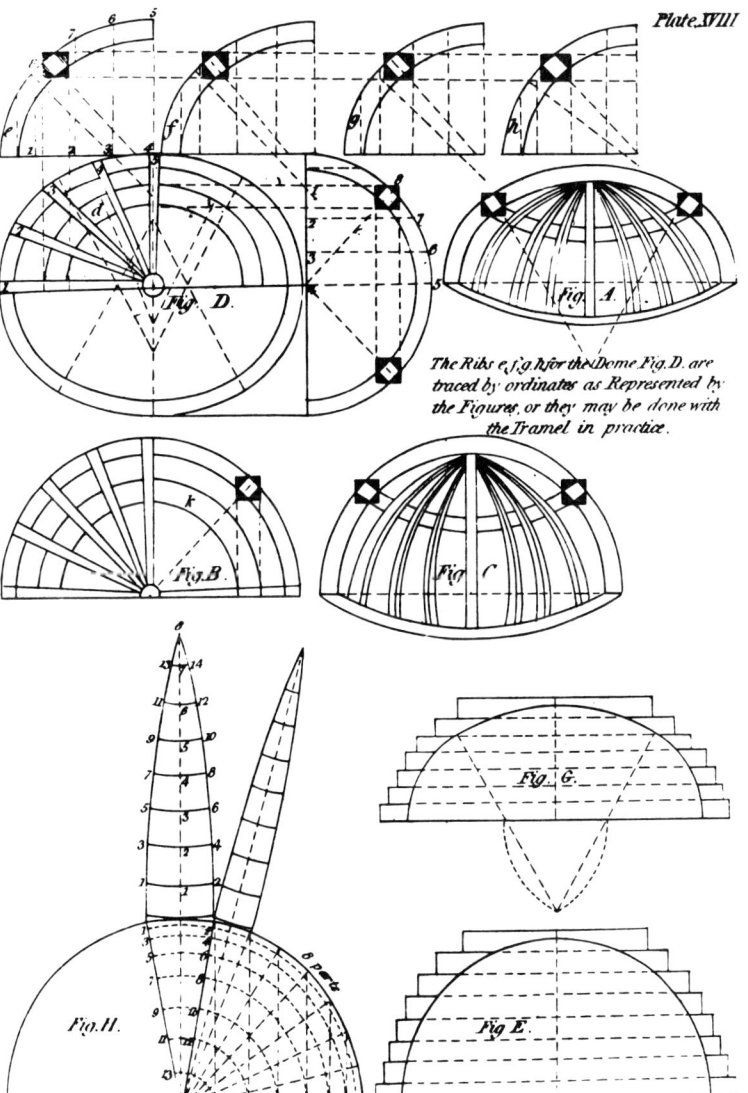

III-C-24.

D. Public and Private Architecture"

III-D-1.
Sebastiano Serlio, Book VI: *Delle habitationi di tutti li gradi degli uomini*, [(a) ms. Avery Library, Columbia University, New York, c. 1541-47, ed., Myra Nan Rosenfeld, *Sebastiano Serlio on Domestic Architecture*, Cambridge, Mass., 1978;
(b) ms. Bayerische Staatsbibliothek, Munich (Cod.icon. 189), c. 1547-51, ed., Marco Rosci, *Sebastiano Serlio, il sesto libro delle habitationi di tutti li gradi degli uomini*, Milan, 1966 (2v.)].

In his *Regole*, presenting the plan of his foreseen complete treatise, Serlio announced a "sixth book" on "dwellings." Developing graphically a suggestion of Vitruvius (*De architectura*, VI, 7), he conceived a double progression, from "la casa del povero contadino" to "l'habitatione regale per villa," and from the "casa del povero artefice" to "la casa del re dentro la citta." From a first manuscript on paper (a) begun likely in Fontainebleau c. 1541 but left unfinished c. 1547, probably in connection with the death of his protector, François I, he achieved a second version on parchment (b), which he sold to Jacopo Strada. Neither version was published. A French printed edition, undertaken in France in the seventeenth century, apparently did not succeed (one copy is known in the Bibliothek Albertina).

In the Venetian editions of Serlio's complete works (1600, 1618, 1619), the *libro estraordinario* became the *Sesto libro*, but the real Book VI, known from the first manuscript (a), left in the French royal architect's hands, had a strong influence on Jacques Androuet Du Cerceau's *Livre d'architecture*, and on Pierre Le Muet's *Manière de bastir pour touttes sortes de personnes*.

Claude Mignot

III-D-2
Jacques Androuet du Cerceau the Elder (1515?-1585, architect, decorator, engraver), *Premier livre d'architecture*, Paris, Benoît Prévost, 1559 (pub. simult. in Latin, *De architectura*).
Second livre d'architecture, Paris, André Wechel, 1561.
Troisième livre d'architecture, Paris, 1572 (facs. ed. of all three books, *Les trois livres d'architecture*, Ridgewood, 1965).

The founder of a dynasty of architects, engravers and decorators who worked in France during the sixteenth and seventeenth centuries, Du Cerceau was probably born in Paris. He travelled to Italy c. 1530-1533, where he studied the monuments of antiquity and newly built Roman architecture. Upon his return to France, he resolved both to disseminate the knowledge of ancient architecture and to propagate the art of the Italian Renaissance in his native land. Not surprisingly, he is known principally for his many published works — the books on architecture, the inventions of ornament and furniture designs, and above all, *Les plus excellents bastiments de France*. His role as an architect is more difficult to pinpoint, though his name has been linked to the designs of the châteaux of Verneuil, Charleval, and the Maison Blanche in Gaillon, because of certain stylistic analogies. Examining his work as an ensemble, Du Cerceau emerges as more than a superb virtuoso surveyor and draftsman, for his oeuvre is our chief source of information on the great architecture of the French Renaissance. In fact, much of the total patrimony of this architecture is transmitted to his progeny and to his son-in-law, Salamon De Brosse, who assured the perpetuity of the architectural distinction of the family.

The *Premier livre* is Du Cerceau's first major contribution to architectural literature. Dedicated to Henri II, it marks the beginning of relationships with the royal family. It sets forth a series of plans and facade elevations of fifty different town houses for "those who wish to build, whatever their means." Perhaps the earliest practical handbook, analogous to Serlio's unpublished Book VI in circulation at that time, this volume was of value not only to masons, carpenters and other workers, but also intriguing to all who then as now delight in the portrayal of buildings.

Dedicated to Charles IX, the second book is comprised primarily of architectural details — fireplaces, attic windows, doors, fountains, wells, and pavilions to enhance the interior as well as the exterior of the building — and including ten different designs for as many tombs. Du Cerceau presented this work of "many useful necessary inventions to . . . embellish all sorts of buildings."

Written at Montargis, a Huguenot sanctuary, where Du Cerceau found refuge under the patronage of Renée de France, Duchess of Ferrara, the third book is in the practical genre of the first book. It provides plans for country houses and their surroundings. In the dedication to Charles IX, Du Cerceau requests (because of his age and the state of his health) the means to complete future books on the great buildings of the kingdom.

Naomi Miller

III-D-2.

III-D-2.

III-D-3.

Jacques Androuet du Cerceau the Elder, *Les plus excellents bastiments de France*, Paris, the author, 1576-1579 (2 v.) (later eds., Paris, 1607, 1648, 1868-70) (facs. ed., Farnborough, 1972).

Du Cerceau's monumental opus, among the masterpieces of printed books, provides an unparalleled source for our knowledge of the great buildings of sixteenth-century France, since altered or destroyed. Probably begun under the aegis of Henri II, publication was delayed by the Religious Wars. Volume I, originally dedicated to his great friend and benefactress, Renée de France, was rededicated after her death in 1575 to Catherine de' Medici, with thanks to God for a respite from wars " . . . to contemplate here a part of the most beautiful and excellent buildings with which France today is still enriched." Each volume is composed of fifteen châteaux, both royal and private. A brief text is followed by a series of engraved plates — plans, elevations, illustrations in perspective, and details. Factors taken into account include the topography of the site, the materials used, the history of the construction, the architecture of the building, the plan of its gardens and surroundings, and the state of its preservation; as also medieval origins, chronological data, and patronage.

Naomi Miller

III-D-4.

Pierre Le Muet (1591-1669, architect), *Manière de bastir, pour touttes sortes de personnes*, Paris, Melchior Tavernier (printer for the King), 1623 (facs. ed., Aix-en-Provence, 1981).

A native of Dijon, Le Muet was employed in his youth as an executor of architectural models for Salomon de Brosse. The chief concern of his early career was military architecture — Richelieu commissioned him to fortify several towns in Picardie — but he later became a leading architect of Parisian town houses, such as the Hotels Davaux (1640-1650), Dassy (1642), Tubeuf (1650), and De Luynes (1650-1657). In addition, he completed the Palais Mazarin (1616). With Gabriel Le Duc he carried out the dome, vaulting, and decorative furnishing of the Val-de-Grâce after the death of Lemercier in 1655. His publishing interests extended to translations of Palladio and Vignola: *Traité des cinq ordres d'architecture dont se sont servis les Anciens, traduit du Palladio* (editions 1645, 1647, 1682); *Règles des cinq ordres d' architecture de Vignolle, revueuës, augmentées et reduites de grand en petit format* (editions 1632, 1657, 1671).

The purpose of the *Manière de bastir* (1623) was to make available to bourgeois patrons and *amateurs* essential information on the urban residence. The basic format had been used earlier by Androuet du Cerceau in his first *Livre d'architecture* (1559) and by Delorme in his *Nouvelles inventions pour bien bastir* (1561): a series of plans and elevations with commentaries for a range of houses both simple and complex. Le Muet elaborated on the work of his predecessors by broadening the scope of the dwellings and addressing patrons of modest income who could not afford an architect. Thus many of the designs are for *maisons* consisting of little more than a narrow facade lacking special architectural embellishment, and concealing a single major chamber on each floor. The second edition of 1647 was expanded to include examples of aristocratic *hôtels* with courtyards, gardens, and dependencies which Le Muet himself had constructed. The book was in some respects complemented by Louis Savot's *Architecture françoise* published in 1624, which discussed building practices in Paris. There were further Paris editions of the *Manière* in 1647, 1664 (with supplementary plated on roof types), and 1681, c. 1728. A translation by Robert Pricke was published in London in 1670-5 and 1679.

Robert Neuman

III-D-5.

Josef Furttenbach (1591-1667), architect, architectural theorist), *Architectura civilis*, Ulm, Jonam Saurn, 1628.

Josef Furttenbach the Elder was one of the most prolific architectural theorists of the German Baroque, and his writings give a complete overview of the technical knowledge of his day. Furttenbach was sent to Italy at the age of 14 and his ten-year stay there profoundly influenced his later buildings and writings. After his return to his native Germany Furttenbach began to practice architecture and was made city architect of Ulm in 1631. Although there are a number of buildings by Furttenbach in and around Ulm his most important work was as an architectural theorist. Beginning with the *Architectura civilis* in 1628 Furttenbach published a long series of highly practical treatises on all types of architecture, public and private.

The *Architectura civilis*, like the rest of Furttenbach's writings, disdains pure theory. Furttenach was not interested in impractical discussions of proportions or mathematics. Instead, the slim *Architectura civilis*, comprising only 78 pages, gives practical details about the construction of an astonishing range of structures, including palaces, zoos, grottoes, fountains, houses, churches, monasteries, hospitals, cemeteries and leprosaria. As with most of Furttenbach's books there are a large number of illustrations in the *Architectura civilis*. These include both overall views, plans and sections and specific details of building construction. The buildings and even the language of the *Architectura civilis* exhibit the strong Italian influence which dominated Furttenbach's early works.

William J. Diebold

III-D-4

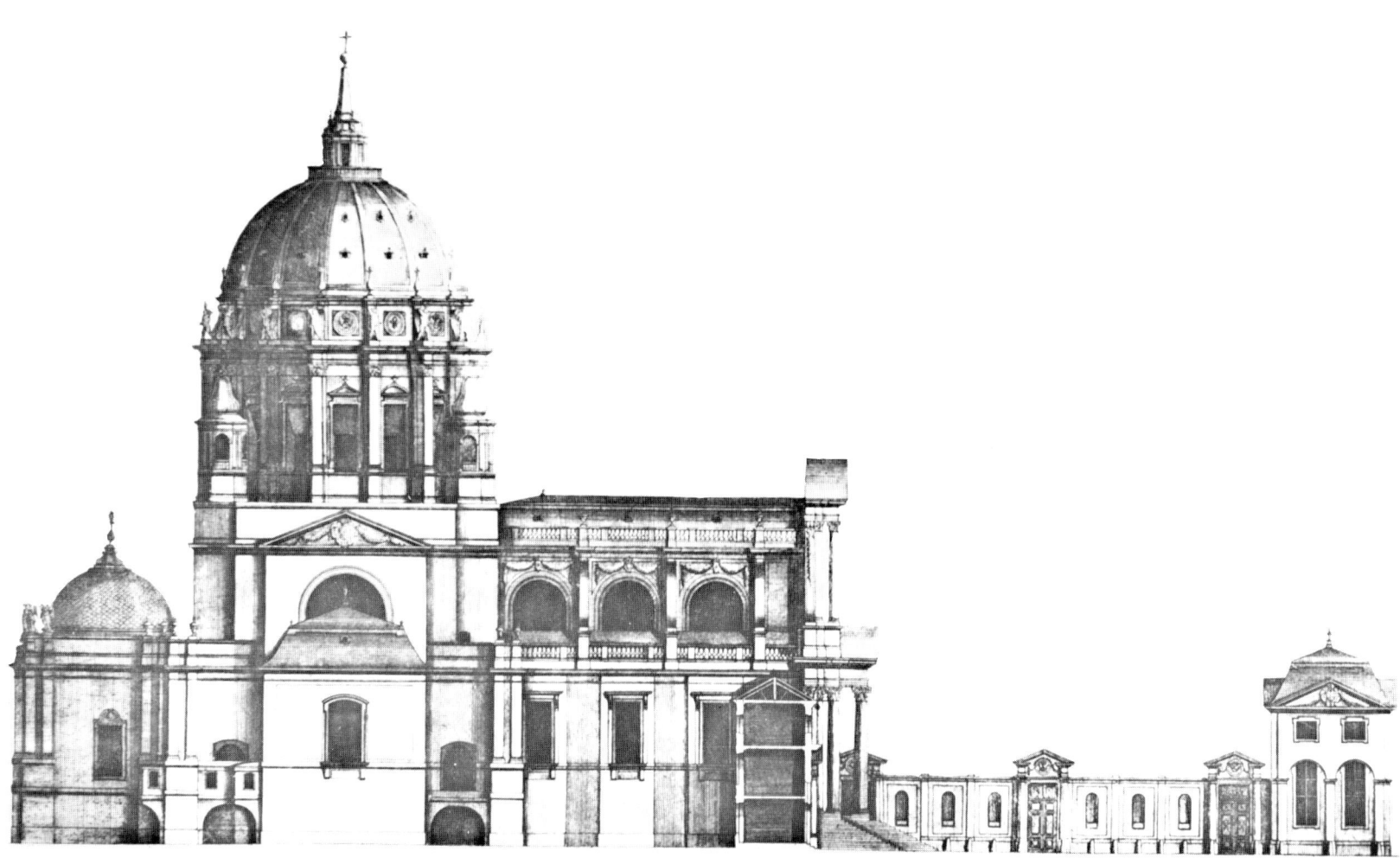

III-D-8.

III-D-6.

Francesco Borromini (1559-1667, architect) [Virgilio Spada], *Opus architectonicum Equitis Francisci Boromini (Opera del Cav. Francesco Boromino, Cavata da suoi Originali, cioè l'Oratorio e Fabrica per l'Abitazione de' PP. dell'Oratorio di S. Filippo Neri di Roma),* Rome, Sebastiano Giannini, 1725 (facs. ed. London, 1965).

Francesco Borromini came to Rome as a young man and worked for his kinsman Carlo Maderno, first as a worker in stone at St. Peter's and later as draftsman and trusted assistant. It was only in the 1630's that he began to receive independent architectural commissions, and in 1637 he was named architect of the Congregation of S. Filippo Neri, charged with the design of a new oratory and monastery adjacent to the church of S. Maria in Vallicella. The *Opus architectonicum* is a publication of that project.

Although bearing Borromini's name as author and written in the first person, the *Opus architectonicum* was actually composed by Virgilio Spada, a member of the Congregation, later cardinal and advisor to Innocent X, and advocate of Borromini and his architecture. Internal evidence provides a date of 1648 for the text, although the letter of dedication (addressed to the Spanish envoy Marchese di Castel Rodriguez) is dated 1658 and the volume was not acutally published until 1725. The parallel Latin and Italian texts are complemented by a great many illustrations of the oratory and monastery — plans, sections, views, and abundant details — which, in spite of a few inconsistencies, provide a thorough record of the building. In the text Borromini (speaking through Spada) explains many points of the complicated design, emphasizing its practicality, revealing some of his attitudes toward design in general, and insisting on the importance of originality. His model is Michelangelo, "first among architects," who, according to Borromini's preface, declared that "whoever follows others never advances beyond them."

Patricia Waddy

III-D-6.

III-D-7.

Antoine Le Pautre (1621-1679, architect), *Desseins de plusieurs palais,* Paris, the author, 1652 or 1653 (facs. of 1681 ed., Farnborough, 1966).

Le Pautre, a Parisian architect, published the *Desseins de plusieurs palais* as a book of engravings with a brief preface. It appeared at a critical moment in his career, when his vocabulary was changing from an austere idiom for Jansenist patrons to a full Baroque style intended to appeal to the court circle of Cardinal Mazarin. The *Desseins* is dedicated to the Cardinal, and includes the architect's early executed buildings (Hôtel de Fontenay-Mareuil, Chapelle de Port-Royal), which contrast markedly with his bold, ideal designs for châteaux, hôtels, city gates, fountains, ceilings, and ornament. In his preface, the architect asserts that his aim is not to rehash architectural theory but simply to present his designs. The publication by an architect of a volume entirely devoted to his projects had precedents in the French tradition (J.A. du Cerceau the Elder), but the inclusion of designs in contrasted styles dramatized Le Pautre's stylistic revolution.

In 1681, two years after his death, there appeared *Les oeuvres d'architecture d'Anthoine Le Pautre* (Paris, Jombert, n.d.), a reissue of the plates of the *Desseins* with an extensive, anonymous text generally attributed to Augustin Charles Daviler (1653-1700), who had recently returned to France (1680) from studies in Italy. The text is arranged as commentaries on each of the château, hôtel, and church designs. Extremely detailed, the commentaries reveal how a sympathetic but classically-oriented architect-theoretician of the Louis XIV period viewed Le Pautre's (mostly) Baroque projects.

Robert W. Berger

III-D-7.

III-D-8.

Jean Marot (c. 1619-1679, architect, engraver), *Recueil des Plans, Profils et Elévations des plusiers Palais, Chasteaux, Eglises, Sepultures, Grotes et Hostels batis dans Paris* (le Petit Marot), Paris, n.d. (btwn 1654-1660) (facs. ed., Farnborough, 1969).

Born in Paris into a family of artists, Marot had a successful career as an architect; although a Huguenot, he held the title "architecte du roi." His reputation, however, was based on his architectural engravings. In addition to the *Recueil* he published a collection of engravings known as the "Grand Marot," *Le magnifique Château du Richelieu, Le Château de Madrid*, and *Le Château du Louvre*. He also provided engravings for Le Muet's *Maniere de bâstir* as well as for the French translations of Palladio, Vignola and Scamozzi.

The "Petit Marot" consists of a set of engravings in a small format without a text. It presented contemporary buildings by many of the leading architects of the period — Salamon de Brosse, François Mansart, Louis Le Vau, Jacques Lemercier, along with designs by Marot himself. In many cases this book provides the only record of the designs of these buildings. After acquiring the plates between 1727 and 1738, Mariette published an edition of "Petit Marot" which was to complement his *Architecture Françoise*.

Steven Frear

III-D-9.

Jean Marot, *Le grand ouevre d'architecture de Jean Marot*, (le Grand Marot), Paris, n.d. (c.1665) (facs. ed., Paris, 1967).

This collection of engravings was first published during the architect's lifetime around 1665. In a larger format than his previous publication, it again presented contemporary buildings and designs by the leading architects of the day. The collection ends with some Greek and Roman temples. These last engravings, perhaps commissioned by the Perraults, were based on measurements made in Baalbek, nonetheless the illustrations were inaccurate.

Between 1725 and 1727 Marot's grandson sold the copper plates of this series to Jean Mariette who published them under the title *L'architecture françois, ou Recueil des plans, elevations, coups et profils des églises, palais, hôtels & maisons particulières de Paris, & des chasteaux & maisons de campagne ou de plaisance des environs, & de plusieurs autre endroits de France*. Although published first and unnumbered, this volume of Marot's engravings was the fourth volume of Mariette's *Architecture Françoise*.

Steven Frear

III-D-10.

Jean-François Félibien des Avaux (1658-1733, connoisseur, historiographer), *Les Plans et les Descriptions de deux des plus belles Maisons de Campagne de Pline le Consul avec des Remarques sour tous ses bâtiments, et une Dissertation touchant l'architecture antique & l'architecture gothique*, Paris, 1699 (later eds., London, 1707; Amsterdam, 1736; and under the title *Delices des maisons de campagnes appelées le Laurentin et la maison de Toscane*, Venice, 1755).

Son of André Félibien, sieur des Avaux, Jean-François succeeded his father in the posts he held: Historiographer of the Royal Buildings, counselor of the King, treasurer of the Académie des Inscriptions et Belles Lettres. In 1715 he was made secretary of the Académie Royale d'Architecture. In addition to the *Plus Belles Maisons* he published *Recueil historique de la vie et des ouvrages des plus célèbres architectes*, 1687 and *Description de la nouvelle église des Invalides*, (1702).

The title provides a full description of the contents of the book. Félibien begins with plans and a description of Pliny the Younger's Laurentian villa, taken from Pliny's Latin letters, followed by the text of Pliny's letters in Latin and in French translation with a commentary included. Scamozzi's description of the villa follows in Italian, again with French translation on the same page. The same format is used for the Tuscan villa. In the *Dissertation* Félibien considers how and why renaissance superseded gothic, and the part played by the *Hypnertomachia* in that process.

Steven Frear

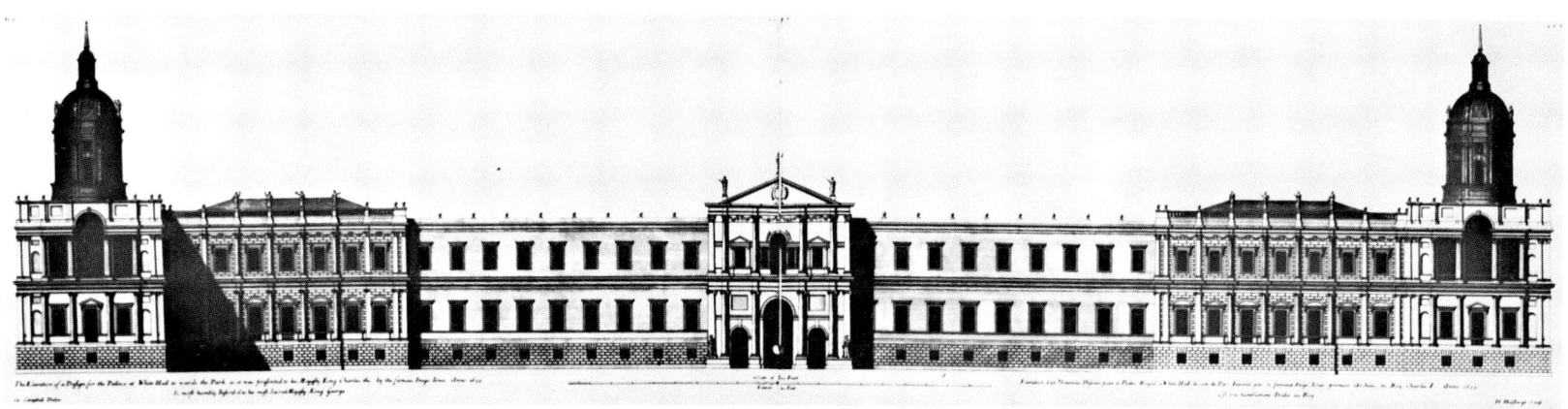

III-D-12.

III-D-11.

Paul Decker (1677-1713, architect), *Fürstlicher Baumeister oder: Architectura Civilis*. Augsburg, Jeremias Wolf, 1711, 1713, 1716 (3v.) (facs. ed., Hildesheim, 1978).

Decker, unlike many other authors of architectural treatises, was much more of an architect than a theoretician. In 1699 he travelled to Berlin to study with the great architect Andreas Schluter and in 1722 he was made Director of Buildings for the Mark of Brandenburg-Bayreuth. Decker's architectural style is characterized by a courtly refinement and an exuberance, undoubtedly derived from his master, that is not found in the work of other German theorists such as Josef Furttenbach the Elder. It is not surprising that Decker's interest in architectural practice is reflected in his two books on architecture, the *Fürstlicher Baumeister* and the *Ausführliche Anleitung zur Civilbaukunst*, (Nuremberg, no date), where the pictures are much more important than the text. Decker wished his books on architecture to serve as modelbooks, and the *Fürstlicher Baumeister* is known to have influenced Balthasar Neumann, Decker's celebrated contemporary.

As the foreword to the *Fürstlicher Baumeister* notes, Decker intended to show "How great princes and lords can conveniently construct palaces with their courts, gardens, grottoes, orangeries as well as how to decorate them in the modern manner." The *Fürstlicher Baumeister* is essentially a pattern book for the house of a noble, and each plate of Decker's work shows one section of a model palace. The third part of the *Fürstlicher Baumeister* illustrates an imperial palace, rather than a house for a noble, and it is not surprising that this part is more idealized and less practically oriented than are the first two parts of the book.

William J. Diebold

III-D-12.

Colin Campbell (1676-1729, lawyer and architect), *Vitruvius Britannicus*, London, the author, 1715, 1717, 1725, 1767, 1771 (5v.) (facs. ed., New York, 1967).

Campbell was born into the Scottish nobility and received a liberal education, probably graduating from the University of Edinburgh in 1695. He held many public offices in England including chief clerk and deputy surveyor (1718), architect to the Prince of Wales (1719), Surveyor of Greenwich Hospital (1726). He was also associated with wealthy patrons such as Lord Burlington, Horace Walpole and the Earl of Pembroke.

Campbell's role in the spread of the Palladian movement in England is epitomized in his work, *Vitruvius Britannicus*. Contemporaneous with Leoni's translation of Palladio's *I Quattro Libri*, Campbell's work was a folio of one hundred engravings of classically styled buildings in Britain. The brief introduction constitutes the only text in the book and is directed to a nationalistic plea for recognition of the great British architects, including Wren, Hawksmoor and Vanbrugh, and, most notably, Inigo Jones. Campbell's book came at a time when Wren's long ascendancy was beginning to fail and he advocates the superiority of "antique simplicity" over the "affected and licentious Baroque." Campbell's less advertised intent in producing this book was to promote his own designs. After the plates of Inigo Jones' works (considered the best English Classicism), Campbell inserted one of his own buildings, Wanstead House, near London, to advertise himself "as the purest, most classical architect of the day." The essential characteristic of *Vitruvius Britannicus* is that it was readily accessible and understandable to a large British audience and went far to initiate, by example and imitation, the Jones/Palladio revival that England was to enjoy.

Elise M. Quasebarth

III-D-11.

III-D-12.

III-D-13.

Johann Bernhard Fischer von Erlach (1656-1723, architect), *Entwurff einer historischen Architektur*, Vienna, 1721 (facs. ed., Ridgewood, 1964).

By 1694, Fischer von Erlach was already in Rome where he was part of the circle of artists around the classicizing painter, Carlo Maratta, and, more importantly, associated with that master of high Baroque architecture, Carlo Fontana and his students. Among the latter, Filippo Juvara seems to be of special importance and his *Superga* evokes analogies with the *Karlskirche*. Most significant for the subsequent formulation of the *Entwurff*, however, was Fischer's membership in Queen Christine of Sweden's "court in exile." At the Accademia Arcadia he met Bellori and the Jesuit polymath from Fulda, Kircher. Upon returning to the Austrian court after his Italian journey (ca. 1685), he rapidly became the most successful architect in the German lands of the day. His activities included the *Pestsäule* (1687), being tutor in architecture for the King of Hungary (1689), and architect for the Imperial Triumph of Joseph II and for the first project for the imperial palace at Schönbrunn (1690).

The *Entwurff* (underway at least since 1712, and probably conceived earlier) represents a new kind of treatise on architecture, one grounded in comparative cultural studies and based on information gleaned from the travel accounts of Nieuhof, DuHalde, Chardin, and the erudite compendia of Athanasius Kircher. For the first time, Assyrian, Egyptian, Phoenician, Persian, Arabian, Turkish, Chinese, and Japanese monuments are placed on equal footing, and the contributions of Greeks and Romans, perforce, are set in a broad cultural perspective and rendered relative. Construed neither as a biographical work (Vasari) nor as a text on building technology (Vignola, Serlio, Palladio, Scamozzi), the *Entwurff* represents a prescient and ecumenical comparative study of styles. Significantly for the developing aesthetic interests of the Baroque era, the world's major architectonic "wonders" then known — including natural colossi (Mt. Athos configured as Alexander the Great) and primitive "ambiguous" marvels (Stonehenge) – are enthusiastically evaluated against the background of *their* historical context. The treatise is organized into five books or chapters with a French and German text composed by Karl Gustav Heraeus, Director of the Imperial Collection of Medals and Coins, to accompany the engravings drawn by Fischer and his son. A measure of its success is that it was reprinted several times, twice with an English translation.

Barbara Maria Stafford

III-D-14.

Jean Mariette (1660-1742, engraver, editor, publisher), *L'Architecture Françoise ou Recueil des Plans, Elévations, Coups et Profils des Maisons Royalles, de quelques Eglises de Paris, et de Châteaux et Maisons de Plaisance situées tant aux environs de cette ville qu'en d'autres endroits de France, baties nouvellement par les plus habiles Architectes, & levées & mesurées exactement sur les lieux*, Paris, C.A. Jombert, 1727 (2nd ed., 1738) (facs. ed., Paris, 1927-9, 3v.).

Mariette was born into a prominent Parisian publishing family. He studied painting with his brother-in-law J.B. Corneille and was advised by Le Brun to devote himself to engraving. After taking over the family business he published an edition of Langlois's *L'Architecture à la Mode*, Daviler's *Cours d'Architecture* and the 1738 edition of the "Petit Marot."

Mariette's *Architecture Françoise* continues the tradition of the publication of contemporary buildings in France. The collection of engravings was to fill five volumes; the first two volumes presented contemporary Parisian hotels along with châteaux and church facades. The third volume on interior decoration provided an excellent document on the transition from the late Louis XIV style to the height of the Rococo. A reprint of the "Grand Marot" was counted as the fourth volume, and the fifth volume in a larger format, dated 1738, illustrated the Louvre, Versailles and several other royal residences. J.F. Blondel had a large part in the completion of this product; in his *Discours* he credits himself with not only the engravings, but with the design of the plates themselves. Not surprisingly many of these plates appear in Blondel's *L'Architecture Françoise* of 1752.

Steven Frear

III-D-15.

Robert Castell (?-1729, classical scholar), *The Villas of the Ancients Illustrated*, London, the author, 1728 (facs. ed., New York, 1982).

Castell is known only as the author of this work, an attempt at theoretical restoration of ancient Roman villas based on the descriptions of classical authors. The original Latin is accompanied side-by-side with an English translation, and comments by Castell. Elaborate plates by P. Fourdrinier show the villas and their surroundings which have similarities to English landscape gardening designs. The work treats Pliny's Laurentian and Tuscan villas and those described by Varro and Columella. The practice of the ancients on their country estates, as revealed by Castell, provided sanction for combining pleasure and profit in rural retirement. The beautiful folio edition, dedicated to Lord Burlington, was produced for only 116 subscribers. A less elaborate "trade edition" omitted the Latin text. Castell was imprisoned for debt in 1728 where he died of smallpox. He was preparing a translation of Vitruvius which was "pretty far advanced" in November 1727.

Elizabeth Lambeth

Der Macedonische Berg Athos in Gestalt eines Riesen, wie der Dinocrates, des Großen Alexanders Architect, solchen Bau angegeben. *Vitruv. Præfat. L.2. Strabo. L.13*

Le Colosse du mont Athos en Macedoine selon le dessein qu'en forma Dinocrate Architecte du grand Alexandre. *Vitruv. Præfat. L.2. Strabo. L.13*

III-D-16.

[Gilles Tiercelet], *Architecture moderne ou l'art de bien bâtir pour toutes sortes de personnes*, Paris, Jombert, 1728 (2nd ed., 1764) (2 v.) (facs. ed., New York, 1968).

Long attributed to Charles-Etienne Briseux, this book, as Wolfgang Herrmann has demonstrated, contains work by the little known architect Gilles Tiercelet. In 1726 the publisher Claude Jombert purchased a collection of designs of different houses by Tiercelet which he used for the first edition. His son Charles-Antoine Jombert published an enlarged version in 1764. Following the example of Pierre Le Muet's *Manière de bien bâtir* (3rd ed. 1663), this book provided examples of urban homes which could be built on a full range of lot sizes. The authorship of the volume, which also includes discussions of *la distribution,* construction, preparing *le devis,* measuring, and building law and building practice in Paris, is unknown.

Richard A. Etlin

III-D-17.

James Gibbs, *A Book of Architecture, containing Designs of Buildings and Ornaments,* London, W. Innys & R. Manby, 1728 (facs. ed., New York, 1968).

The *Book of Architecture,* a handsome folio published at the height of Gibbs' career, served as a personal advertisement and a counterblast to the Whig-biased *Vitruvius Britannicus* from which Gibbs' work had been rigorously excluded. Its novelty and effect derive however not so much from the record it provides of the churches, houses and public buildings which Gibbs has designed, but from the numerous variants for steeples, garden buildings, chimney-pieces, monuments, etc., which as Gibbs pointed out in his Introduction, 'may be executed by any Workman who understands Lines, either as here Design'd, or with some Alteration, which may be easily made by a person of Judgment.'

John Newman

III-D-18.

Johann Jacob Schübler (1689-1742, architect, architectural theorist), *Synopsis architecturae civilis eclecticae, oder, Kurtzer Entwurff von denen nöthigen Partial-Bergriffen welche . . . den ganzen Umfang der Civil-Bau-Kunst vorstellig machen,* Nurnberg, J.C. Weigels, 1732-1735.

Schübler was the author of numerous theoretical works, including a study of the Temple of Solomon. Developing an architecture rooted in a rigorous control of proportions, Schübler's designs, above all those for interior decoration, are based on complex mathematical calculations.

Dora Wiebenson

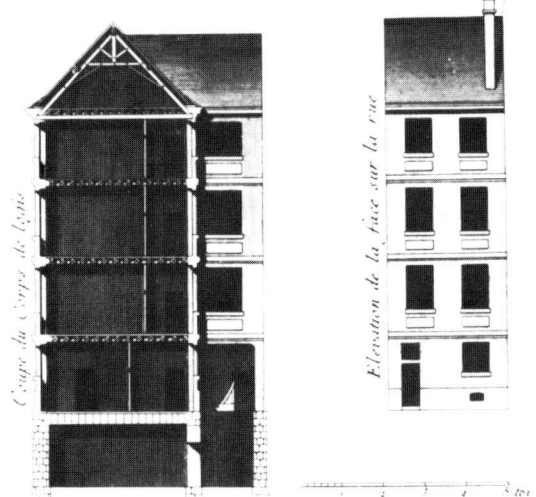

III-D-16.

III-D-17.

III-D-19.

Juste Aurèle Meissonnier (1693?-1750, ornamentalist, sculptor, decorator, architect, goldsmith), *Oeuvre*, Paris, the author, 1723-1735 (facs. ed., New York, 1969).

Meissonnier was born in Turin and died in Paris. In his youth he went to France where he held the patent as "orfèvre de roi" in 1724. Two years later, he became "dessinateur de la chambre et du Cabinet du roi" under Louis XV. He worked in Paris until his death where he was a foremost exponent of the exuberant rococo, gleaned largely from his native Piedmont. Known for his fantastic garden architecture and festival décor and the pseudo-organic character of his ornamental designs, he was cited by Jacques-François Blondel in 1774 as one of "the three initial inventors of the picturesque genre" — the most extreme phase of eighteenth century French décor. His obituary in the *Mercure de France* noted with displeasure that "he had been seduced by the taste of Borromini."

This giant folio is quite rare in its complete state; it includes 118 designs on 72 leaves together with the title page and the portrait of the artist. A frontispiece features a figure with the tools of his art, displaying a plaque on which is etched Iconographia, Orthographia, Sciographia, Scenographia, Idolographia, and Megalographia. Many collections of Meissonnier's designs for ornament and architecture are presented. There are marvelous patterns for silver candelabras, panelled ceilings, tables, watch cases, salt cellars, mirrors, setpieces, a grand fountain, and a porcelain inkstand. Among the most intriguing architectural projects are the plan of the Maison du Sieur Brethous shown in its surroundings, with site plan, elevations, and details; the elegant rococo salon of the Princess Sartorinski in Poland; the cabinet of M^r le Comte Bielenski, Grand Marshall of the Polish crown, executed in 1734. The architectural wonders of this magnificent tome are reserved for the last folios. Here are the well-known projects for the Church of St. Sulpice in Paris, dated 1726, including the elevation and facade in plan, and projects for its high altars and chapel, and for the altars of St. Aignan in Orléans, dated 1730.

Naomi Miller

III-D-20.

Jacques-François Blondel, *De la distribution de maisons de plaisance, et de la décoration des édifices en général*, Paris, Chas. Ant. Jombert, 1737-1738 (facs. ed., Farnborough, 1967) (2v.).

Blondel's first published work, this book was also known by the title *Traité d'Architecture dans le goût Moderne*. Directed to the architect, the student and "the lover of building," it was written during the great domestic architecture building boom of the eighteenth century in France. Blondel guided the reader through several country houses of his own design. These houses for the very rich illustrated the principle of 'convenance' in the planning of the house; this was determined by social custom and reason. This book was published in two volumes with most of the plates designed by the author. The first volume includes the site plans, plans and elevations of the houses and gardens. Volume two contains details of the gardens and a section on interior decoration.

Steven Frear

III-D-19.

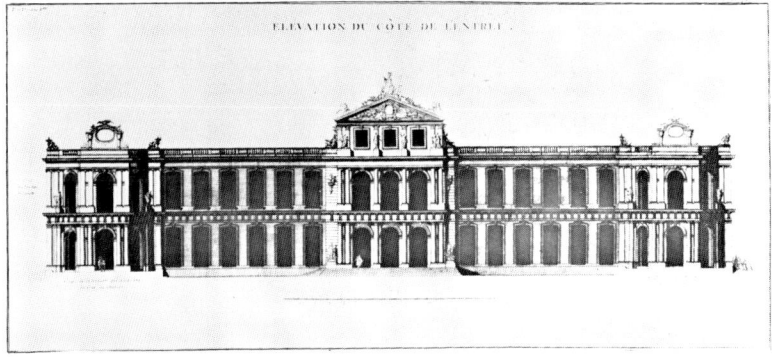

III-D-20.

III-D-21.

Charles-Etienne Briseux, *L'Art de bâtir des maisons de campagne où l'on traite de leur distribution, de leur construction, et de leur décoration,* Paris, chez Prault pere, 1743 (2v.) (facs. ed., Farnborough, 1966, 2v.).

French architects in the second quarter of the eighteenth century were proud of the advances in *la distribution,* the arrangement of rooms, in their urban and country houses. Domestic architecture was celebrated as more commodious than in the past as a given amount of space was provided with more rooms which were also now designed according to specific uses. Briseux's *L'Art de bâtir* provides seventy models of these new homes to cover the entire range of clients from the *bourgeois* to the *seigneur.* This format follows the example of Jacques-François Blondel's *De la Distribution des maisons de plaisance, et de la décoration des édifices en général.*

Richard A. Etlin

III-D-22.

Germain Boffrand (1667-1754, architect), *Livre d'architecture contenant les principes généraux de cet art et les plans, elevations et profils de quelques-uns des batimens faits en France & dans les pays etrangers, par le Sieur Boffrand,* Paris, Guillaume Cavaliere pere, 1745 (facs. ed., Farnborough, 1969).

Boffrand entered the royal architectural office under the direction of Jules Hardouin-Mansart and after 1700 he became independent as an architect of Paris town-houses and as court-architect in Lorraine. It was only after Mansart's death (1708), that he was received in the Academy of Architecture (immediately in the First Class), where in 1710 he presented his first *mémoire* (on the proportions of cornices in apartments). After 1720, Boffrand became involved much more with administration, engineering and decoration (and later on with town-planning) than with architecture proper; in those years his interest in theory and academic activities grew. He became the leading man in the Academy's theoretical discussions and his essays were generated mainly as contributions to the planned publication of the Academy's proceedings, of which he was the editor: his regular interventions on the question of *toise* began in 1718, on the *Us et coutumes de Paris dans le bâtiment* in 1725; in 1734 he first presented his essays on the *bon goût* and on the application of Horace's poetics to the architecture; from 1742 on he continuously worked on the planned edition. His book *Description de ce qui a été pratiqué pour fondre en bronce d'un même jet la Figure équestre de Louis XIV élévee par la Ville de Paris dans la place Louis le Grand en 1699* was approved by the Academy in 1742 and issued in 1743.

As he does as an architect, so with his book Boffrand bridges somehow the gap between the Louis XIV-period and early Neo-classicism (he was the only member of Mansart's school to publish an ambitious book). He presents no coherent theory, but four essays plus a choice of his own works with commentary (18 works in 70 plates). The short essay on interior decoration is of minor interest; in the other on the proportions of superimposed orders he applies optical principles proposing a visual instead of the real diminution of height. The most important essays, read and discussed several times in the Academy and repeated even after his death till 1771, are those on the *bon goût* and on the Horatian poetics as applied to architecture. Boffrand declares himself strongly in favor of building on the foundations of tradition and against fashion; *bon goût* — more or less synonymous with *bon sens, jugement* and *convenance* — includes nearly all architectural principles and is more important than the professional instruments. Boffrand's theorizing is main-line French and was certainly influential as being intended for both the lay and scholarly reader (both French and Latin text are included) in a non-specialist way, but did not have real consequences in theory. Even his passage on the *caractères* — important for the insistence on the term and its wider understanding justified by the literary origin — does not constitute in itself a major source for the *architecture parlante.*

Jörg Garms

III-D-23.

Laurids Lauridsen de Thurah (1706-1759, architect), *Den Danske Vitruvius,* Copenhagen, E.H. Berlings, 1746-9 (2v.) (facs. ed., Copenhagen, 1967, 3v.).

Widely travelled, designing in the sophisticated International Classical Baroque manner, Thurah became court architect in 1733, and would profit from the revival of building activity in Denmark. His *Danske Vitruvius,* begun in 1735, was doubtless inspired by Campbell's British version. In its two volumes Thurah displays the Danish kingdom's architectural achievements. Volume I is devoted to the principal royal and public buildings of Copenhagen, Volume II to Danish country castles.

Dora Wiebenson

III-D-23.

III-D-24.

Daniel Garrett (?-1753, architect, draughtsman, clerk of works), *Designs and Estimates of Farm-houses, etc. for the County of York, Northumberland, Cumberland, Westmoreland and Bishoprick of Durham*, London, J. Brindley, 1747 (later eds., 1759, 1772).

Garrett, a London-trained architect with an extensive North Country clientele, was one of Burlington's protégés, assisting him with many early building projects. In 1727 he was given a subordinate post in the Office of Works as "Laborer in Trust" at Richmond New Park Lodge where his immediate superior was Roger Morris. Garrett was a conscientious disciple of Burlington, designing his houses in a straight-forward Palladian style. However he used rococo plasterwork in interior design and designed several Gothic buildings in the manner of William Kent. His work included the Masoleum at Castle Howard, the rebuilding of the house at Kirtlington Park, Oxon., and the remodelling of Wallington Hall, Northumberland.

Garrett's thin folio volume was the first publication devoted entirely to farmhouses, traditionally excluded from the hierarchy meriting architectural consideration. Ten designs of Palladian massing in a plain style, with detailed estimates for building in brick or stone, offered examples of good architecture to landowners. Plates were by Remi Parr, engraver largely of architectural views for books. Garrett choses between ornament and practicality by stating: "Ornament is rather a profusion than a useful Branch (of architecture), but Convenience above all should be the Builder's principal Care . . . " The format developed by Garrett of recording each design in plan and elevation, delineating uses and sizes of rooms, and presenting price estimates for all phases of construction would be adopted in later house publications. The change in recognition of this class of building was occasioned in part by an increased need for farmhouses due to enclosure, and to the English Palladian's academic efforts to simplify and regularize architectural principles, applying them to all buildings regardless of size or function. Garrett would state that "structure should be justly composed and appropriated to the use it is intended for . . . but regularity is a necessary in both" the palace and the cottage.

Elizabeth Lambeth

III-D-25.

William Halfpenny, *A New and Compleat System of Architecture*, London, John Brindley, 1749.

This is one of several house publications undertaken by Halfpenny, including estimates, plans and elevations for country houses, and perhaps inspired by the success of Garret's book of 1747. The pedestrian nature of Halfpenny's designs and their execution bely his preface on the nature of beauty; " . . . simplicity is the basis of beauty; as decoration is of magnificence; harmony is the result of the first, and proportion elegantly composed is the certain effect of the latter . . . "

Elise M. Quasebarth

III-D-26.

William Halfpenny, *Useful Architecture in Twenty-one Designs*, London, Robert Sayer, 1752 (first section printed in 1750 as *Designs for Farmhouses*, and succeeding sections issued in 1751 and 1752) (later eds., 1755, 1760).

The conception and execution of this publication is similar to that of *A New and Compleat System of Architecture*. The format is surely taken from Garrett's work, although Halfpenny's subjugation of graciousness to contrived utility lays to rest any doubt about why more of these designs were not built. However, the successive reeditions attest to the popularity of this type of farmhouse manual, which surely was used, as Garrett intended his to be, to give models for gentlemen building tenant farms on their country estates.

Dora Wiebenson and Elise M. Quasebarth

III-D-27.

Robert Morris, *Rural Architecture: consisting of Regular Designs of Plans and Elevations for Buildings in the Country, in which the Purity and Simplicity of the Art of Designing are variously exemplified. With such Remarks and Explanations as are conducive to render the Subject Agreeable*, London, the author, 1750 (repub. as *Select Architecture*, London, 1755 and 1757) (facs. ed., London, 1971; New York, 1973).

III-D-27.

III-D-27.

Rural Architecture contains forty-one designs, most of which are consistent with the ideas Morris expressed in two of his earlier books, *Lectures on Architecture* and *An Essay in Defense of Ancient Architecture*. Many of the designs were produced years earlier for a book that was never published. Daniel Garrett, author of *Designs and Estimates of Farm Houses* (1747), had inspected the designs prior to publication and may have encouraged Morris. Morris himself felt the designs were worth publishing to encourage the use of the Grecian and Roman styles, which were being neglected in favor of the frivolous Gothic and Chinese styles. Each plan and elevation is presented as an aesthetic composition without room labels and measurements. The simple geometrical designs were especially influential in the United States, where both Thomas Jefferson and Peter Harrison owned and used copies.

Richard Ryan

III-D-28.

Jacques-François Blondel, *Architecture Françoise, ou recueil des plans, elevations, coupes et profils des églises, maisons royales, palais, hôtels and edifices . . . châteaux et maisons de plaisance . . . avec la déscription de ces edifices and des dissertations utiles and interessantes sur chaque espèce de bâtiment*, Paris, C.A. Jombert, 1752-1756 (facs. ed., Paris, 1904-1905).

This book represents a survey of French architecture from the early reign of Louis XIV to the time of publication. Blondel provided descriptions and critical comments on the buildings described; these added together form an illustrated exposition of Blondel's architectural theories. The nucleus of this collection is the set of engravings from Mariette's *L'Architecture Françoise*, which were acquired by the publisher Charles-Antoine Jombert after Mariette's death in 1742. Five hundred plates were used along with selections from the "Grand Marot" and the "Petit Marot." Blondel compared his book to *Vitruvius Britannicus* and found it to be superior. His work was to remain popular throughout the late eighteenth century.

Steven Frear

III-D-29.

William and John Halfpenny, *Chinese and Gothic Architecture Properly Ornamented*, London, Robert Sayer, 1752 (facs. ed., New York 1968).

The conception and execution of this publication is similar to many of Halfpenny's works on domestic architecture. Here, however, he presents houses with Palladian massing and Gothic/Chinese details. He rationalizes this dichotomy in the preface: " . . . there is nothing more acceptable and advantageous to the Public in General than Invention and Variety of Construction . . . We would not be understood to aim at eclipsing the munificence of Roman Architecture, but justly to promote Each Gothic and Roman in their proper situations; for whatever Denominations they go under, if Gracefulness and true Symmetry are found in the Structure, they will be sufficient bars to any . . . Aspersions . . . " In this book the reader can see the early development of the Gothic Revival where the details of a building determined the style and the plan, more conservative, remained classical.

Elise M. Quasebarth

III-D-30.

Jean-François de Neufforge (1714-1791, architect, engraver), *Recueil Elémentaire d'Architecture contenant plusieurs études des ordres d'architecture d'après l'opinion des anciens et le sentiment des modernes*, Paris, L'auteur, 1757-1768, 1772-1780 (suppl.) (facs. ed., Farnborough, 1967, 9v. in 3).

Born in Belgium of an old but impoverished aristocratic family, Neufforge went to Paris in 1738 to pursue a career in architecture. It is believed that he was a pupil of Jacques-François Blondel and P.E. Babel, the engraver. Neufforge's career floundered until 1755 when he began working on his *Recueil Elémentaire*. This was to occupy him for the rest of his life. As an engraver he was to provide 18 plates for J.D. LeRoy's *Ruines des plus beaux monuments de la Grèce* (1758).

Following the format of a traditional pattern book, Neufforge was to include examples of all types of buildings of varying sizes to suit rich and poor clients. In the eventual nine volumes containing nine hundred

III-D-29.

III-D-30.

plates the range of buildings was much wider than any previous pattern book; included were designs for lighthouses, prisons, theatres and churches. This work received enthusiastic reception from the press and the endorsement of the Academy. It has been seen as a popularization of the "gout grec," however, Neufforge's designs are rather clumsy and heavy-handed and seem to have more to do with sixteenth century Italy than with the elegance of eighteenth century France.

Steven Frear

III-D-31.

Marie-Joseph Peyre (1730-1785, architect), *Oeuvres d'architecture*, Paris, Prault et Jombert, 1765 (2nd ed., 1795) (facs. ed., Farnborough, 1967).

A student of J.F. Blondel, Peyre won the *grand prix d'architecture* in 1751. He went to Rome in 1753 and along with Moreau-Desproux and De Wailly, measured the thermae of Diocletain and Caracalla. Aside from the publication of his *Oeuvres*, Peyre's career was not distinguished; in 1767 he was made a member of the Académie and Contrôleur des batiments de Choisy-le-Roi. His most significant built works were the Maison de Neubourg and the Théâtre Français, undertaken with the collaboration of De Wailly.

The nineteen engravings with text that comprise the book include the plans of the thermae Peyre measured for his Rome *envoi*, a design for academical buildings, and his designs for the Maison de Neubourg and the Hôtel de Condé. These were highly influential on the development of Neoclassicism in France and affected the works of important architects such as Gabriel, Ledoux, Victor Louis, Chalgrin and Rousseau.

Steven Frear

III-D-32.

John Crunden (1745-1835, architect, surveyor), *Convenient and Ornamental Architecture*, London, the author and Henry Webley, 1767 (later eds., 1770, 1785, 1788, 1791, 1805, 1815).

Crunden was born in Sussex and worked in London as the assistant to a master-builder who was the father of architect Henry Holland. He exhibited designs at the Society of Artists in 1776 and 1777. He is best known as the author of a number of popular pattern books which show him to be a designer of no great talent working within the British Palladian tradition.

Convenient and Ornamental Architecture provided designs and functions for houses for all classes of society. As Crunden stated in his introduction, the intention of the publication was "calculated both for town and country, and to suit all persons in every station of life." Unlike Garrett and Halfpenny, Crunden chose not to include building estimates in his publication.

Elise M. Quasebarth

III-D-33.

Thomas Rawlins (active 1743-1780, stonemason), *Familiar Architecture*, Norwich, published by the author, 1768 (later eds., 1789, 1795).

Rawlins was born in Norwich, the son of a weaver. Although he exhibited architectural designs at the Society of Artists and at the Royal Academy, he is best known as a monumental stonemason.

Familiar Architecture provides designs and estimates for houses in the Palladian mode and has some affinity to the work of James Paine. Like many of the house publications, this book was intended to serve as a substitute for an architect in areas where professional assistance was not readily available. Rawlins provides a building with a triangular plan in an apparent effort to refute statements of Isaac Ware and William Chambers to the effect that this geometric shape was not suitable for building plans. The design also indicates a possible link with the French theorist, Laugier, who proposed such a plan for a church in his *Essai sur l'Architecture* (1753). *Familiar Architecture* is a pretentious work that was parodied by Peacock in *Nutshells* (1785) for its eccentricities of plan and measurements.

Elise M. Quasebarth

III-D-33.

III-D-34.

Robert Adam (1728-1792, architect, entrepreneur, author), *The Works in Architecture of Robert and James Adams . . . Les ouvrages d'architecture de Robert et Jacques Adam*, London, Printed for the authors, 1773-1779 (2 v.) (facs. ed., London and New York, 1975).

Adam, the son of a prominent Scots architect and builder, was born in Kirkaldy, Fife, Scotland. He attended the University of Edinburgh, but left without a degree to join his father's office. From 1754-1758 he toured the continent, studied drawing and antiquities in Rome under the tutelage of the French Neoclassical architect and draftsman Charles-Louis Clérisseau, met many of the future leaders of the international Neoclassical style, including G.B. Piranesi, and with Clerisseau measured and drew the Place of Diocletian at Split, Dalmatia. In 1758 he returned to London and began an architectural practice with his brothers James and William. His work at Harewood (1758-1771), Kedleston (1759-1770), and Syon House (1760-1769) established an Adam Style of Neoclassical planning and ornament that affected English, Continental, and Colonial design for decades. He was made Architect of the King's Works and Fellow of the Royal Society in 1761. In 1764 he published *Ruins of Spalatro* on the work at Split, and, in 1773-1779, the influential *Works in Architecture*. Although he practiced architecture until his death, his reputation declined in the early 1780's, and most of his later work was done in Scotland.

The Works in Architecture of Robert and James Adams was first published in five parts in English and French, 1773-1778, and issued as a single volume in 1778. A second volume was published in 1779. A third volume of previously uncollected designs was issued posthumously in 1822. Containing plans and elevations of churches, country and city houses, designs for ceilings, chimneybreasts, gardenseats, organs, candelabra, mirrors, ruined bridges, and furniture, it was the most comprehensive presentation of stylistically unified designs ever published in Britain. Among the aristocratic and wealthy class, it was seminal in popularizing Neoclassical ideas of interior planning and the Adam Style of ornament, and in freeing English design from the Palladians' austere interpretation of the classical idiom.

Bradley Barker

III-D-35.

John Wood, the younger (1728-1781, architect, writer), *A Series of Plans for Cottages or Habitations of the Labourer*, London, J. Taylor, 1781 (later eds., 1792, 1806, 1837) (facs. ed., Farnborough, 1972).

Wood was the younger son of John Wood, the architect of Bath. He became his father's assistant in 1749. Following the death of the elder Wood in 1759, Wood completed the residential Circus begun by his father, adding the Royal Crescent and New Assembly rooms to the development of central Bath. These developments represent a synthesis of Palladian design and baroque urban planning. In addition to his work in and around Bath, Wood completed public and domestic buildings in the Palladian manner in Bedford, Kent, Surrey, Sussex, London, and Ireland.

A Series of Plans for Cottages or Habitations of the Labourer is a collection of designs for one to three room cottages for country or town labourers. Wood's concern with rural housing, and the format of presentation of plan, elevation, designation of room use, and estimation of construction costs, is similar to earlier house publications associated with the Palladian movement. But where earlier books were concerned with raising the quality of the design of farmhouses and estates of the minor gentry and rural middle class, Wood's sole concern was, "The necessity there was of improving the dwellings of the poor labourer . . ." The book was one of several contemporary publications on the house that recognized the squalid state of the housing of the poor. It was offered to landowners who wished to improve the condition of tenant housing. That a climate receptive to such improvement existed, seems to indicate a growing consciousness among the gentry of the need for reform, and a new participation of the architect as a generator of reform.

Bradley Barker

III-D-36.

James Peacock (c. 1738-1814, architect), *OIKIDIA, Nutshells: Being Iconographic Distributions for Small Villas; chiefly upon Economical Principles . . . by Jose MacPacke, a bricklayer's labourer*, London, the author, 1785.

Peacock was employed in George Dance's office from the late 1760's until his death, and was from 1771 Dance's assistant as Clerk of the Works to the City of London. He published several works on architectural subjects, the most important, *OIKIDIA*, under the anagrammatic pseudonym of "Jose MacPacke." It contains "iconographic distributions" (plans) for thirteen small houses, with a satiric commentary and measurements, providing a parody of earlier house publications, especially Robert Morris's *Rural Architecture* and Thomas Rawlins's *Familiar Architecture*. Peacock, an architect who, like Wood, was concerned with social and economic issues, assumes here the trade of a bricklayer, (Rawlins was a mason) and contrasts his humble octavo with a folio edition (which Rawlins had produced). He shows only plans and gives dimensions only to the "best" rooms, possibly in reference to Swan's procedures. He suggested that his designs could be used by "gentlemen of large fortune" to "erect little villages of this kind" and he includes proportional tables which sarcastically exaggerate refinement by application of proportional themes, such as are found in Morris's *Lectures*. A lengthy appendix which addresses the relations between clients and their architects or builders, is "sensible on matters of fact and sardonic about contemporary architectural practice and taste." Peacock pointed the way for a new group of small house publications by indicating designs for small houses intended for those of limited means who had previously been city dwellers.

Elizabeth Lambeth

III-D-37.

John Plaw (c. 1745-1820, bricklayer, master-builder, architect, writer), *Rural Architecture; or Designs from the Simple Cottage to the Decorated Villa*, London, Taylor, 1785 (later eds., 1794, 1796, 1800, 1802, 1804) (facs. ed., Farnborough, 1971).

In 1759 John Plaw was recorded as an apprentice to Thomas Kaygill, a bricklayer. By 1768, when he was awarded a premium by the Society of Arts for a drawing of Inigo Jones's Banqueting House, he was described as an 'architect and master-builder in Westminster'. He exhibited sketches at the Society of Artists in 1773, 1790, and 1791, and at the Royal Academy after 1775. In 1791 he was elected president of the Society of Artists. He published three books of designs for picturesque cottages, villas and farms, and executed many of his designs before emigrating to Prince Edward Island in Canada in 1810.

Rural Architecture was a popular and influential book. Published in 1785, it was republished with additional designs in 1794, 1796, 1800, 1802, and 1804. Unlike an earlier class of cottage publications which was socially conscious and concerned with housing reform, utility, and economy of construction, *Rural Architecture* concentrated almost entirely on the picturesque character of vernacular architecture and rustic building materials. Plaw's book was the first of a class of house publications in which the house was illustrated in a picturesque landscape, the plan was subordinated to the picturesque effect of elevation, and the newly developed medium of acqua-tint was used to give a picturesque character to his illlustrations. All these devices, introduced in *Rural Architecture*, became, in the work of Malton, Elsam, Gandy, Nash, Loudon, and others, standard elements in the picturesque conception of the small house.

Bradley Barker

III-D-38.

George Richardson (1736?-1817?), draftsman, engraver, drawing-master, architect, author), *New Designs in Architecture*, London, the author, 1792.

Richardson is first recorded described as an apprentice, probably a draftsman, in the office of John Adam in Edinburgh. From 1760 to 1763 he travelled as a draftsman with James Adam on Adam's Grand Tour of Europe. He continued in Adam's employment for several years in England and may have been responsible for the Adam ceilings at Kedleston Hall. Richardson began his own practice in 1765, but built little. Three churches in the Gothic style and one Neoclassical church have been attributed to him. He apparently made his living from his books of designs and a practice as a drawing master. He published eleven books, including a treatise on the Orders, a number of books of classical ornament, and *New Vitruvius Britannicus*, a two volume compendium of late eighteenth century British architecture.

New Designs in Architecture, dedicated to the Earl of Gainsborough, was subscribed to by the aristocracy, the gentry, and the wealthier class of professionals and merchants. Unlike earlier English books on the small house, it was unconcerned with innovation in plan form or reform of the housing of the poor. It is concerned with the ornamental and picturesque aspect of small house design. Like Plaw, Richardson uses the acquatint engraving, a process that produces a misty effect, to develop the picturesque aspect of shape, texture, and massing as applied to a variety of house types, including thatched cottages, villas, and townhouses. Few of the designs are original, many taken from Adam's books of designs. Although Richardson was primarily concerned with ornament and picturesque design, *New Designs* includes a short section dealing with room function, dimensions, building materials, and specifications.

Bradley Barker

III-D-37.

III-D-39.

Sir John Soane (1753-1837, architect), *Sketches in Architecture, containing Plans & Elevations of Cottages, Villas, and other useful Buildings*, London, J. Taylor, 1793, (2nd ed., 1798) (facs. ed., Farnborough, 1971).

The son of a bricklayer, Soane entered the office of George Dance, the younger, the City Surveyor, through the good offices of the latter's assistant, James Peacock. Admitted to the Royal Academy Schools (1771), and assistant to Henry Holland (1772-78), he then, having attracted the attention of William Chambers, was awarded the King's Travelling Scholarship enabling him to tour Italy with R.F. Brettingham. Appointed to the surveyorship of the Bank of England (1788) through the influence of William Pitt, he was appointed to be the Clerk of the Works at Whitehall (1791). In 1806 he succeeded George Dance as Professor of Architecture at the Royal Academy, delivering elaborately illustrated letters from 1809-1836. Interested in architectural education, he did much to raise the standards of architectural practice. He was offered the Presidency of the Royal Institute of British Architects at its founding in 1834, and was recognized as the father of his profession when he was presented a Gold Metal in 1835.

Sketches is Soane's third published collection of designs. It includes eight cottages "for the laborious and industrious part of the community," villas for persons of moderate fortune, and garden structures. They are notable for their small scale and picturesque surroundings, including elements such as tree trunks decorated with vines and thatched roofs. According to Soane, he published the *Sketches* because he was "induced to offer another publication on the same subject (of *Plans, Elevations, and Sketches of Buildings*), but on a smaller scale . . . calculated for the real uses and comforts of life, and such as are within the reach of moderate fortunes." Soane describes, as did Wood, the necessary conveniences for cottage dwellers, such as raised ground floors, dry and airy situations, and a good supply of water, and much attention is paid to the site and picturesque effect.

Elizabeth Lambeth

III-D-40.

James Malton (?-1803, architectural draftsman, topographical artist, author), *An Essay on British Cottage Architecture*, London, Hookham and Carpenter, 1798, (facs. ed., Farnborough, 1972).

James Malton was the son of an architectural draftsman and writer on perspective. He worked for a time in Ireland as an architectural draftsman in the office of James Gandon. In the 1790's he moved to London where he worked as a topographical artist. He published *A Descriptive View of Dublin* in 1797. Malton exhibited topographical views and architectural designs at the Royal Academy. He published two books of architectural designs. Although he called himself an architect, he built nothing.

An Essay on British Cottage Architecture, presented the cottage as, " . . . a small house in the country; of odd, irregular form, with various, harmonious colouring, the effect of weather, time, and accident; the whole environed with smiling verdure . . . a cheerful dwelling of the careless rustic . . ." Earlier writers had applied the Palladian style to the cottage in an effort to improve the 'hovels' of the poor. Malton invented a romanticised conception of the cottage, for the pleasure of "the substantial farmer or affluent gentleman" His conception of the cottage replaced the classical diction that Kent, Wood, and Peacock had brought to the type, with a picturesque vernacular idiom of thatch, half-timber, and diamond-paned windows, applied to (for the first time in a house publication) an asymmetrical form. His book, published as the romantic ideal was gaining currency, contributed greatly to giving the cottage an image of picturesque respectability.

Bradley Barker

III-D-39.

III-D-40.

III-D-41.

Etienne-Louis Boullée (1728-1799, architect, theoretician, educator), *Architecture, essai sur l'art* (ms. 9153, Bibliothèque Nationale, Paris) (eds. H. Rosenau, London, 1953; P. de Montclos, Paris, 1968; Eng. trans., H. Rosenau, London, 1973).

Boullée studied first, and importantly, with the painter of *russeries*, Jean-Baptiste Pierre, and later, relunctantly it seems, in the architectural school of Blondel. Already by the 1750's he was active as a practicing architect, primarily, but not exclusively, of Parisian *hôtels*, and as an inspiring teacher at the Ecole des Ponts et Chaussées. Subsequently, he played an active role in the Académie de l'Architecture where he was a member since 1762. The latter part of his career, however, was not similarly blessed with numerous public or private commissions. In light of this, it was in the decade immediately preceding the revolution that he concentrated upon the *Essai*, composed of "painterly" and "poetic" drawings of imaginary sites and of "visionary" musings to accompany them on architecture, art, and their formative role in the intellectual development and collective progress of an ideal society.

The dating of the manuscript remains problematic. While the *Essai* remained unpublished until modern times, it seems to have been written in consecutive sequences late in Boullée's career, and he died before completing it; nevertheless, it also appears to incorporate material written at an earlier date. Thus it offers a conceptual framework to interpret his entire work, for completed and projected architecture alike. The leitmotif of this treatise — reflecting some of the most important cultural concerns of his day — is nature, embodied in the creation of an *architecture des ombres* and an *architecture ensevelie*, and the modern architect's complex relationship to its various manifestations in a post-Newtonian and highly scientifically conscious age. A no less important subtheme might well be identified as the aesthetic investigation of how the Enlightenment ideal — known to him through the writings of Diderot, the shapers of the *Encyclopédie*, Bailly, Romé de L'Isle, Chenier — of the marriage between art and science might become a reality. Further, his emphasis on formal simplicity, symmetry, and functionalism, perhaps best embodied in the Cenotaph for Newton (1784), looks back to, while simultaneously advancing, the Baconian ideal of a classical "plain" style suitable for scientific discourse and the clear transmission of an object's true *caractère*. The visual and speculative daring of the *Essai*, therefore, does not set him apart from, but roots him in, his time.

Barbara Maria Stafford

III-D-42.

Richard Elsam (fl. 1793-1825, architect, author), *An Essay on Rural Architecture*, London, E. Lawrence, 1803 (facs. ed., Farnborough, 1972).

Elsam's date of birth is unknown. He exhibited some designs at the Royal Academy between 1797 and 1807. He was employed as an architect in the Barracks Department of the War Office until 1803. His career as an architect was undistinguished; he was let go by a number of clients for poor estimation of building costs. Curiously, he wrote two books on construction estimating, *The Gentleman and Builder's Assistant* (1808), and *The Practical Builder's Perpetual Price Book* (1825). He also wrote *Hints for improving the Condition of the Peasantry, with Plans, Elevations and Descriptive Views of Characteristic Designs for Cottages* (1816), and *A Brief Treatise on Prisons* (1818).

An Essay on Rural Architecture, is to some extent a polemic on Malton's concept of the rustic cottage as a small house of odd, irregular, vernacular character. Elsam countered that, "The peasant's cot, and the farm-house . . . are not, to my conceptions, proper models of imitations for persons of fortune, who are desirous of building themselves rural retreats, which may be erected to convey the idea of cottages . . . " He suggested that a vernacular combination of, " . . . brick, wood, plaster, or brick noggin, dashed to insinuate the effects of age . . . contribute to impress the mind of the spectator with the idea of poverty, rather than with a just notion of its cheerful and independent inhabitants." While he retained Malton's romantic association of the cottage with cheerful simple living, independence, and the picturesque landscape, he proposed a 'genteel Cottage', allowing thatch and casements, but of uniform materials and symmetrical plan and massing. Additionally, he proposed an association of style with social class, suggesting that the Gothic, Greek, and Roman 'styles' were the most appropriate expressions of gentility for the rural house.

Bradley Barker

III-D-43.

Claude-Nicolas Ledoux (1736-1806, architect, theorist), *L'Architecture considérée sous le rapport de l'art, des moeurs et de la législation*, Paris, chez l'auteur, 1804 (facs. ed., Paris, 1961; Hildesheim, 1980).

Ledoux was one of the most prolific neoclassical architects and theorists of the late eighteenth century. His works include the Hôtel d'Hallwyl (1766), Hôtel de Montmorency (1769), Hôtel Guimard (1770-1771), Hôtel de Thélusson (1776-1783) in Paris as well as the theater of Besançon (1775). Named inspector general of saltworks in Lorraine and Franche-Comté in 1771, Ledoux constructed the saltworks of Chaux at Arc-et-Senans (1774-1779). In 1784, he began the construction of a new tax wall around Paris with forty-seven monumental toll gates or *barrières* for the Fermiers Généraux.

Ledoux's book presents his principle work in the context of a literary and social Utopia. The text opens with a traveler's arrival at the pastoral world of Chaux where the saltworks along with an idealized agricultural community have realized a prosperous and harmonious society. The combined houses and workshops for each profession are given an expressive architectural form on the exterior while the interiors are arranged so that four families re-enact Rousseau's social contract around a communal hearth as a daily ritual. The actual buildings at the saltworks present a heavy set and rusticated nether-world while the houses for the agricultural guards and the barrel makers as well as the cemetery and even the ideal plan of Chaux are imbued with a cosmological symbolism. This architecture prompted a skeptical nineteenth century critic to coin the phrase *l'architecture parlante*.

Richard A. Etlin

III-D-44.

Joseph Michael Gandy (1771-1843, architect, architectural draftsman, painter, writer), *Designs for Cottages, Cottage Farms, and Other Rural Buildings; including Entrance Gates and Lodges,* London, John Harding, 1805 (facs. ed., Farnborough 1971).

Gandy was the son of an employee of White's Club in London. In 1787 he entered the office of the architect James Wyatt. In 1787 he began studies at the Royal Academy, where he won the Gold and Silver Medals. In 1794, the owner of White's Club sent him to Rome to study at the Academy of St. Luke. He returned to England in 1797 and found a place in the office of John Soane. He practiced architecture intermittently from 1800 to 1810, but received few commissions. A painter, he showed 112 paintings at the Royal Academy, among them many fantasies of monumental architecture in the tradition of Piranesi, but sold few. Chronically in debt, Gandy lived on occasional commissions to illustrate Soane's designs in watercolor. He died in poverty.

Designs for Cottages and *The Rural Architect* are in a class of house publication that recognized the need to improve the housing of the poor. By the time of Gandy's publications, the reformist attitudes of the earlier publications had become public policy. In the introduction to *Designs for Cottages,* Gandy states that, "The idea of the following work was suggested . . . in the valuable Publication issued under the direction of the Board of Agriculture . . . replete with observations dictated by the soundest policy, and originating in the humane desire of increasing the comforts and improving the condition of the Labouring Poor." Gandy's preference for elemental geometrical forms is similar to Wood's for Palladian cottage designs, but his combination of the Palladian manner with such picturesque devices as the tree-trunk column, asymmetrical massing, and natural landscape setting, as well as much of Malton's vocabulary, is a striking reconciliation of rational and romantic principles of design.

Bradley Barker

III-D-43.

List of Abbreviations

AB	*Art Bulletin*
AH	*Architectural History*
Alessi Convegno	*Galeazzo Alessi e l'architettura del cinquecento. Atti del convegno internazionale di studi,* Genoa, 1975.
BSHAF	*Bulletin de la Société de l'histoire de l'art français*
BCISAAP	*Bollettino di Centro Internazionale di studi d'architettura Andrea Palladio*
GBA	*Gazette des Beaux-Arts*
Guarini Convegno	*Guarino Guarini e l'internazionalita del Barocco. Atti del convegno internazionale promesso dall'Accademia delle scienze di Torino* (1968), Turin, 1970 (2v.)
JSAH	*Journal of the Society of Architectural Historians*
JWCI	*Journal of the Warburg and Courtauld Institutes*
SDA	*Studi e documenti di architettura*
Vittone Convegno	*Bernardo Vittone e la disputa fra classicismo e barocco nel Settecento. Atti del convegno internazionale promesso dall'Accademia delle scienze di Torino nella ricorrenza del secondo centenario della morte di B. Vittone* (1970), Turin, 1972 (2v.)
Wittkower Essays	*Essays in the History of Architecture presented to Rudolf Wittkower,* London, 1967 (ed., D. Fraser, et al.).

BIBLIOGRAPHY

General

Comolli, A. *Bibliografia storico-critica dell'architettura civile ed arti arti subalterne*, Rome, 1788-1792 (4v.) (facs. ed., Milan, 1964-5).

Fichet, F. *La Théorie architecturale à l'age classique*, Brussels, 1979.

Germann, G. *Einfuhrung in die Geschichte der Architekturtheorie*, Darmstadt, 1980.

I: Vitruvius Discovered

Ackerman, J.S., "Architectural Practice in the Italian Renaissance," *JSAH*, 1954, 3-11.

——————. "Ars sine scientia nihil est: Gothic Theory of Architecture at the Cathedral of Milan," *AB*, 1949, 84-111.

——————. *The Cortile del Belvedere*, Città del Vaticano, 1954.

Alvise Cornaro e il suo tempo (exhibition catalog), Padua, 1980.

Andrea Palladio: il testo, l'immagine, la città (exhibition catalog), Vicenza, 1980.

Barbieri, F. *Vincenzo Scamozzi*, Verona, 1952.

Benzine, J. *Walther Ryff und sein literarisches Werke; eine Bibliographie*, Hamburg, 1959.

Betts, R. "On the Chronology of Francesco di Giorgio's Treatises: New Evidence from an Unpublished Manuscript," *JSAH*, March 1977, 3-14.

Blunt, A. *Artistic Theory in Italy, 1450-1600*, Oxford, 1966.

——————. "The Hypnerotomachia Poliphili in Seventeenth-Century France," *JWCI*, 1937-38, 117-137.

——————. *Philibert de l'Orme*, London, 1958.

Brenzoni, R. *Fra Giovanni Giocondo veronese, Verona 1435-Roma 1515*, Florence, 1960.

Buddensieg, T. "Bernardo della Volpaia und Giovanni Francesco da Sangallo," *Romisches Jahrbuch für Kunstgeschichte*, 1975, 89-108.

——————. "Criticism of Ancient Architecture in the Sixteenth and Seventeenth Centuries," *Classical Influences on European Culture, A.D. 1500-1700*, Cambridge, 1976 (ed. R.R. Bolgar), 335-348.

Carunchio, T. "Dal VII Libro di S. Serlio: 'XXIII case per edificar nella villa' lettura integrata del VII libro manoscritto e dell'edizione a stampa," *Quaderni dell'istituto di storia dell'architettura*, 1975, nos.127-132, 95-126.

Cervera, Vera, L. *El codice de Vitruvio hasta sus primeras versiones impresas*, Madrid, 1978.

Cevese, R. *I modelli della mostra del Palladio*, Venice, 1976.

Ciapponi. L. "Appunti per una biografia di Giovanni Giocondo da Verona," *Italia medievale e humanistica*, 1961, 131-158.

——————. "Vitruvius," *Catalogus translationem et commentariorum* (ed. F.E. Cranz and P.O. Kristeller), Washington, D.C., 1976 (3v.), III, 399-409.

Coffin, D. "Pirro Ligorio on the Nobility of the Arts," *JWCI*, 1964, 191-210.

Dinsmoor, W.B. "The Literary Remains of Sebastiano Serlio," *AB*, 1942, 55-91, 115-154.

Du Colombier, P. "Jean Goujon et le Vitruve de 1547," *GBA*, 1931, 155-178.

Ericsson, C.H. *Roman architecture expressed in sketches by Francesco di Giorgio Martini*, Helsinki, 1980.

Fiocco, G. "La lezione di Alvise Cornaro," *BCISAAP*, 1963, 33-43.

Forsman, E. "Falconetto e Palladio," *BCISAAP*, 1966, 52-57.

——————. "Palladio e Vitruvio," *BCISAAP*, 1962, 31-42.

Gadol, J. *Leon Battista Alberti; Universal Man of the Early Renaissance*, Chicago, 1969.

Hamberg, P.G. "Vitruvius, Fra Giocondo and the City Plan of Naples," *Acta Archaeologica*, 1965, 105-125.

Herrmann, W. *The Theory of Claude Perrault*, London, 1973.

Hersey, G. *Pythagorean Palaces: Magic and Architecture in the Italian Renaissance*, Ithaca, 1976.

Hoffman, V. "Brunelleschis Architektursystem," *Architectura*, 1971, 54-71.

——————. "Sebastiano Serlio's Venetian Copyrights," *The Burlington Magazine*, 1973, 512-516.

Horster, M. "Skizzenbucher der Renaissance nach Antiken," *Archäologischer Anzeiger*, 1975, 427-432.

Howard, D. "Four Centuries of Literature on Palladio," *JSAH*, Oct. 1980, 224-241.

"Il Filarete," *Arte Lombardia*, 1973 (nos. 38-39).

Juřen, V. "Fra Giovanni Giocondo et le début des études Vitruviennes en France," *Rinascimento*, 1974, 101-115.

——————. "Un traité inédit sur les ordres d'architecture et le problème des sources du *Libro IV* de Serlio," *Monuments et mémoires publiés par l'Académie des Inscriptions et Belles-Lettres*, 1981, 195-239.

Kambartel, W. *Symmetrie und Schönheit; über mögliche Voraussetzungen des neueren Kunstbewussteseins in der Architekturtheorie Claude Perraults*, Munich, 1972.

Krinsky, C.H. "Cesariano and the Renaissance without Rome," *Arte Lombarda*, 1971, 211-218.

——————. "Seventy-Eight Vitruvius Manuscripts," *JWCI*, 1967, 36-70.

Lang, S. "Sforzinda, Filarete and Filelfo," *JWCI*, 1972, 391-397.

"Leon Battista Alberti," *Architectural Design*, 1979 (nos. 5-6).

Lesuer, P. "Fra Giovanni Giocondo en France," *BSHAF*, 1931, 115-144.

Lucke, H.K. *Alberti Index*, Munich, 1975-76 (4v.).

Mandowsky, E., ed. *Pirro Ligorio's Roman Antiquities*, London, 1963.

Marconi, P. "Un progetto di città militari: l'VIII libro inedito de Sebastiano Serlio." *Controspazio*, 1969, no.1, 51-59; nos.4-5, 52-59.

Marías, F. and A. Bustamente Garciá. *Las ideas artísticas de El Greco*, Madrid, 1981.

McKean, J.M. "Sebastiano Serlio," *Architectural Association Quarterly*, 1979, 14-27.

Olivato, L. "Galeazzo Alessi e la trattatistica architettonica del rinascimento," *Convegno Alessi*, 131-146.

Onians, J. "Alberti and ΦΙΛΑΡΕΤΗ: A Study in their Sources," *JWCI*, 1971, 96-114.

_____. "The Last Judgement of Renaissance Architecture," *Journal of the Royal Society of Arts*, October 1980, 701-718.

Palladio (exhibition catalogue), Vicenza, 1973.

Palladio (exhibition catalogue), London, 1975.

Palladio e Verona (exhibition catalogue), Verona, 1980.

Pallucchini, R. "Profilo di Vincenzo Scamozzi," *BCISAAP*, 1961, 89-101.

Pellati, C.F. "Giovanni Sulpicio da Veroli," *Atti de 2 Congresso nazionale di studi romani* (1930), Rome, 1931, III, 382-386.

Pepper, S. and G. Hughes. "Fortification in late Fifteenth Century Italy: the Treatise of Francesco di Giorgio Martini," *British Archaeolotgical Reports*, 1978 (suppl. ser. 41).

Puppi, L. "Il tratto del Palladio e la sua fortune in Italia e all'estro," *BCISAAP*, 1970, 257-272.

_____. *Scrittori Vicentini d'architettura del secolo XVI*, Vicenza, 1973.

_____. "Vincenzo Scamozzi, trattatista, nell'ambito della problematica del Manierismo," *BCISAAP*, 1967, 310-329.

Ricci, C. "Vitruvio nel Medio Evo e nel Rinascimento," *Bollettino de Instituto Nazionale di Archeologio e storia dell'Arte*, 1932, 111-132.

Rosci, M. *Il trattato di architettura di Sebastiano Serlio*, Milan, 1966.

Rosenfeld, M.N. "Sebastiano Serlio's Drawings in the Nationalbibliothek in Vienna for his *Seventh Book on Architecture*," *AB*, Sept. 1974, 400-409.

Saalman, H. "Early Renaissance Architectural Theory and Practice in Antonio Filarete's *Tratatto di Architettura*," *AB*, March 1959, 89-106.

Scaglia, G. "Autour de Francesco di Giorgio Martini, ingénieur et dessinateur," *Révue de l'art*, 1980, 7-25.

_____. "A Translation of Vitruvius and Copies of Late Antique Drawings in Buonaccorso Ghiberti's *Zibaldone*," *Transactions of the American Philosophical Society*, 1979.

Schmidt, D. *Untersuchungen zu den Architekturekphrasen in der Hypnerotomachia poliphili*, Frankfurt am Main, 1978.

Schweikhart, G. *Le antichità di Verona di Giovanni Caroto*, Verona, 1977.

Semenzato, C. "Gian Maria Falconetto," *BCISAAP*, 1961, 70-77.

Spencer J.R. "Filarete and Central-Plan Architecture," *JSAH*, 1958, 10-18.

Tafuri, M. *L'architettura del Manierismo nel Cinquecento europeo*, Rome, 1966.

The Drawings of Andrea Palladio (exhibition catalog), Washington, D.C., 1981

Vagnetti, L. "2000 anni di Vitruvio," *SDA*, 1978, no.8.

Vagnetti, L. and Marcucci, L. "Per una consienza Vitruvianna," *SDA*, 1978, no.8, 11-184.

Verga, C. "Francesco Gaffurio e Giambattista Caporali: due umanisti tra musica e architettura," *Archivi storico lodigiano*, 1964, 18-26.

Walcher-Casotti, M. *Il Vignola*, Trieste, 1960.

Westfall, C.W. *In this most perfect Paradise: Alberti, Nicholas V, and the Invention of Conscious Urban Planning in Rome, 1447-55*, University Park, Pennsylvania, 1974.

_____. *The Two Ideal Cities of the Early Renaissance*, New York, 1967.

Wilkinson, C. "The New Professionalism in the Renaissance," *The Architect* (ed. S. Kostof), New York, 1977, 124-160.

Wischermann, H. "Castrametatio und städtebau im 16. Jahrhundert: Sebastiano Serlio," *Bonner Jahrbücher*, 1975, 171-186.

Wittkower, R. *Architectural Pinciples in the Age of Humanism*, London, 1949.

_____. "Giacomo Leoni's edition of Palladio's 'Quattro libri dell'architettura'," *Arte Veneta*, 1954, 310-316.

_____. *Palladio and Palladianism*, New York, 1974.

Zander, G. "Le invenzioni architettoniche di Giovanni Battista Montano," *Quaderni dell'istituto di storia dell'architettura*, 1958 (no. 30) and 1962 (nos. 49-50).

Zorzi, G. "La Preparazione de 'I Quattro Libri dell'Architettura'," *I disegni delle antichità di Andrea Palladio*, Venice, 1959, 145-159.

II: Architects and Amateurs

Blunt, A. "Roman Baroque Architecture - the Other Side of the Medal," *Art History*, 1980, n.1, 61-80.

Cavallari Murat, A. "Aggiornamento tecnico e critico nei trattati vittoniani," *Vittoni Convegno*, I, 457-600.

_____. "Struttura e forma nel trattato architettonico del Guarini," *Guarini Convegno*, I, 451-496.

Egbert, D.D. "From the Founding of the Académie Royale d'Architecture to the Revolution," *The Beaux-Arts Tradition in French Architecture, Illustrated by the Grands Prix de Rome*, Princeton, 1980, 11-35.

Fagiolo, M. "La 'geosofia' del Guarini," *Guarini Convegno*, II, 179-204.

Ferrero De Bernardi, D. "Il Conte Ivan Caramuel di Lobkowitz, Vescova di Vigerano," *Palladio*, 1965 (I-IV), 91-110.

Gengaro, M.L. "Il valore dell'architettura nelle teoria settecentesca padre Carlo Lodoli," *L'arte*, 1937, 313-317.

Grassi, L. *Razionalismo architettonico dal Lodoli a G. Pagano*, Milan, 1966.

Habicht, V.C. "Architekturtheorie," *Reallexikon zur deutschen Kunstgeschichte* (O. Schmidt, ed.), I, 959-992, Stuttgart, 1937-67

_____. "Die deutschen Architekturtheoretiker des 17. und 18. Jahrhunderts," *Zeitschrift für Architektur und Ingenieurwesen*, 1916, 1ff, 261ff; 1917, 209ff; 1918, 157ff, 201ff.

Harris, J. *Sir William Chambers, Knight of the Polar Star*, London, 1970.

Herrmann, W. "Antoine Desgodets and the Académie Royale d'Architecture," *AB*, 1958, 23-53.

_____. *Laugier and Eighteenth-Century French Theory*, London, 1962.

_____. "The Problem of Chronology in Claude-Nicolas Ledoux's Engraved Work," *AB*, 1960, 191-210.

_____. "Unknown Designs for the 'Temple of Jerusalem' by Claude Perrault," *Wittkower Essays*, 143-158.

Kaufmann, E., Jr. "Memmo's Lodoli," *AB*, 1964, 159-175.

Kernodle, G. "Joseph Furttenbach the Elder, 1591-1667," *The Renaissance Stage: Documents of Serlio, Sabbattini and Furttenbach* (B. Hewitt, ed.), Coral Gables, 1958, 178-251.

Maltese, C. "Guarini e la Prospettiva," *Guarini Convegno*, I, 557-572.

Marconi, P. "Guarino Guarini ed il Gotico," *Guarini Convego*, I, 613-635.

Mauclaire, P. and C. Vigoureux. *Nicolas-François de Blondel, Ingénieur et Architecte du Roi (1618-1686)*, Laon, (1938).

Middleton, R. "The Abbé de Cordemoy and the Graeco-Gothic Ideal: A Prelude to Romantic Classicism," *JWCI*, 1962, 278-320; 1963, 90-123

_____. "Jacques-François Blondel and the *Cours d'Architecture*," *JSAH*, 1959, 140-148.

Nyberg, D. "The 'Mémoires critiques d'architecture' by Michel de Frémin," *JSAH*, 1963, 217-224.

_____. "*La Sainte Antiquité*: Focus of an Eighteenth-Century Architectural Debate," *Wittkower Essays*, 159-169.

Oechslin. W. "Osservazioni su Guarino Guarini e Juan Caramuel de Lobkowitz," *Guarini Convegno*, I, 573-595.

_____. "Premesse all'architettura rivoluzionaria," *Controspazio*, 1970, n.1-2, 2-15.

Pérouse de Montclos, J.M. "Charles-François Viel, architecte de l'Hôpital Général et Jean-Louis Viel de Saint-Maux, architecte, peintre et avocat au Parlement de Paris," *BSHAF*, 1966, 257-269.

Pevsner, N. "Apollo or Baboon," *Architectural Review*, December 1948, 271-279.

Prozzillo, E. *Francesco Milizia teorico e storico dell'architettura*, Naples, 1971.

Ramirez, J.A. "Guarino Guarini, Fray Juan Ricci and the 'Complete Salamonic Order'," *Art History*, 1981, n.2, 175-185.

Reuther, H. "Das Modell des salomonischen Tempels im Museum fur Hamburgische Geschichte," *Niederdeutsche Beitrage zur Kunstgeschichte*, 1980, 61-193.

Rykwert, J. "Lodoli on Function and Representation," *Architectural Review*, July 1976, 21-26.

_____. *The First Moderns: The Architects of the Eighteenth Century*, Cambridge, Mass., 1980.

Semrau, M. "Zu Nikolaus Goldmann's Leben und Schriften," *Monatshefte für Kunstwissenschaft*, 1916, 349-361; 463-473.

Summerson, J. "The Mind of Wren," *Heavenly Mansions and Other Essays on Architecture*, London, 1949.

Saxon, A.H. *Giuseppe Galli-Bibiena's "Architetture e prospettive,"* Vienna, 1969.

Tafuri, M. "Retorica e sperimentalismo: Guarino Guarini e la tradizione manierista," *Guarini Convegno*, I, 667-704.

Taylor, R. "Architecture and Magic: Considerations on the Idea of the Escorial," *Wittkower Essays*, 81-110.

_____. "Hermetism and Mystical Architecture in the Society of Jesus," *Baroque Art: The Jesuit Contribution* (ed. R. Wittkower and I.B. Jaffe), New York, 1972, 63-97.

_____. "El Padre Villalpando y sus ideas estéticas," *Academia. Anales y Boletin de la Real Academia de San Fernando*, 1952, no.2, 3-65.

Vidler, A. "Architettura, gestione, principi etici/Architecture, Management, Morals," *Lotus International*, XIV, 1977, 4-20.

Wiebenson, D. *Sources of Greek Revival Architecture*, London, 1969.

Wilton-Ely, J. *The Mind and Art of Giovanni Battista Piranesi*, London, 1978.

Wittkower, R. "Federico Zuccari and John Wood of Bath," *JWCI*, 1943, 220-222.

_____. "Piranesi's Architectural Creed," *Studies in the Italian Baroque*, London, 1975.

_____. "Piranesi's 'Parere su l'Architettura'," *JWCI*, 1938-39, 147-158.

III: The Elements of Architecture

A. The Orders

Bury, J.B. "The Stylistic Term 'Plateresque'," *JWCI*, 1976, 199-230.

Ehrmann, J. "Hans Vredeman de Vries (Leeuwarden 1527-Anvers 1606)," *GBA*, 1979, 13-26.

Forssman, E. *Dorisch, jonisch, korinthisch: Studien über den Gebrach der Saulenordnungen in der Architektur des 16.-18. Jahrhunderts*, Stockholm, 1961.

_____. *Säule und Ornament; Studien zum Problem des Manierismus in den Nordischen Saulenbuchern und Vorlageblattern des 16. and 17. Jahrhunderts*, Stockholm, 1956.

Harris, E. "Batty Langley: A Tutor to Freemasons (1696-1751)," *Burlington Magazine*, May 1977, 327-335.

Lotz, W., Walcher Casotti, *et al. La vita e le opere di Jacopo Barozzi da Vignola 1507-1573*, Vignola, 1974.

Miller, N. "A Volume of Architectural Drawings Ascribed to Jacques Androuet du Cerceau, the Elder, in the Morgan Library," *Marsyas*, 1962-64, 33-41.

Pérouse de Montclos, J.M. "Le Sixième Ordre d'architecture, ou la pratique des ordres suivant les Nations," *JSAH*, 1977, 223-240.

Puppi, L. "Profilo di Ottavio Revese Bruti," *BCISAAP*, 1961, 121-131.

Summerson, J. *The Classical Language of Architecture*, London, 1964.

Thomson, D.A. "Architecture et humanisme au XVIe siecle, le Premier Livre d'Architecture, de Julien Mauclerc," *Bulletin Monumental*, 1980, 7-40.

Von May, E. *Hans Blum Von Lohr am Main, Ein Bautheoretiker der deutschen Renaissance*, Strasbourg, 1910.

Weissman, A.W. "Simon Bosboom," *Oud-Holland*, 1907, 1-8.

B. Geometry and Perspective

Argan, G.C. "The Architecture of Brunelleschi and the Origins of Perspective Theory in the Fifteenth Century," *JWCI*, 1946, 96-121.

Bartoli, M.T. "Orthographia, Ichnographia, Scenographia," *SDA*, Sept. 1978, no.8, 197-208.

Baltrusaitis, J. *Anamorphoses ou perspectives curieuses*, Paris, 1955.

Carter, B.A.R. "Perspective," *Oxford Companion to Art*, London, 840-861.

Descargues, P. *Perspective*, New York, 1977, (trans., I.M. Paris).

Edgerton, S.Y. *The Renaissance Rediscovery of Linear Perspective*, New York, 1975.

Emiliani, M.D., ed. *La prospettiva rinascimentale: codificazioni e trasgressione*, Florence, 1980.

Ivins, W.M. *On the Rationalization of Sight, with an Examination of Three Renaissance Texts on Perspective*, New York, 1938.

Kaufmann, T.C. "Perspective of Shadows: the History of the Theory of Shadow Projection," *JWCI*, 1975, 258-287.

Kitao, T.K. "Prejudice in Perspective: a Study of Vignola's Perspective Treatise," *AB*, 1962, 173-199.

Klein, R. "Pomponius Gauricus on Perspective," *AB*, 1961, 211-230.

Oechslin, W. "Geometry and Line. The Vitruvian 'Science' of Architectural Drawing," *Daidalos*, 1981, I, 20-35.

Panofsky, E. "The History of the Theory of Human Proportions as a Reflection of the History of Styles," *Meaning in the Visual Arts*, New York, 1955, 55-107.

_____. *Die Perspektive als symbolische Form*. (Vorträge der Bibliothek Warburg, 1924-1925).

Poudra, N.G. *Histoire de la perspective, ancienne et moderne*. Paris, 1864.

Sanz Serrano, M.J. *Juan de Arfe y Villafañe, y la custodia de Sevilla*, Seville, 1978.

Vagnetti, L. "Cosimo Bartoli e la teoria mensoria nel secolo XVI," *Quaderno dell'Istituto di Elementi di Architettura e Rilievo dei Monumenti dell'Universita di Genoa*, 1970, no.4, 109-164.

_____. "De naturali et artificiali perspective," *SDA*, 1979.

White, J. *The Birth and Rebirth of Pictorial Space*, London, 1967.

_____. "Developments in Renaissance Perspective," *JWCI*, 1949, 58-79; 1951, 42-69.

Wittkower, R. "The Changing Concept of Proportion," *Idea and Image: Studies in the Italian Renaissance*, 1978, 109-123.

C. Technology

Ferriday, P. "Francis Price: Carpenter. A Bicentenary," *Architectural Review*, Nov. 1953, 327-328.

Mueller, W. "The Authenticity of Guarini's Stereotomy in his *Architettura Civile*," *JSAH*, 1968, 202-208.

_____. "Guarini e la Stereotomia," *Guarini Convegno*, I, 531-556.

Pérouse de Montclos, J.M. *L'Architecture à la francaise*, Paris, 1982.

Wiebenson, D. "Building Technology in France (1685-1786)," *JSAH*, 1980, 312-315.

D. Public and Private Architecture

"L'Art de bâtir à la campagne selon J-F Blondel," *Connaissance des Arts*, March 1976, 74-81.

Berger, R. "Antoine Le Pautre and the Motif of the Drum-without-the Dome," *JSAH*, 1966, 165-180.

Breman, P. and D. Addis. *Guide to "Vitruvius Britannicus,"* New York, 1972.

Conner, T.P. "The Making of *Vitruvius Britannicus*," *AH*, 1977, 14-30.

Connors, J. *Borromini and the Roman Oratory: Style and Society*, New York, 1980.

Esdaile, K.A. "The Small House and its Amenities in the Architectural Handbooks: 1749-1847," *Transactions of the Bibliographical Society*, XV, 1917-19, 115-132.

Etlin, R. "'Les Dedans': Jacques-François Blondel and the System of the Home c. 1740," *GBA*, April 1978, 137-147.

Fischer, M. *Die frühen Rekonstruktionen der Landhäuser Plinius' des Jüngeren*, Berlin, 1962.

Forster, K. "Back to the Farm: Vernacular Architecture and the Development of the Renaissance Villa," *Architectura*, 1974, 1-12.

Girouard, M. "English Art and the Rococo," *Country Life*, 13 Jan., 1966, 58-66; 27 Jan., 1966, 188-190; 3 Feb., 1966, 224-227.

Herrmann, W. "The Author of the 'Architecture Moderne' of 1728," *JSAH*, 1959, 60-62.

Humbert, M. "Serlio: il *Sesto Libro* e l'architettura borghese in Francia," *Storia dell'arte*, 1981 (no. 43), 201-240.

Kaufmann, E. "The Contribution of Jacques-François Blondel to Mariette's *Architecture Française*," *AB*, 1949, 58-59.

Kunoth, G. *Die historische Architektur Fischer von Erlach*, Dusseldorf, 1956.

Mauban, A. *L'Architecture françoise de Jean Mariette*, Paris, 1945.

_____ . *Jean Marot, architecte et graveur parisien,* Paris, 1944.

Miller, N. "A Volume of Architectural Drawings ascribed to Jacques Androuet Du Cerceau the elder, in the Morgan Library, New York," *Marsyas: 1962-1964,* 33-41.

Mordie, M.M. "Picturesque Pattern Books and Pre-Victorian Designers," *AH,* 1975, 43-59.

Nachmani, C.W. "The Early English Cottage Book," *Marsyas,* 1968-69, 67-76.

Pérouse de Montclos, J.M. "De la villa rustique d'Italie au pavillon de banlieue," *Révue de l'art,* 1976, 23-36.

_____ . *Etienne-Louis Boullée, 1728-1799, de l'architecture classique à l'architecture révolutionnaire,* Paris, 1969 (abr. transl., New York, 1974).

Portoghesi, P. "'L'Opus Architectonicum' del Borromini," *Wittkower Essays,* 128-133.

Robinson, J.M. "Model Farm Buildings of the Age of Improvement," *AH,* 1976, 17-31.

Saboya, M. "Claude-Nicolas Ledoux et son utopie sociale," *L'Information d'histoire de l'art,* 1970, 136-318.

Teyssot, G. "Cottages et pittoresque: les origines du logement ouvrir en Angleterre," *Architecture, Mouvement, Continuité,* 1974, no.34, 26-37.

Wiebenson, D. "A Document of Social Change: The Small House Publication," *English Art and Aesthetics in the 18th Century,* Los Angeles, 1983, (ed. R. Cohen).

_____ . "'L'Architecture terrible' and the 'Jardin Anglo-Chinois," *JSAH,* 1968, 136-139.

INDEX

Accolti, P. **III-B-11**, **III-B-15**
Adam, R. I-27, II-30, II-32, **III-D-34**, III-D-38
Arfe, J. de. **III-B-5**
Alberti, L.B. **I-1**, I-2, I-3, I-10, I-15, I-24, I-28, II-2, II-6, II-31, II-40, III-A-1, III-A-28, III-B-6
Aldrich, H. **II-15**
Barbaro, D. I-9, I-13, **I-21**, I-30, I-33, **III-B-7**
Bartoli, C. **I-15**, **III-B-6**
Bassi, M. **III-B-9**
Bertin, D. **I-19**
Bibiena, F.G. **II-16**, II-B-24, **III-B-30**
Blondel, F. I-31, **II-6**, II-9, II-10, II-24, II-30, III-A-19, III-A-20, III-C-14
Blondel, J.F. **II-27**, II-30, **II-36**, **II-38**, II-39, II-40, III-D-14, III-D-19, **III-D-20**, III-D-21, **III-D-28**, III-D-30, III-D-31, III-D-41
Blum, H. **III-A-3**, III-A-9, III-A-10
Boffrand, G. II-39, **III-D-22**
Borromini, F. II-35, **III-D-6**, III-D-19
Bosboom, S. **III-A-18**
Bosse, A. **III-A-15**, III-B-16, III-B-17, **III-B-20**, **III-B-21**, III-C-7, **III-C-8**
Boullée, E.-L. II-39, **III-D-41**
Branca, G. **II-3**, II-22
Briseux, C.-E. **II-24**, II-29, III-B-28, III-D-16, **III-D-21**
Bullant, J. **III-A-8**
Bullet, P. II-12, **III-C-14**, III-C-17
Campbell, C. **III-D-12**
Caporali, G.B. **I-9**
Capra, A. **II-8**
Caramuel de Lobkowitz, J. **II-7**, II-11
Castell, R. **III-D-15**
Cataneo, P. **I-22**
Cesariano, C. di L. **I-7**, I-8, I-9, I-10, I-11, I-16, I-21
Chambers, W. II-29, **II-30**, II-32, II-36, II-40, III-D-33, III-D-38
Chéreau, J. **III-C-2**
Colonna, F. **I-3**, I-10

Cordemoy, J.L. de **II-14**, II-24, II-40
Courtonne, J. **III-B-28**
Cousin, J. **III-B-3**
Crunden, J. **III-D-32**
Daviler, C.A. II-10, **II-12**, II-28, II-29, II-30, III-A-16, III-A-31, III-D-7, III-D-14
Decker, P. **III-D-11**
De La Rue, J.B. **III-C-16**
Delorme, P. I-13, **I-24**, II-11, III-A-25, **III-C-1**, III-C-2, III-C-3
Derand, F. **III-C-9**, III-C-16, III-C-27
Desargues, G. II-11, III-A-15, III-B-26, **III-B-17**, III-B-19, III-B-20, III-B-21, **III-C-7**, **III-C-8**, III-C-9, III-C-19, III-C-27
Desgodets, A.B. **II-10**, II-17, **III-C-17**
Dietterlin, W. **III-A-9**
Dubreuil, J. **III-B-19**, III-B-20, III-B-26
Du Cerceau, J.A. III-A-5, III-A-6, **III-B-10**, III-D-1, **III-D-2**, **III-D-3**, III-D-4, III-D-5
Durantino **I-8**, I-10
Elsam, R. **III-D-37**, **III-D-42**
Félibien des Avaux, A. II-13, **III-C-12**, III-C-13, III-D-10
Félibien des Avaux, J.F. **III-D-10**
Filarete **I-2**
Fischer von Erlach, J.B. **III-D-13**
Francine, A. III-A-5, **III-A-12**
Fréart de Chambray, R. II-10, II-19, **III-A-14**
Frémin, M. de. **II-13**
Frézier, A.F. II-14, II-40, III-C-7, III-C-9, **III-C-20**, **III-C-21**, III-C-23
Furttenbach, J. **III-D-5**, III-D-11
Galiani, B. **I-33**, II-40
Gallaccini, T. **II-2**, II-35
Gandy, J.M. III-D-37, **III-D-44**
Gardet, J. **I-19**
Garrett, D. II-29, **III-D-24**, III-D-27, III-D-32
Gerbier, B. **II-4**
Gibbs, J. **III-A-26**, III-C-18, **III-D-17**
Giocondo, G. **I-6**, I-8, I-10, I-17, I-21, I-23, I-24, III-A-1

Giorgio Martini, F. di. **I-4**, I-22
Goldmann, N. **II-5**
Guarini, G. II-7, **II-11**, II-31, III-B-24
Halfpenny, W. **III-A-22**, **III-A-23**, **III-B-29**, **III-C-15**, **III-D-25**, **III-D-26**, **III-D-29**, III-D-32
Hondius, H. **III-B-14**
Indau, J. **III-A-21**
Jamnitzer, W. **III-A-6**, **III-B-8**
Jeaurat, E.-S. **III-B-31**
Jousse, M. **III-C-5**, **III-C-6**, III-C-9, III-C-27
Labacco, A. **I-18**
Laet, I. de. **I-30**
Lambert, J.H. **III-B-32**
Lamy, B. **III-B-26**
Langley, B. **III-A-24**, **III-A-27**, **III-A-29**, **III-A-30**, **III-C-15**, III-C-24
Laugier, M.A. I-33, II-14, II-14, **II-25**, II-26, II-29, II-32, II-38, II-40, III-D-33
LeBlond, J. **II-12**, **III-A-20**
Le Camus de Mézières, N. II-38, II-39, **III-C-25**
Leclerc, S. I-31, **II-17**, II-30, **III-B-22**, **III-B-23**, III-B-31
Ledoux, C.N. II-38, III-D-31, **III-D-43**
Le Muet, P. **III-A-13**, III-A-17, **III-D-1**, **III-D-4**, III-D-8, III-D-16
Le Pautre, A. I-31, **III-D-7**
Lodoli, A. **II-26**, II-40
Malton, J. **III-D-40**, III-D-42
Malton, T. III-B-12, III-B-19, III-B-27, **III-B-33**, III-D-37
Mariette, P.-J. II-12, III-A-20, III-D-8, III-D-9, **III-D-14**, III-D-28
Marot, J. III-A-20, **III-D-8**, **III-D-9**, III-D-14, III-D-28
Martin, J. **I-10**
Mauclerc, J. **III-A-10**, III-A-17, III-B-11
Meissonnier, J.A. **III-D-19**
Memmo, A. **II-26**, II-35
Menand, **III-C-23**, III-C-28
Monge, G. III-B-17, **III-B-34**, III-C-7

Monroy, J.F. **III-C-26**, III-C-27

Montano, G.B. **I-27**

Morris, R. **II-19**, **II-20**, **II-21**, **III-D-27**, III-D-36

Moxon, J. III-B-14, **III-C-13**

Nativelle, P. **III-A-25**

Neufforge, J.F. de **III-D-30**

Niceron, J.F. **III-B-18**

Ouvrard, R. **II-9**, II-24

Pain, W. **III-C-24**

Palladio, A. I-13, I-20, I-21, I-22, **I-25**, I-27, II-6, II-10, II-15, II-19, II-29, II-30, II-37, III-A-11, **III-A-13**, III-A-14, III-A-15, III-A-16, III-A-22, III-A-23, III-A-25, III-A-28, III-A-31, III-B-5, III-B-9, III-C-18, III-C-22, III-C-24b, III-D-4, III-D-8, III-D-12, III-D-14

Peacock, J. III-D-33, **III-D-36**, III-D-39, III-D-40

Pèlerin, J. **III-B-1**

Perrault, C. **I-31**, **I-32**, I-33, II-6, II-10, II-14, II-24, II-30, II-31, II-36, II-40, III-A-14, **III-A-19**, III-C-12, III-D-9

Peyre, M.-J. **III-D-31**

Pfalz-Simmern, J. II. **III-B-2**

Philander, G. I-10, I-13, **I-14**, I-16, I-17, I-30, III-A-7

Pini, E. **II-34**

Piranesi, G.B. **II-32**, III-D-34

Plaw, J. **III-D-37**, III-D-38

Pompei, A. **III-A-28**

Pozzo, A. **III-B-25**

Price, F. **III-C-18**

Pricke, R. III-A-10, III-A-12, III-A-16, **III-A-17**, III-B-19, III-D-4

Rawlins, T. **III-D-33**, III-D-36

Revesi Bruti, O. **III-A-11**

Revett, N. **II-33**, III-A-31

Richardson, G. **III-D-38**

Rieger, C. **II-28**

Riou, S. **III-A-31**

Rusconi, G.A. I-13, **I-20**

Ryff, W. **I-11**, **I-23**

Sagredo, D. de, **III-A-1**

Salmon, W. **III-C-19**

Sambin, H. **III-A-5**

Savot, L. **III-C-4**, III-C-14, III-C-17, III-D-4

Scamozzi, V. **I-26**, II-6, II-12, **III-A-16**, III-A-18, III-A-25, III-A-31, III-D-8, III-D-10, III-D-13

Schubler, J.J. **III-D-18**

Séguin, C. **III-C-27**

Serlio, S. I-10, **I-12**, I-14, I-17, I-22, I-23, I-24, I-25, I-27, II-10, III-A-1, **III-A-2**, III-A-3, III-A-4, III-A-6, III-A-7, III-A-9, III-A-28, III-B-5, III-B-7, III-B-9, III-B-12, III-C-2, **III-D-1**, III-D-2, III-D-13

Shute, J. II-4, **III-A-7**

Simonin, **III-C-28**

Sirigatti, L. **III-B-11**

Soane, J. **III-D-39**, III-D-43

Stuart, J. **II-33**, III-A-31

Sulpitius, I. **I-5**

Swan, A. **III-C-22**, III-D-36

Taylor, B. **III-B-27**, III-B-33

Thurah, L.L. de, **III-D-23**

Tiercelet, G. II-29, **III-D-16**

Tolomei, C. **I-13**, I-20

Torija, J. de, **III-C-10**

Troili, G. **III-B-24**

Ubaldo del Monte, G. **III-B-12**

Vandelvira, A. de, **III-C-3**

Vaulezard, I.D. de, **III-B-16**

Viel de Saint-Maux, J.L. **II-41**

Vignola, G.B. da, I-13, II-13, II-30, **III-A-4**, III-A-25, III-A-28, III-A-31, **III-B-4**, III-B-9, III-D-4, III-D-8, III-D-13

Villalpando, J.B. **II-1**

Villeneuve, P.P.A.B. de, **II-22**

Viola Zanini, G. **I-29**

Visentini, A. **II-35**

Vitruvius Pollio, M. I-1, I-3, I-4, **I-5**, **I-6**, **I-7**, **I-8**, **I-9**, **I-10**, **I-11**, I-13, I-14, **I-16**, **I-17**, I-19, **I-20**, **I-21**, I-24, I-28, **I-30**, **I-31**, I-32, **I-33**, II-2, II-6, II-9, II-11, II-15, II-40, III-A-1, III-A-2, III-A-4, III-A-6, III-A-7, III-A-9, III-A-15, III-A-28, III-A-31, III-B-7, III-C-12, III-D-1, III-D-12, III-D-15, III-D-23

Vittone, B.A. II-11, **II-31**, II-35

Vredeman de Vries, H. III-A-5, **III-A-6**, III-A-9, **III-B-13**

Ware, I. **II-29**, II-30, III-B-11, III-D-33

Wilsford, T. **III-C-11**, III-C-26

Wood, J. **II-23**, III-D-35

Wood, J. (the younger) **III-D-35**, III-D-36, III-D-39, III-D-40, III-D-43

Wotton, H. **I-28**, I-30, II-4

Wren, C. **II-18**, III-A-26, III-D-12